# Bhagavad Gita's *Guide to* CORPORATE DHARMA

**Ashok Kumar Bhatia** is a speaker, blogger and occasional author. He loves talking about management, P.G. Wodehouse, Bollywood, and life in general. After working in senior management in industrial groups, including Tata and HCL, for over 35 years, in 2021, he joined the UK-based Conscious Enterprises Network to help care for our planet.

His first book, *Surviving in the Corporate Jungle*, was a practical guide for CEOs and managers to navigate the corporate world. In the book in your hands, he highlights how the timeless wisdom of the Bhagavad Gita can help us achieve our career goals. He also stresses the importance of being ethical in one's business practices.

Ashok Kumar Bhatia's detailed profile and writings can be accessed at:

LinkedIn: https://www.linkedin.com/in/ashokkumarbhatia
Blogs: https://ashokbhatia.me

*Praise for the book*

Ashok Bhatia, through his excellent book, propounds an alternative path that draws on the spiritual aspect of what is regarded as the foremost 'religious book' in the Asian context, the *Bhagavad Gita*. Differentiating between the 'mind and intellect', he has used an ancient spiritual text to convey his message very simply, and with humour.

**Dr Bharat Nain,** Arbitrator and Management Consultant,
PhD, MBA, BE(Mech), FSIArb, MCIArb, Pune, India

Ashok Bhatia paints a wide canvas of the kind of strategic and tactical issues business owners and managers face in their routine lives. With a calm objectivity, he demonstrates how the same could be resolved by imbibing what the scripture says. The undercurrent is essentially that of following high values and ethics in management, so a business may run on a sustainable basis.

**Late Dr (Prof.) G.P. Rao,** Founder-Chairman, SPANDAN, India,
Former Senior Professor and Founding Head,
Department of Management Studies,
Madurai Kamaraj University(1981–1997)

This book motivates me to look at the bigger picture in life, while at the same time remaining connected to my inner self. Using many examples of the kind of challenges we face in our careers, it makes us appreciate the deep wisdom contained within the *Gita*. The book, even though rooted in ancient Indian wisdom, has a global appeal.

**Mohan Arumugham,** Global Technology Leader, Transformation and
Innovation, GE Power, USA

A creative interpretation of the *Gita*, this book would be immensely useful to our GenNext who wish to lead a happier and more fulfilling life, helping them to achieve their career goals more effectively and efficiently.

**Dhanpat Raj Dhariwal,** Global Mentor to CEOs,
Ex-President, Birla White (A division of Ultratech Cement,
Aditya Birla Group), and Ex-CEO, Thirumalai Chemicals Ltd (India and
Malaysia)

The book is a great primer for CEOs and managers who are keen to get a basic grasp of the universal concepts highlighted in this unique scripture from India. The timeless lessons enshrined in the *Bhagavad Gita* have been innovatively presented by Ashok, with limited doses of subtle humour of a British kind.

**P.R. Ganguly,** Member, Industrial Advisory Board, Manufacturing
Department, Cranfield University, England,
Ex-Deputy Chairman and Managing Director, Grenson Shoes Ltd, UK

# Bhagavad Gita's *Guide to* CORPORATE DHARMA

## Timeless Strategies to Navigate the Corporate Jungle

ASHOK KUMAR BHATIA

RUPA

Published by
Rupa Publications India Pvt. Ltd 2026
161-B/4, Gulmohar House,
Yusuf Sarai Community Centre,
New Delhi 110049

*Sales centres:*
Bengaluru Chennai
Hyderabad Kolkata Mumbai



P-ISBN: 978-93-5352-043-4
E-ISBN: 978-93-5352-051-9

First impression 2026

10 9 8 7 6 5 4 3 2 1



Printed in India

*This book is dedicated to the loving memory of Usha Bhatia, my late wife, who remained a karma yogini throughout her life.*

# Contents

# A Note of Gratitude


The book in your hands would not have taken its present shape without the support and encouragement I received from various individuals who volunteered to read through the manuscript and guide me on several fronts. My heartiest thanks go out to:

- Mr Ashok Narayan, IAS (retired), who has authored several books on the *Bhagavad Gita*, Lord Krishna and Radha. Most of the English translations of the verses of the *Bhagavad Gita* that appear in this text were done by him as part of his detailed commentary on the scripture called *My Stray Thoughts on Srimad Bhagavad Gita*.
- Mr Kul Bhushan Khullar, an expert in textiles and business management, and a scholar of the *Bhagavad Gita* and Vedantic studies, who—despite several other professional commitments—made invaluable suggestions towards enriching the contents.
- Mr H.C. Verma, an expert in supply chain management and logistics, and well-versed in the nuances of the *Bhagavad Gita*, provided essential support.
- Mr C.S. Dwivedi, vice president of Manufacturing and Corporate Planning at HCL Infosystems Limited, who continually encouraged me despite his own professional preoccupations.
- Mr Sitanath Nandi, an expert in IT security, who provided essential technical information for select chapters.
- Mr Dominique Conterno, an IT and AI expert and the co-founder of Conscious Enterprises Network, UK, who helped improve the contents of some chapters.
- Late Mr Upendra Ratra, a Puducherry-based artist, who provided most of the illustrations. One of the

illustrations, viz. SQ, was done by Mr Sanket Bhatia, founder of ProDecipher and SensorX, two Switzerland-based start-ups.

- All the business leaders and academics who went through the manuscript and offered their insights.
- Ms Sneha Shoney, a freelance editing professional who did the preliminary edits of the manuscript.
- Ms Saswati Bora, Ms Padma Pegu, Ms Kausalya Saptharishi, Ms Srilagna Majumdar and the supporting team at Rupa Publications, who helped improve the contents and ensured that the book reaches you in perfect form.
- Above all, to the many souls who make up my family in this mortal life. Without their support, this work would not have seen the light of the day.

The following texts were consulted for the translation of verses and as inspiration for commentary:

- Chakravarty, Ajanta E., *The Geeta and the Art of Successful Management*, Rupa Publications, New Delhi, 1996.
- *Krishna.com*, 'Bhagavad-gita As It Is Summary', n.d., https://tinyurl.com/p9xdbrsf. Accessed on 7 November 2025.
- Narayan, Ashok, IAS (Retired), *My Stray Thoughts on the Srimad Bhagavad Gita.*
- *Srimad Bhagavad Gita*, https://tinyurl.com/4bscavrv. Accessed on 7 November 2025.
- Swami Chinmayananda, *The Holy Geeta: Commentary by Swami Chinmayananda*, Central Chinmaya Mission Trust, India, 2000.

# With Malice towards None

While endeavouring to connect the dots between the business world and the tenets of the *Bhagavad Gita*, the book quotes a few examples of certain corporate houses based in India and abroad. Many of these are based on media reports, as interpreted in a subjective manner by the author.

The intention is neither to eulogize some of the corporate houses mentioned, nor to denigrate a few others for their apparent lack of wisdom in handling a specific business challenge. It is merely to advance an argument in relation to a specific tenet of the revered scripture.

# Foreword from a Business Leader

It brings me immense joy to introduce this insightful book by Ashok Bhatia, which delves into the profound teachings of the *Bhagavad Gita* within the dynamic realm of the corporate world. As a long time practitioner of Transcendental Meditation and a student of values and human systems design, I have long recognized the transformative power of this ancient text.

However, it was only after writing the book *Managing from the Heart* and then co-authoring the book *One Wholesome World* that the immense practical relevance of the *Bhagavad Gita* in today's times became so clear. In this book, Ashok has brought out the timeless wisdom of the *Bhagavad Gita* in the context of life in the 'corporate jungle' to hopefully help turn it into a 'corporate garden'.

Without pontificating, Ashok brings out the challenges and dilemmas that CEOs face in their day-to-day lives. He then connects these with wit and topical examples to the wisdom of the *Bhagavad Gita*.

This book is timely and relevant. We are in the midst of 'the great turning'—a time of radical upheavals, disruptions and change. We are also in an age where we expect our leaders to be compassionate—for themselves, for others and for the environment. To respond appropriately, leaders need a calm and creative mind. This forms the foundation of the clarity, conviction and courage that they need to act wisely.

As an accomplished author, blogger and speaker on management topics, Ashok Bhatia brings a wealth of experience to his writing. You will notice that every single verse from the *Bhagavad Gita* that he discusses in this book is illustrated with real-life examples from the corporate world. These come from his vast experience as a corporate generalist, as a consultant, a serial entrepreneur, a social worker and an accomplished speaker in the fields of training and skill development.

In my professional life, having worked with the Tatas before turning into a leadership coach, it became clear to me that the source of all values is the infinite silence, emptiness, love and freedom of the real Self. When we see the same Self in others, and all of life as a manifestation of one energy, compassion and care for all emerges naturally. The source becomes the fountain of *Humata* (Good Thoughts), *Hukhta* (Good Words) and *Hvarshta* (Good Deeds)—the foundational principles of Zoroastrianism and also the house of Tatas.

When everything around us is in a state of incessant flux, it helps to have an inner anchor of peace and steadfastness. This comes from an inner connection with one's true Self.

As a leader, I have often experienced a huge improvement in my productivity and speed on days that I have meditated in the morning. Not only do I work faster, with more fluency, but also find intuitive answers to vexing queries which keep popping up spontaneously. Regular meditation does result in a huge increase in efficiency.

Going through the *Bhagavad Gita* is like an invitation to transcend the temporal, and in so doing, becoming one with the wholeness of life. It is such wholesome or 'soulful' leaders, as Ashok refers to them, who can take our organizations, social systems and our planet to a glorious new destiny. Such leaders do not really do anything. They are like the autonomous cars of the future, as Ashok beautifully describes in this book, free of the delusion of an 'I-Am-the-Doer' syndrome from which most CEOs and managers seem to suffer. There is truly no one inside. Things happen through such leaders. They become instruments of the larger evolutionary dance of life. Their compassion and open-heartedness weave the magic of action through apparent inaction. This paradox is explained in Chapter 4, Verse 18 of the *Bhagavad Gita* which Ashok utilizes to demonstrate the promise of what he calls 'contemplative downtime'. It is one of the many verses in this scripture which deal with the paradoxical nature of reality.

This book is not an armchair read for people who are retired. It is a manual for skilful action for leaders in the marketplace, for educators who would like to bring out the true meaning of education, to awaken students to the magnificence and creative power that lies dormant in each one of us.

As a manual for the kind of leadership that the world needs today in all areas, the essence of this book can be captured by the last—and my own favourite—verse of the *Bhagavad Gita*:

> यत्र योगेश्वरः कृष्णो यत्र पार्थो धनुर्धरः ।
> तत्र श्रीर्विजयो भूतिर्ध्रुवा नीतिर्मतिर्मम || 18.78 ||
>
> *Where there is Sri Krishna, the Lord of Yoga, where there is Partha, the wielder of the bow, there are surely fortune, victory, prosperity and policy. Such is my view.*

I hope that this book will become a primer for leaders, professionals, teachers, teacher-educators, students of management and professional developers, helping raise the bar across the world to learn, teach and practise the art of wholesome and soulful leadership in action.

May the wisdom of the *Bhagavad Gita* inspire and enliven us all towards wholesome thoughts, words and actions.

**—Arun Wakhlu**
Founder, Executive Director and
Chief Mentor, Pragati Leadership, Pune, India
www.pragatileadership.com

# Blessings from a Spiritual Leader

The *Bhagavad Gita* does not belong to any particular religion, community or ethnicity. Indeed, it is a way of life. Anyone who has read it soon realizes that it lays the foundation for an aspirant whose consciousness is suitably awakened to follow any spiritual path.

We humans are a proud lot, admiring our intellectual prowess and analytical abilities, but when it comes to transforming ourselves and evolving into more humane members of the society, we happen to be slow learners. Reining in our egos and desires is a difficult thing for us to do. Most of the time, the desire for more governs our thought processes, both at the individual and the corporate level. Being able to let go and detach does not come easily to us. All this leads to a build-up of distress, burnout, and feelings of emptiness, despite the material success we might externally enjoy in life. Our inner being craves a higher sense of purpose and meaning, seeking the real source of happiness and joy within. The coronavirus pandemic is perhaps nature's way of gently telling us where we are going wrong, and what we really need to do to get our priorities right.

This book demonstrates the relevance of the eternal knowledge of the *Bhagavad Gita* to business leaders and managers. It cites typical instances from the world of management, and then guides the reader to a relevant verse of the scripture, thereby making the underlying message easier to grasp. One concept it touches upon is the importance of crafting and following a value-based strategy. Also, the benefits of letting go of attachments in the life of a CEO are explored in detail. Karmic theory is viewed through a modern technological lens as an operating system of human beings, and the supremacy of *sattvic karma* over our idea of destiny is covered.

This book also explores the challenges that management faces with the onset of the Industrial Revolution 4.0. It highlights the need to deploy both emotional and spiritual intelligence in order to navigate the choppy waters of advances in artificial intelligence, machine learning, blockchain and the like. The concept of the soul is explained based on the analogy of driver-less cars, which are already on the horizon.

A unique feature of the book is the humour and light-hearted way in which the author conveys deep and serious messages, without being preachy. Even still, he recommends a dose of one chapter a day, so that the reader does not suffer from intellectual dyspepsia!

For leaders and managers who keep the giant wheels of commerce and economics running in our society, this book may open new windows, and persuade them to base their decisions on both a mindful and heartful approach. They would then be able to balance their material and spiritual compasses, to steer their businesses in a more sustainable manner.

There are many parallels between the teachings of the *Bhagavad Gita* and the Heartfulness Way of meditative practices that we recommend. The purpose of these practices, as well as the process of meditation, is described in detail in Chapter 6 of this unique scripture. In fact, the whole approach to individual growth and advancement is meditation-based. The *Gita* highlights the importance of absolute surrender to the Divine, just as Heartfulness practitioners are encouraged to do. The *Gita* speaks of doing self less work, treating oneself as a mere instrument of the Divine. In the Heartfulness Way, we have the same concept, described as Constant Remembrance.

As someone who was an integral part of the pharmaceutical industry in the USA for over three decades, I could easily relate to the business challenges described by the author here. And the way he brought to light solutions from a 5,500-year-old scripture from India is praiseworthy.

This book has been designed to arouse our curiosity about the real meaning of the *Bhagavad Gita*. I hope that it will persuade many of us to delve deeper into this scripture's timeless messages to humanity.

I wish this unique attempt of the author every success.

—**Kamlesh Patel** (fondly referred to as Daaji),
Global Guide, Heartfulness Institute,
Kanha Shanti Vanam, Hyderabad, India
www.heartfulness.org

# From: The Author, To: The Reader

There is a good chance that you are twiddling your thumbs trying to figure out how *Bhagavad Gita*, a stream of knowledge close to 5,500 years old, could help you in your business or career.

As a conscientious manager who is always trying to expand her horizon of knowledge, you may already have a copy of this scripture adorning your well-stocked bookshelf. However, much like Sisyphus, whenever you pushed your rock of comprehension up the slope of its esoteric contents, it somehow kept rolling back. Having tried to go through it a few times, you might have decided to place it back on the shelf with a sigh of exasperation.

Alternately, having vaguely heard of this scripture, you could be one of those sceptics who hold *Gita* to be a suitable guide only for those who possess a defeatist attitude; a guide to come up with lame excuses as to why they could not crack a particular target. Moreover, how could you be expected to achieve your goals while practising detachment?

Or, you could be taking a jaundiced view of some of the basic concepts proposed in this scripture—an everlasting soul, reincarnation, accumulation of *karma*, devotion to a supreme power leading to complete surrender, and the like.

In the book in your hands, an attempt has been made to demystify *Gita* and address the above-mentioned concerns. Hopefully, some of you who come across this compilation might get enthused to pick up the original scripture and relish a swim in its scintillating waters.

Let us consider some of the challenges CEOs face in a volatile business environment.

## The Mixed-bathing Challenge

Those who aspire to occupy a C-suite keep an ear to the ground. But the real fun begins when they end up occupying one. Soon, they realize the perils of trying to swim in the Zambezi River on the Dark Continent. To their utter horror, they discover that mixed-bathing practices are in vogue and that their dip is being shared by a couple of young crocodiles. What leaves them literally cold in the feet are the penetrating and unfriendly eyes of some of the crocodiles swimming alongside, who take a jaundiced view of their habitat being infested with a juicy specimen of the tribe of *Homo sapiens*. Quite a few others are gleeful, drooling over a good source of their daily vitamins.

These crocodiles might as well be representing the kind of challenges C-suite occupants typically face—business goals, quarterly guidelines, macroeconomic shocks, dark clouds of wars and geopolitical tensions, pandemics, investor pressure, ethical dilemmas, redesigning business processes given newer frontiers of technology opening up, the advent of retaining high-octane performers, compliances of all kinds, burnouts, employee morale, to cite only a few.

## Business Leaders of the Future and Compassionate Capitalism

The business environment is amid a rapid flux of multiple transitions. The past is no longer a reliable playbook for how the future will unfold. At the macro level, leaders face such challenges as climate change, biological threats, cyberattacks, reshaping of global supply chains and changing demographics.

Increasingly, a realization is dawning that the model of capitalism followed so far has outlived its utility. Income and wealth disparities have only increased. So has the gap between access to healthcare, education, and other social welfare parameters. Thus, there is a conscious move towards a more humane kind of capitalism where the ends are as important as the means. Organizations are now talking about a triple bottom line, that of financial, social and environmental results. Thus, desirable traits of business leaders and CEOs are changing, from autocratic to a more democratic and benevolent kind.

There is a need for business leaders who can steer their businesses using not only a commercial but also a spiritual compass. Compassionate decision-making has often resulted in improvements of running businesses more efficiently and effectively.

Enlightened businesses have invariably used a judicious mix of commercial and spiritual tenets to run their operations. If the former puts a premium on bottom lines, the latter tries to limit the greed for profit. Just the way commercial considerations act like an accelerator in organizations, spiritual tenets play the role of a brake, thereby avoiding many disasters that could pop up on the highway to growth. Many of our Indian business leaders—J.R.D. Tata, Ardeshir Godrej, Verghese Kurien and R.K. Talwar, to name only a few—have guided their businesses thus. The last two, famous for the 'milk revolution' and the growth of the State Bank of India respectively, have spoken of the influence of *Bhagavad Gita* on their actions.

In an era when technological developments are redefining the way businesses interact with their stakeholders, there is much that CEOs and managers can learn from the *Bhagavad Gita*. It is a do-it-yourself 'Manual of Motivation'. Its language is pregnant with symbolism at times. But it has rich lessons to offer for the day-to-day conduct of business.

The lessons it offers doesn't just apply to professionals who seek a sense of inner contentment in their work at an individual level. It goes a step further and paints a wide rainbow of colours which indicate the broad contours of what could be alluded to as 'Corporate Dharma'.

## Of Jackals, Cobras, Giraffes, Elephants and Tortoises

To run a business well, wily jackals, cobras and wolves are required, but so are friendly giraffes, brainy elephants and wise tortoises. If one represents the warp of the business fabric, the other assumes the role of the weft.

If the leader herself happens to be a spiritually inclined person, focused on steering the ship of business successfully towards its purpose and goals, but without running into a collision with massive icebergs hiding major compromises with core values and ethics, she would attain the exalted status of a *conscience keeper* for the entire business.

## The *Gita*'s Relevance in Our Technology-infested Times

Industrial Revolution 4.0 (or even beyond) and the onset of artificial intelligence notwithstanding, humans cannot be wished away. Yes, with each leap of technological faith, their role in society is set to evolve. But one wonders if the psychology of the individual would ever vanish from the face of our planet. Human ambitions, desires, greed, jealousy, anger, and attachment to things and people on the material plane would continue to govern the behaviour of not only the developers of these advances but also the values and intentions of business leaders who decide how to use them.

Hapless consumers, whether industrial or otherwise, run a much higher risk of facing concerns over data privacy, 24x7 connectivity leading to rapid burnouts and the perennial need for making rapid-fire decisions based on a steady input of processed information which is at a CEO's fingertips. Agility needs to go hand in hand with wisdom.

In the years to follow, a likely spin-off of the advent of AI would be the availability of extra time in the hands of managers of all hues, sizes and shapes. A conscious choice would need to be made as to the utilization of this time. The smart ones would surely like to use it for bouts of introspection.

This is a clear indication of the continued—and even heightened—relevance of the kind of sage advice that Lord Krishna dishes out to a befuddled Arjuna in the *Bhagavad Gita*.

**Some Words of Caution**

By no stretch of imagination can the contents of this book be said to be exhaustive. These are the result of a selective reading of the *Bhagavad Gita* through the foggy lens of someone who has a limited understanding of the art and science of management. Moreover, if you imagine me to be an expert in *Bhagavad Gita*, rattling off *shloka*s in Sanskrit at the drop of a hat, you may be disappointed. This scripture is like an ocean of profound concepts at the bottom of which one is apt to find pearls of unparalleled wisdom and rich mineral deposits of immense value to the person who wishes to live her life to the fullest.

One would also be wrong in presuming that this scripture has ready-made solutions to a CEO's problems. In any case, it does not offer a quick band-aid kind of advice. It offers long-term solutions which involve hard work on the part of one who has made up one's mind to transform oneself from within. Looking at the same situation with a different lens, as it were. It prompts one to rewire oneself and lead a peaceful life. Calling it a do-it-yourself self-help kit may make better sense.

An effort has been to make this book a lighter read. However, a speedy consumption of its contents could lead one to suffer from intellectual dyspepsia. The same is better savoured in a leisurely manner, perhaps while cruising along in a pressurized metal tube some 35,000 feet above the ground, supported by some charming crew members who ensure a steady supply of your favourite tissue restorative, while some soothing music is playing into your earphones.

While on terra firma, the recommended dose for hassled and sleep-deprived CEOs would be a single chapter a day, preferably devoured around dinner time. This would surely induce a kind of boredom which would cure them of their insomnia.

Senior managers with frayed nerves could go up to two chapters a day, preferably before breakfast. Changes in their workplace behaviour might soon make their bosses consider the option of handing out a pink slip to the enlightened souls.

To readers who are brave enough to ignore such risks, let me wish a delightful and instructive foray into this humble offering of yours truly.

If you like it, tell those you admire and love.

If you end up despising it, gift it to someone you hate.

If either of these sounds too much of an ask, you always have the option of aiming your hard copy at the nearest waste-paper basket, or, if in possession of a soft version, simply pressing the delete button!

# A Management Summary of the Book

This book endeavours to cover many of the salient features of the *Gita* in a business-friendly manner. Here is a bird's eye view of its contents.

**Key Concepts Covered**

- The core characteristics of a manager's proficiency—knowledge, skills and attitudes—have been, respectively, likened to the three kinds of yogas covered in the *Gita*, namely, *Gyan Yoga*, *Karma Yoga* and *Bhakti Yoga*.
- The plight of befuddled CEOs and the potential solutions the *Gita* provides.
- Values followed by organizations have been held to be the virtual 'souls' of businesses. These are indestructible and can survive the harsh slings and arrows of the business environment.
- The concept of reincarnation has been held to be akin to job hopping, thereby focusing on the question of retaining people.
- The karmic theory is presented as an operating system of human beings.

**A Few Mundane Concerns Addressed**

- The way equanimity and inner resilience can be used to burst the stress bubble within which CEOs often operate.
- The importance of developing an inner connection with one's true Self.
- The importance of teamwork based on what the *Gita* says.
- The perks and perils of practising detachment.

- The art of attaining (and retaining) happiness and inner peace.
- The role of ego and the need to live and work in the present.
- Techniques of controlling desires and anger.
- Managing conflicts and office politics.
- Creating wealth and generating profits is not a taboo.
- Why procrastination and hypocrisy deserve to be avoided.
- Doing work and getting work done, while maintaining work-life balance.
- How inertia and procrastination lead to corporate scams.
- The perks and perils of perfection.
- Controlling the wild horse called mind.
- Communication dos and don'ts; maintaining positive relationships.
- Handling major disasters in life and career. Free will and destiny.
- Shoring up one's Spiritual Quotient.
- Can *Gita* enable CEOs to handle the challenges posed by the Industrial Revolution 4.0?

Towards the end of the book, you will find a summary of the book in simple language in the form of an imaginary address by Lord Krishna to Harvard students.

The example of an autonomous car of the future has been used to demonstrate the 'I-Am-the-Doer' delusion from which most CEOs and managers suffer.

The book also captures in brief the original chapter scheme of the *Gita*.

The book tries to not be preachy. Rather, it highlights the kind of dilemmas CEOs and managers face in their day-to-day lives and then goes on to point out what the *Gita* says regarding these.

At the micro/individual level, it shows professionals how to transform the way they look at things. At the macro level, it speaks of the *dharma* that corporates can follow to ensure that their businesses invariably enjoy a brand positioning which is unique in the industry they happen to operate in.

It is more in the genre of a self-help book, stoking a spirit of enquiry and nudging the reader towards picking up and going through the original scripture itself!

# 1

# Introduction: Sacred Scriptures of India

There are indeed times when the chips are down, and CEOs end up facing mighty challenges in their careers. A macroeconomic shock could have wiped out a major chunk of the market demand. A raging pandemic might have shot down many expansion and diversification plans in industries. An innovative product launched in the market could have drowned, like the infamous Titanic, thanks to customers' negative perception. A critical merger and acquisition negotiation might have gone off track, leading to a change in the business strategy. A senior team member groomed by the CEO could have made a bloomer, causing serious embarrassment with the prospect of his being dished out a pink slip looming large. Advances in technology might be leading to severe disruptions in the way the business operates. Customers might be demanding a higher level of compliance with environmental, social and governance norms. Employees may be protesting against the lack of gender diversity in the company's hiring and promotion practices. Regulators might be snapping at her heels, asking for compliance with stricter norms of corporate governance.

While roaming around in the corporate jungle, CEOs often come across grizzly bears who try to undermine whatever they plan. When hard-working CEOs propose a business diversification plan, there is never a shortage of detractors who pull them down. They prick holes in the plans. They point out the flaws which they claim to be of a serious nature. Their bearish stance on the proposals may stem from genuine concerns or simply a lack of faith in the person presenting them. They could also have a political reason and a score to settle. CEOs then

C.E.O
BUSINESS PLAN
SALES

face a dilemma. They could choose to present facts and figures which support their proposals and come out firing with their hunting rifles; or look out for improved prospects in some other corporate entity and thereby manage to escape a mauling or two inside the board room.

At such times, a mood of despondency envelops a CEO. Dark clouds hover over the career horizon. Her soul is in torment. It is at times such as these that the person seeks solace. There is an inner urge to search for wisdom and truth.

However, the search for eternal wisdom and truth could start even in times when one is feeling content, when the mind is at rest, when flowers are in full bloom, when God is believed to be in heaven and when all is well with the world.

Whatever be the trigger making one yearn to understand the deeper layers of life, sacred scriptures from India offer just the kind of lessons one is seeking. First and foremost are the *Veda*s, which could be justifiably referred to as the core of the spiritual and psychological soft power of India. Then there are the *Upanishad*s, which capture the highest spiritual knowledge and experience that India can offer to the world.

India also has the *Purana*s, *Itihasa*s, *Tantra*s, *Dharma Shastra*s and *Sutra*s, besides the innumerable works of religious poetry in regional languages.

## *Ramayana* and *Mahabharata*

Among Indian scriptures, the *Ramayana* and *Mahabharata* happen to be the most popular narratives. Both are rich in mature thought and contain teachings of a political, religious, ethical and social nature. Both of these showcase, in a relatively simple language than that of the Vedas and the Upanishads, the Indian idea of dharma or righteousness.

Both appeal to the soul as well as to the imagination of an intelligent mind. Even illiterates find gems of wisdom in these two epics. In this unique fabric, philosophy, ethics, morals, social concepts, political thoughts and administrative justice form the warp, whereas heroic tales, human emotions, poetry, aesthetics, fiction, romance and villainy form the weft.

These epics showcase a highly developed sense of ethics and values, social and cultural realities of a distant past, besides intellectual and philosophical refinement. Lay persons could draw several life lessons from both these works. So could professionals of all hues.

## Sanskrit, the Supreme Language

Sanskrit is the language which forms the bedrock of a vast majority of these works. An intimate feeling of the language helps in understanding the multi-layered narratives better. One acquires a heightened sensitivity towards the shades of style and the context in which a statement is being made.

In today's inter-connected world, one may not know Sanskrit but can still savour a fraction of the fragrant nectar of knowledge offered by any of the Indian scriptures.

The *Bhagavad Gita* is composed in Sanskrit, the classical literary language of ancient India. In his book *Being One: The Vision and Way of the Bhagavad Gita*, Danish scholar Jens Gnaur says:

> The 700 stanzas of the Gita are composed in an intricate sophisticated semantic and linguistic pattern like a beautiful Persian carpet that exudes a profound harmony out of a multitude of carefully balanced colours and variations of themes.

## The *Bhagavad Gita*

### *The Song Celestial*

The *Bhagavad Gita* forms an integral part of the *Mahabharata*, appearing in its 'Bhishma Parva'. It comprises 18 chapters. Broadly speaking, this unique composition touches upon four kinds of yoga—Karma Yoga (The Yoga of Action), Gyan Yoga (The Yoga of Knowledge), Bhakti Yoga (The Yoga of Devotion) and *Raj Yoga* (The Yoga of the Kings). (Yoga is a term which is often confused with physical practices of a certain kind. However, the term is used here in the sense of describing a communion, specifically the communion of an individual soul with the Divine.)

The Upanishads articulate the philosophical principles concerning mankind, world and God. The *Gita* could be said to be a management summary of these. It explains the way human beings can practise these subtle philosophical principles in their mundane lives.

What makes this scripture so special is the unique manner in which it combines philosophical insight and spiritual depth with poetic beauty and conceptual clarity.

### *An Effective Balm for the Anguished Soul*

The reality is that modern people, even if they are unconscious of it, require consolation, a buffer against and an escape from the disappointment and turmoil of earthly life, as much as people in any other period ever did, quite possibly more so. People in the old world, at least, could admit without shame their need for consolation. More often, with the spotlight of social media invariably upon one, the modern people are denied even that.

A hapless modern aspirant, mentally fatigued by ceaseless efforts to keep the wolf away from the door, and the perennial pressure of putting up a pretence of being happy through the wide array of sensory gratifications offered by consumer-oriented market forces, aided and abetted by 24x7 connectivity, richly deserves to win a reprieve for herself and her loved ones. To cast off the shackles of this new kind of slavery is not an easy task. Often, she is apt to find that of the rainbows she is chasing, one has suddenly turned and bitten her in the leg.

Overall, the *Bhagavad Gita* excels at providing the reader with at least two important spiritual benefits: a tender consolation from the sufferings of the world, and some insight regarding why one suffers in the first place. In the end, one finds that this work of erudite scholarship is an effective balm for an anguished soul.

Project this into a future replete with technological advances, and one would realize the increasing relevance of the scintillating and wisdom-laced advice which is merely to be plucked, savoured and imbibed from the low-hanging juicy fruits which line up both sides of the sunlit streets of this scripture.

### *Soulful Management*

One of the basic concepts enunciated by Krishna in the *Bhagavad Gita* is that of the everlasting nature of the soul.

The concept of a soul now finds a resonance even in modern management literature. In his book *The 8th Habit*, Stephen R. Covey urges professionals to pay heed to their 'inner voice'. While proposing the whole person paradigm, he speaks of the four dimensions of a person—spirit, body, heart and mind.

## The Need for Spiritual CEOs and Managers

Peter Drucker, the renowned management expert, says that:

> The individual needs the return to spiritual values, for he can survive in the present human situation only by reaffirming that man is not just a biological and psychological being but also a spiritual being, that is creature, and existing for the purposes of his Creator and subject to Him.

The time for the emergence of spiritual CEOs and managers is already upon us! In an era when technological developments are redefining the way businesses interact with their stakeholders, there is much that CEOs and managers can learn from the *Bhagavad Gita*. Its language is pregnant with symbolism at times. However, it has rich lessons to offer for the day-to-day conduct of business.

A lay manager could be tempted to pick up any commentary based on the lessons contained in this great work of wisdom. She could be excused for putting it down after eagerly reading the first few chapters, only to find it difficult to grasp. She might even conclude that it lacks practical relevance in today's technology-driven business environment. Tools like AI, big data and blockchain offer her little help in making sense of it. As a result, she may mistakenly believe that she isn't intelligent enough to navigate its pristine depths.

This stream of knowledge is said to be close to 5,500 years old. However, time has not robbed it of its relevance as it gives us clear tips on controlling our minds and thoughts, reining in our senses, transcending our queen-size egos, striving to achieve perfection in whatever we do, practising equanimity, and cultivating a habit of introspection and meditation. Ultimately, it is about living a happier and healthier life.

# 2

# Of Knowledge, Skills and Attitudes

One of the basic concepts of modern management theories of Western origin is that of the three attributes: knowledge, skills and attitudes. If knowledge captures the facet of 'what' needs to be done, skills define 'how' it can be done. Additionally, attitudes define 'why' a thing must be done.

On the other hand, the *Bhagavad Gita* proposes the concept of three kinds of yoga: Karma Yoga (Action Orientation), Gyan Yoga (Knowledge Orientation) and Bhakti Yoga (Devotion Orientation). By way of an overview, it presents the concept of Raj Yoga [The Yoga of the Kings (read CEOs!)].

## The Term 'Yoga' Demystified

The term 'yoga' here does not indicate the kind of body-contorting exercises which many of us undertake these days to remain fit. Rather, it indicates a communion with a supreme power, or, let us say, the ways in which all three facets—what, how and why—are handled perfectly.

The basic concept of yoga is captured by Lord Krishna thus:

योगस्थ: कुरु कर्माणि सङ्गं त्यक्त्वा धनञ्जय |
सिद्ध्यसिद्ध्यो: समो भूत्वा समत्वं योग उच्यते || 2.48 ||

*Established in yoga, O winner of wealth, perform actions renouncing attachment and remaining even in success and failure. Evenness (of mind) is called yoga.*

Smart CEOs and managers who are endowed with this quality of evenness of mind handle successes and failures with level-headedness. Success does not lead to a ballooning of their egos.

Rather, it is subject to a pitiless analysis, to identify the critical factors which enabled the success to come through. Likewise, failure does not disturb them unduly; a root cause analysis is done and corrective steps are taken to avoid future disasters.

**The Western and the Eastern Approaches**

There are quite a few similarities in these two seemingly diverse approaches to management.

Broadly speaking, Karma Yoga is about doing things skilfully, by putting one's best foot forward in achieving results, but without either getting frustrated by failures or getting intoxicated with successes (both of which reduce efficiency as well as effectiveness in reaching one's goals). Work gets done when one has a definite purpose behind it. The emphasis here is on doing one's best within the given constraints, while remaining aware that the outcome is ultimately beyond one's control.

Gyan Yoga exhorts us to acquire knowledge and apply it for the good of all.

Bhakti Yoga motivates us to be devoted to a supreme power which, in the realm of management and leadership, could be interpreted in terms of an attitude of devotion and loyalty to the basic values which drive an organization, and not to one's superiors. One of the perks of following the path of Bhakti Yoga is that one's ego remains on a tighter leash.

Raj Yoga is not a term that the scripture uses explicitly. But throughout the narrative, one finds this to be the underlying current of thought. It elaborates upon the way business leaders and CEOs need to conduct themselves. It nudges them towards the overall goal of doing the right things the right way, keeping the overall good in mind. It highlights the need for a person to strive for spiritual progress and indulge in such practices as meditation and the study of scriptures to realize the ultimate reality of the self within each one of us. It helps one attain a state of perfect harmony where all distinctions and contradictions disappear.

The approach of Lord Krishna across the entire text is like that of a compassionate and patient teacher of mathematics. Nowhere does He force any concept on Arjuna. He solves the complex equation of life in steps, allowing Arjuna to keep interrupting and questioning Him at all steps, till the time all his doubts fade away and he picks up his arms with renewed vigour and enthusiasm.

### Karma Yoga: Excellence in Action

From a management point of view, perhaps the most relevant are the concepts espoused under the overall umbrella of Karma Yoga. Here, Lord Krishna emphasizes the importance of selfless action, free of its rewards and gains. A state of inaction is held to be another form of action itself. In any case, inaction is neither desirable nor feasible.

कर्मेन्द्रियाणि संयम्य य आस्ते मनसा स्मरन् |
इन्द्रियार्थान्विमूढात्मा मिथ्याचार: स उच्यते || 3.6 ||

यस्त्विन्द्रियाणि मनसा नियम्यारभतेऽर्जुन |
कर्मेन्द्रियै: कर्मयोगमसक्त: स विशिष्यते || 3.7 ||

*He who sits, restraining the organs of action, (but) dwelling in his mind on the objects of senses, self-deluded, is said to be a hypocrite.*

*But he who, controlling the senses with the mind, without attachment engages the organs of action in the yoga of action, he excels, O Arjuna.*

### Gyan Yoga: Keeping Your Saw Sharpened

The concepts enshrined under Gyan Yoga are also highly relevant for management professionals. This is because one of the major challenges in their careers is to keep unlearning, so the process of real learning can never cease. For example, those who are fearful about their prospects of earning a decent living in the era of Industrial Revolution 4.0 urgently need to re-skill in order to remain relevant amid a structurally shifting job market. Smart professionals always keep an open mind. They strive to keep abreast of latest technological developments. To use a phrase deployed by Stephen R. Covey, 'they keep their saws sharpened.' They keep learning from their failures as well as from their successes.

According to the *Bhagavad Gita*, the following are the traits of learned persons; anything else is ignorance:

> Absence of pride, flamboyance, non-violence, patience; simplicity, worship of the teacher, purity, stability, self-control; dispassion towards the objects of the senses and absence of ego also, seeing the miseries of birth, death, old age and diseases; non-attachment and absence of feeling of possession in son, wife, home and so on; always being even-minded in favourable and unfavourable circumstances; a firm devotion to myself through exclusive yoga, resorting to solitude and non-involvement with company of persons; the constancy of the knowledge of self, perception of the essence of knowledge—all this is called knowledge. What is other than this is ignorance.

(Verses 13.7–13.11, discussed in some detail in Chapter 38: 'When Life Hurls Big Rocks at One: Part 1')

## Bhakti Yoga: A Devotion to the Purpose of the Organization

When it comes to Bhakti Yoga, the terms loyalty and devotion—to a superior as well as to the company—spring to one's mind. But in the absence of a truly charismatic business leader of the stature of Lord Krishna, blind devotion could perhaps lead to a catastrophe in one's profession. A sense of misplaced loyalty often becomes an excuse for senior managers to remain in their comfort zones. Accepting fresh challenges does not come easily. Their skill sets start getting rusty. Much like stones which do not roll, they start gathering moss.

The relevance of Bhakti Yoga lies elsewhere. If the focus were to shift from an individual to a collective value system, or even to a super-ordinate goal, a sense of commitment and loyalty towards the same makes eminent sense. When one's inner values find a resonance with the corporate values, a synergy is found. For someone at the top of the organizational pyramid, this is essential. If this does not happen, an unceremonious exit could soon follow. At the lower levels of management, this resonance is highly desirable. It results in a deeper sense of harmony. Managers can identify with their organization's goals. Their capacity to deliver better results improves. Much like the ace archer Arjuna, a manager is likely to keep hitting the bull's eye more often.

The limitation here is that like all things transient, a professional's devotion and loyalty remain dependent on her tenure in any given organization. Once a separation takes place, the loyalty changes to the next outfit which has offered a broader platform for the professional to function from.

The implication is that the concept of Bhakti Yoga is as relevant for employees as it is for entrepreneurs who are fired with missionary zeal and are possibly committed to a cause for an entire lifetime. Whether they operate in the social sector or in the anti-social sector (read business!), the devotion they display towards the cause they are committed to is exemplary.

The downside is that such individuals often run the risk of developing queen-size egos over time. They could then start expecting their team members to be personally devoted to them, with the devotion towards the cause coming a distant second. They could then end up being surrounded by 'yes-persons', often leading to their own downfall.

Lord Krishna touches upon devotion as:

समः शत्रौ च मित्रे च तथा मानापमानयोः |
शीतोष्णसुखदुःखेषु समः सङ्गविवर्जितः || 12.18 ||

तुल्यनिन्दास्तुतिर्मौनी सन्तुष्टो येन केनचित् |
अनिकेतः स्थिरमतिर्भक्तिमान्मे प्रियो नरः || 12.19 ||

*Even to foe and friend, in honour and dishonour, in heat and cold, happiness and misery, (is) free from attachment, balanced in praise and censure, reticent, satisfied with anything, without attachment to the place of residence, whose intellect is firmly fixed on Me, and who is full of devotion to Me—such a devoted person is dear to Me.*

## Raj Yoga: Moving to a State of Self-actualization

In Chapter 9, *Gita* cautions us to abhor blind faith, thereby telling us to avoid sycophancy at all costs. Moreover, in real life, we see that religion, particularly the ritualistic version of it, often tends to divide humanity and leads to conflicts. Spirituality, on the other hand, has the potential to unite us. CEOs who take this path and evolve to 'a state of self-actualization', to borrow a term from Maslow's 'Hierarchy of Needs', would tend to take a holistic view of the operations and people under their control, thereby working for the good of all stakeholders. We may call them 'leaders steeped in a higher state of consciousness,' worried as much about the results of the next quarter as about the ESG impact of their businesses.

*Gita* presents the concept of Raj Yoga as an approach to self-perfection and extolls it as a royal secret!

राजविद्या राजगुह्यं पवित्रमिदमुत्तमम् |
प्रत्यक्षावगमं धर्म्यं सुसुखं कर्तुमव्ययम् || 9.2 ||

*This is the king of knowledge, the king of secrets, supremely holy, the best, directly experienced, righteous, easy to practise and imperishable.*

## The *Bhagavad Gita*: A Manual of Motivation

During the great war of Mahabharata, Lord Krishna virtually leads the seven divisions of the Pandava army to a decisive win against the eleven divisions of the Kaurava army. Even before the war begins, He persuades a demoralized Arjuna to take up his arms by enunciating the basic principles of life in the Bhagavad Gita. He acts like a great leader who is capable not only of identifying a worthy follower but also of pulling the latter out of his deep sense of despondency and motivating him to do his duty. He charts a pragmatic path for us to follow—guns ready, targets in sharp focus, chins up, eyes sparkling and morale high.

What follows is an attempt to present it in a way which might appeal to CEOs and business executives alike. The idea is not necessarily to take up a particular verse and interpret it using management jargon. Rather, the approach is to present the kind of challenges one faces in one's profession and then examine the solution/s that the *Bhagavad Gita* may offer to handle the same.

# 3

# When CEOs Are Left Twiddling Their Thumbs

Many a times, CEOs and managers give in to a mood of despondency, much like Arjuna on the battlefield of the *Mahabharata*. It becomes a case wherein the person may approve of the broad general principle of a strategy to be followed or a target to be cracked, but cannot help feeling an internal reluctance to act on the same.

Outside the window of the CEO's corner office, the sun may be shining. The sky may be a clear shade of blue. A gentle breeze may be swaying the trees. Birds may be chirping. But nature fails to provide solace. The mind is boggled. The brow is furrowed. The heart is laden with woe. Confusion and self-doubt reign. A defeatist attitude prevails. Decisions taken in a mental state of this kind merely add to the chaos.

**When the Mind Is Boggled**

CEOs would formulate a business strategy and even go into detailed planning of the steps involved with their team members. But when implementation and execution starts, there is always a chance that they might develop cold feet. Practical considerations, which were latent earlier, suddenly pop up. Some initial steps reveal a chink in the organization's armour, or fresh feedback emerges, altering their perception of reality.

A new product launch could have been conceptualized. Product attributes and design might have been frozen. R&D and Production might have burnt the proverbial midnight oil to come up with bulk samples which would have been successfully

PROFITS

test-marketed. Pricing might have been finalized. Packaging might have been given the go-ahead. Members of the supply chain might have been brought on board.

However, when the launch day dawns, they might wake up all of a twitter, trying to imagine the reaction of a mightier competitor, or discover an environmental challenge or a customer health issue the product may pose, when pushed aggressively in the market.

## Of Corporate Dilemmas

The dilemma facing Arjuna on a battlefield some 5,500 years back was whether to go ahead with a war against his own cousins and senior family members. The corporate world is no different. Here are two of the multiple cases which arose due to in-family disputes and misunderstandings.

### *Of Puma and Adidas*

When brothers Adolf and Rudolf Dassler founded a shoe company in their mother's laundry room in the town of Herzogenaurach, Germany in 1924, little did they imagine that their relations would turn sour during World War II. A split followed in 1948, leading to the emergence of two brands—Puma and Adidas. The two still have rival factories on opposite sides of a river. Rudolf passed away in 1974 at the age of 76, Adolf in 1977 at 78. Never did they reconcile. Both are reportedly buried at opposite ends of the same cemetery.

Both established great brands in their lifetime. But were they inwardly happy and at peace with themselves when they left this world? One can only speculate.

### *The Human Pain behind Raymond*

Back in India, retired tycoon Vijaypat Singhania, entangled in a property dispute with his son Gautam Singhania, concluded thus: 'Love your children and care for them, but don't love them so much that you are blinded.'

He had put his blood, sweat and tears into building a company named Raymond that started as a woollen fabric manufacturer but became a household name in India as it diversified into many products, like suits, shirts, denims, cosmetics, and so on.

Having done this, in 2015, he handed over his shares, worth over ₹1,000 crores, to his son, who, as of October 2024, controls the ₹11,599-crore group. At the core of the dispute between the father and son were their rights over JK House, a family-owned 36-storey redeveloped property in the posh Malabar Hill area of south Mumbai. The father was compelled by the son to move to a rented accommodation, causing him discomfort and mental anguish. Living a hand-to-mouth existence now, one can only imagine his present state of unhappiness.

If one considers the mental state of the businessmen who acted in the manner they did in a given situation, one's mind invariably goes back to the kind of despondency and fatalism experienced by Arjuna, upon surveying the armies facing one another—friends and families at each other's throats. The army of the Kauravas was not only numerically superior but was also led by Bhishma, the grandsire. The futility of a war that had cousins from the same clan fighting on opposite sides left him befuddled, wondering why it should proceed at all, bringing only death and ruin in its wake.

This is how Arjuna expresses himself at the beginning of the Great War, in Chapter 1:

सीदन्तिममगात्राणिमुखंचपरिशुष्यति
वेपथुश्चशरीरेमेरोमहर्षश्चजायते ||1.29 ||

*Seeing these, my kinsmen, gathered to fight, my limbs fail, and my mouth is perched, my body quivers and my hair stands on end.*

गाण्डीवंस्रंसतेहस्तात्वक्चैवपरिदह्यते
नचशक्नोम्यवस्थातुंभ्रमतीवचमेमन: ||1.30 ||

*Gandeeva (Arjuna's bow) slips from my hand and even*

*my skin burns (all over), I am unable to stand, and my mind seems to whirl.*

निमित्तानिचपश्यामिविपरीतानिकेशव|
नचश्रेयोऽनुपश्यामिहत्वास्वजनमाहवे ||1.31 ||

*And I see adverse omens, O Keshava (Sri Krishna), nor do I see good in killing my kinsmen in the battle.*

Luckily, Arjuna has Lord Krishna, a friend, philosopher and guide at hand. How He goes about convincing him and eventually pulling Arjuna out of the deep abyss of despondency is what the *Bhagavad Gita* is about. By the end of the discourse, he confesses to Krishna:

नष्टोमोहः स्मृतिर्लब्धात्वत्प्रसादान्मयाच्युत|
स्थितोऽस्मिगतसन्देहः करिष्येवचनंतव || 18.73 ||

*My delusion is destroyed, and I have gained my memory, through Your grace, O infallible! I stand free from doubt: I will carry out Your word.*

As we are about to discover, this scripture gives us tips as to how to transform ourselves—from a state of confusion and chaos to a state of clarity. Smart CEOs and managers get introduced to fresh ideas and techniques which have the potential to enable them to attain their goals more effectively and efficiently!

# 4

# Of Dilemmas and the Dual Nature of Things

CEOs of today face not only challenges of an economic nature but also emotional upheavals caused by ethical and moral dilemmas involved in decision-making. Even while they are busy in a relentless pursuit of business goals, regulators and NGOs keep giving them the jitters. There are indeed times when self-doubt plagues them. They feel as if they have reached their level of incompetence. They find it difficult to either face a business battle or tone down the targets of economic expansion and business lust which normally drive any business enterprise.

CEOs in the corporate world routinely face dilemmas which arise out of the dual nature of things. Almost all business situations are based on dualities. Often, these lead to the CEOs suffering from an Analysis Paralysis Syndrome.

Peter Drucker, the renowned management expert, frequently touched upon the dualities of freedom and power, authority and responsibility, progress and conservation, good and evil, worldly actions and spiritual fulfilment. He believed in the sanctity of spiritual creation. He considered traditional Christian values to be a type of practical wisdom and an ethical basis for responsible corporate leadership.

Multinationals which operate in a global environment often come across ethical dilemmas. They face situations where there are multiple 'right' answers. Owing to cultural differences, what may be ethically prudent in one country, might turn out to be unethical in another.

For instance, companies located in advanced economies of the world, while sourcing their products from developing countries, may find issues with their suppliers' compliance with such parameters as fair wages, use of child labour, gender parity, environmental pollution, and the like. Such companies might take a jaundiced view of the practice of shelling out 'speed money' to get things done smoothly. Sharing gifts with business partners is another dilemma which keeps cropping up.

By honouring core human values, respecting local traditions and being a good corporate citizen in the countries they operate in, such challenges may get handled effectively.

### The *Bhagavad Gita* for a Befuddled Mind

Coming back to the context of the *Bhagavad Gita*, one finds that Arjuna is smart. He is not only a proficient warrior prince, but also someone who has had the sterling sense of forming a close bond with a great friend, philosopher and guide like Lord Krishna. The *Gita* is all about how Krishna pulls Arjuna out of this sense of despondency and motivates him to do his duty without attachment to the results thereof. Krishna has extraordinary skills in transforming the thinking of His friend's mind, gently steering it towards the task at hand.

It is a human tendency to magnify one's weaknesses and provide some extraneous reasons for justifying one's state of inaction. Also, when one realizes the kind of sacrifices one must make to achieve the goal one has set for oneself, doubts arise about the worth of the goal itself.

> नकाङ्क्षेविजयंकृष्णनचराज्यंसुखानिच|
> किंनोराज्येनगोविन्दकिंभोगैर्जीवितेनवा || 1.32 ||
>
> *I do not desire victory, O Krishna, or kingdom or pleasure.*
> *Of what avail will the kingdom be to us, or enjoyments or*
> *even life, O Govinda!*
>
> येषामर्थेकाङ्क्षितंनोराज्यंभोगाः सुखानिच|
> तइमेऽवस्थितायुद्धेप्राणांस्त्यक्त्वाधनानिच || 1.33 ||

*Those for whose sake we desire the kingdom, enjoyments and comforts are here on the battlefield, having resigned their lives and riches.*

## Handling the Lioness of a Mighty Challenge

When mighty challenges in one's career menacingly stare at one, much like a lioness surprised when running into a hunter in the forest, the hunter, even though he is armed with a rifle, sees no ray of hope in his life. He feels as if his guardian angels have gone off on a long vacation, that too without seeking any prior consent, let alone permission.

At such times, when the fighting option has simply evaporated, the *Bhagavad Gita* gives the hunter a chance to introspect and make an objective assessment of the situation at hand. In the midst of an overwhelming situation, reason returns to its throne. Trees and bushes nearby, which are just a step away and offer a possibility of the flight option getting exercized, get evaluated. The time it would take to load the rifle and shoot the lioness gets assessed. He even weighs the option of smiling and looking into the eyes of the animal, thereby hoping to settle down in a spirit of peaceful coexistence. He thinks of nibbling at some juicy lamb sandwiches after having first shared some with the cub lurking around nearby. Sure enough, a gesture of this kind is apt to make the lioness take a less jaundiced view of the proceedings, enabling the hunter to emerge unscathed from the encounter.

When one has sunk to the bottom of an emotional pit, and the horizon looks bereft of any hope, one can safely find solace, inspiration and guidance in the *Bhagavad Gita*. It speaks in detail about such concepts as detachment, equanimity, and the need to uphold righteousness under all circumstances. It describes in detail the kind of practical steps one can take to handle the harsh slings and arrows of one's life and career.

**From Confusion to Clarity**

Lord Krishna is rather bemused at the state of Arjuna's mind and advises His friend as follows:

> कुतस्त्वाकश्मलमिदंविषमेसमुपस्थितम्।
> अनार्यजुष्टमस्वर्ग्यमकीर्तिकरमर्जुन || 2.2 ||
>
> *Arjuna, from where has this untimely ignorance arisen in you? It is shunned by noble persons, would not bring heaven, nor fame.*

Here are some clues which can assist a befuddled CEO in deciding if the course of action chosen by her is right.

One, we all look up to our own role models in life. It is wise to go back within ourselves and check how such persons, whom we hold in high esteem, would have reacted to the challenge at hand.

Two, checking if we really do want to do it the way we wish to. If one weighs the consequences of one's actions beforehand and finds that the action appears to be doable, there is merit in proceeding ahead. Moreover, if one also finds that one is likely to experience the soft glow of inner bliss once one has acted the way one wishes to—the feeling of having done a good job—one might as well go ahead with it.

Three, by going ahead with a decision of the nature under contemplation, would we be setting a shining example for others who look up to us? If so, having a shot at it would be a good idea!

By checking her proposed actions against these three parameters, a CEO can easily arrive at the right decision which suits her own nature and temperament. The first one takes care of her value system. The second one brings in the need for rationality. The third one takes care of her relationship with the society at large, whether her personal brand equity would get a boost or suffer a dent owing to the proposed action being taken.

In other words, a conscious effort needs to be made to prod the intellect back to its throne, so the situation gets handled objectively, devoid of any distortions caused by a transient emotional turbulence. Dilemmas in career and life, as also the dual nature of things, can be handled better with an approach of this kind.

We now proceed to discover as to how exactly CEOs, who find themselves facing a dilemma and are suffering from Analysis Paralysis, could revive their morale based on some profound advice received from Krishna. They could then be like sad and drooping flowers which perk up when watered with an appropriate mixture of ancient wisdom and knowledge.

# 5

# The Risk of Sweating over the Small Stuff

## The Short Half-life of All Things Material

If Marie Curie had decided to become a human-resource professional at some point of time in her illustrious career, she would surely have had something to say about the half-life of so many things: interpersonal relationships, joys and sorrows, promotions, increments, awards and other recognitions which come one's way all the time. Even insults, abuses and rebukes hurled at managers by their bosses, whether in private or in public, would have been held to be things which have a rather short half-life.

Consider this. When one is about to join a company, a sage-looking junior executive responsible for handling one at the selection stage would invariably paint a rosy picture of the company's operations. One would be shown the kind of awards won by the company while discharging its Corporate Social Responsibility mandate. Bouquets would be highlighted; bricks hurled at the company would be swept under the carpet.

If selected and upon joining, the demo version would continue directly into one's induction period. A honeymoon phase would invariably follow. All would be hunky-dory. Till the day, of course, when the boss would call the new entrant in, look her in the eye and suggest that she start preparing for a bigger challenge—something like camping on Mars and peddling the company's goods and services out there. The scales would then start falling from her eyes. Corporate warts would start becoming visible.

### When Coveted Promotions Turn Sour

Likewise, when a special promotion or increment comes one's way, a short span of happiness and exhilaration is bound to lift one's morale. However, with the passage of time, the recognition may start losing its sheen. Challenges in the new position would weigh one down. Ask a canteen boy who is suddenly promoted to canteen manager. Ask a production supervisor upon whom fate has smiled and who has suddenly found himself promoted to the level of a production manager. Ask a sales representative who finds himself elevated to the rank of a sales manager. There is always a chance that most of such promotes, having found their level of incompetence, would start ruing the day they got promoted. To their utter horror, they would discover that doing a job with their own hands was far easier than getting others to do the same job. Bosses who had originally pushed for the promotion of these souls would be looking sheepish and diffident in such group meetings where the performance, or lack of it, of the promotes would be on full public display. The management may eventually come to regret the decision to confer a promotion on such souls.

### Change Is the Only Constant

Likewise, organizations which are not quick enough to respond to market changes also suffer from a similar half-life phenomenon. Examples like those of Kodak and Nokia abound, where a turnaround strategy was either not taken up, or got taken up only after much water had flown under the bridge and the business had taken a serious hit. If the former did not respond with alacrity to the imminent dawning of a digital photography age, the latter happened to wake up late when it came to smartphones. (In Chapter 27: 'A Jaundiced View of Procrastination and Hypocrisy', we revisit the Kodak case in some detail.)

Countries are also not immune from this phenomenon. Think of a country like India which became independent in 1947. The steel sector was strategic at the time and the state had to step in to supply the economy with the steel it needed. The same was the case with utilities and some other core sectors of the economy.

Cut to the present, when advanced microelectronics, telecom gear, new materials, new technologies for waste management, artificial intelligence and robotics would qualify to be labelled as strategic. The state needs to build capacity in these sectors and exit the ones which have ceased to be strategic. Goes on to show that what defines a strategic sector also has a half-life of its own.

The common thread in all these occurrences is that nothing is of a permanent nature. Life keeps throwing bouquets and brickbats one's way. The impression created on one remains a function of time. That is how we hear wise men say that 'time is a great healer.'

This is not to say that the kind of instances quoted above could always be held to be small stuff. At the time of occurrence, all of these could sound like earthquakes which notch up a score of nine or above on the Richter scale. Some of these could even end up changing the trajectory of one's life and career. But many of these would not be able to withstand the vagaries of time and would be destined to find their way into the dustbin of one's memories.

## Of Reversal of Polarities

Yet another feature of mortal things is what experts in the science of magnetism would thoroughly approve of. This one pertains to the reversal of polarities. A person, an object or even a relationship that happens to be positive at one point in time could easily become negative at another point in time. Of course, the vice versa is also true.

Most people one meets for the first time sound like decent rabbits with some of whom one could nibble lettuce and start a cosy friendship. One could feel as if one could consider settling down with these pious souls. However, with the passage of time, the negative side of their personality starts showing up and the relationship could come under strain. The same person may start looking like a vengeful cat in the garb of a rabbit.

A boss who happens to be a role model could one day metamorphose into a villain in one's career. Over time, unstinted support from her could vanish and assume the sinister shades of vehement opposition to whatever brainy scheme one comes up with. From being a lioness who zealously protects her cub, she could get transformed into a crouching leopard eager to strike.

The underlying reasons could be many. Inwardly shuddering at the junior's competence, she might have developed an inner sense of insecurity. Perhaps she suspects one to be conspiring secretly with a senior she believes to be an enemy of hers. Or a personal issue which might be making her take a dim view of things in general.

Likewise, a much-coveted transfer or promotion could eventually prove to be the proverbial millstone around one's neck. Unforeseen dimensions could open up when handling the situation on the ground. When wisdom dawns, one might realize exactly what the boss meant when she looked you in the eye with a steely gaze and surmised that the only person she thought could gleefully take up a challenge of that nature would be you alone! The glamour which appeared to have been associated with the event gives way to a sense of entrapment. A sense of despondency overtakes one.

This is what the *Gita* has to say on the nature of material things:

मात्रास्पर्शास्तुकौन्तेयशीतोष्णसुखदु: खदा: |
आगमापायिनोऽनित्यास्तांस्तितिक्षस्वभारत ||2.14 ||

*O son of Kunti, contacts (of the senses) with (their)*

> *objects, giving rise to (the experience of) cold and heat, pleasure, and pain, are transient and they come and go. Bear them, O Bharata (without being disturbed).*

As one of the prominent politicians of the last century put it in simple words:

> Our most basic common link is that we all inhabit this planet. We all breathe the same air. We all cherish our children's future. And we are all mortal.
>
> —John F. Kennedy

If everything in the material world is of a transient nature, one might as well ask as to what is eternal, or at the least, longer -lasting, when compared to the kind of small stuff we touched upon here.

In the chapters that follow, namely, 6, 7 and 8, we discuss the importance of values followed by organizations and the very purpose of business. If one looks at business entities that have been alive and kicking for a very long time, and have a shimmering brand equity to boot, one realizes that these are indeed the considerations which are not of a transient nature.

# 6

## The Value of Values

The fact remains that life and career rarely unfold the way one wants them to. Others do not necessarily behave as one would like them to. There are always those who would disagree with one. Things are not handled the way one would expect them to be handled. Some things work out with little effort. Others do not, even with much greater effort. So, if one chooses to fight against this strong undercurrent of life, one is likely to spend much time fighting battles of an insignificant kind. Instead, much like Arjuna, one could eventually choose to fight in a war that is based on the principles of righteousness.

Once one has realized that most material things are transient, it follows that there is no reason for one to sweat over what may be likened to water under the bridge, here now, gone the next instant. One might instead focus one's energy, time and resources on things that have a much longer shelf life.

Hapless CEOs live from one financial quarter to the next. A gentle nudge to their chief financial officer brings about some improvement in the quarterly guidance values. However, there are limits to which receivables can be stretched, inventories can be buoyed up, and expenses deferred to the next quarter. Sweating over the same stuff every quarter takes its own toll on the team's stress levels. A myopic vision gets developed. A long-term value-based view runs the risk of getting relegated to the background.

Business thinkers like Alfred Rappaport are pioneers in developing the principles of values-based management and have suggested practical ways to make long-term shareholder value the essential driver of corporate strategy. His work, *Saving Capitalism from Short-Termism*, is a clarion call for conquering the addiction to short-term profit—and getting on the path to building long-term value.

## Of Things with a Longer Shelf Life: Values, Character, Faith

Which are the things that have a longer shelf life, one may well ask. One's value system. One's character. What one places one's faith in. One's attitude towards life in general. One's capacity to be able to handle the rough and tumble of a management career. One's ability to make decisions based not only on big data analytics but also on intuition.

These are the kinds of things which build the resilience of individual managers as well as organizations to face macroeconomic shocks and market uncertainties with aplomb. Over time, harsh slings and arrows of acareer find it difficult to chip away at these innate qualities of one. Once this core is managed well, external things fall in place most of the time. One's responses to people and circumstances become more refined, thereby improving one's managerial effectiveness. One's personal brand equity acquires a better sheen.

Organizations exist for the purpose of delivering satisfaction to their customers and owners. However, in real terms, these thrive on their value systems which, in turn, determine the way they handle their stakeholders. This goes on to build brand equity which could eventually leave the competition far behind in the marketplace. At times of crisis, customers and distributors chip in. Members of the supply chain offer unequivocal support. Employees pitch in with a helping hand or two. Financial institutions come up with debt-recasting plans. Shareholders also rise to the occasion and contribute in their own way. In general, trust and loyalty levels improve.

The *Bhagavad Gita* highlights the importance of faith in our lives and the latent way it provides a compass that determines the direction of our efforts.

सत्वानुरूपासर्वस्यश्रद्धाभवतिभारत|
श्रद्धामयोऽयंपुरुषोयोयच्छ्रद्धः सएवसः || 17.3 ||

*The faith of all humans conforms to the nature of their mind. All people possess faith, and whatever the nature of their faith, that is verily what they are.*

Our personality is shaped by what we decide to place our faith in. In the case of corporates, the collective personality of like-minded promoters ends up shaping the direction and long-term growth of a business.

Those who develop the conviction that money is of paramount importance, spend their journey of life working towards materialistic goals. Those who place their faith in fame, power and pelf, dedicate their time and energy to chasing C-suites and fancy designations. Those who believe in noble values sacrifice everything to uphold them.

This explains why many businesses end up merely being 'businesses', whereas some make the cut as 'industrialists', trying to give back to society in whichever way they can.

To remain peaceful, one needs to be in equilibrium with one's faith, neither exceeding it nor subverting it.

## The Tata Group: Good Thoughts, Good Words and Good Deeds

Consider the case of the house of Tatas. The group can rightfully boast of a value system which goes back more than 158 years.

The brand equity that the group enjoys is as much about product quality as it is about trust and faith which stakeholders of all hues, sizes and shapes repose in its operations.

Tatas happen to support trusts which are some of the oldest charitable institutions in India. The group has pioneered modern ideas of secular, social services-oriented philanthropy.

### *Investing in the Society*

It is not easy to name another business empire in India which has invested in the social sectors even when no law ever mandated it. Or one which has invested in areas totally unrelated to the core business activities of the group. Iconic institutions like the Indian Institute of Science, the Tata Institute of Fundamental Research, the Tata Institute of Social Sciences, and the National Centre for Performing Arts are but some of the examples which spring to one's mind.

### *An Innate Sense of Decency*

It may also not be possible for us to locate another business house which has gone out of its way to incur a liability out of a sheer sense of decency even when not having a formal agreement to that effect.

In one of his scintillating articles, Arun Maira, ex-member of the Indian Planning Commission and an ex-Tata senior, recounts a 1946 meeting between the KraussMaffei board and J.R.D. Tata and Sumant Moolgaokar on the platform of the bombed-out Munich station. In those times, Indian companies had no way of entering into any agreement with German companies. The Germans requested the Tatas to support their best technicians and their families in India while the Second World War was going on. So, the group learnt metalworking from the best of the best.

He says that many years later, when India had become independent, the German company's headquarters received a letter from the Tatas, asking how much they must pay for the technology KraussMaffei had provided to the group. That letter showed the true spirit of the group—one honours one's debt, even when it is not legally binding, and even when it is not demanded of one.

### *India to Be a Happy Country!*

In a speech made in 1992, when J.R.D. Tata was awarded the

Bharat Ratna, the highest civilian honour in India, he is stated to have remarked thus:

> An American economist has predicted that in the next century India will be an economic superpower. I don't want India to be an economic superpower. I want India to be a happy country.

This statement indicates a core value system which has led to the people-centric policies of the group.

*Zoroastrian Principles*

One may also recall the Tata Finance fiasco in 2001 when a letter alleging some wrongdoings at the company reached the desks of several Tata seniors. Tata Sons could have well adhered to admitting its limited legal liabilities, but Ratan Tata (1937–2024) took a courageous and humane view to publicly declare that the interests of every small investor shall be protected.

In his brilliant book *Six Lenses*, R. Gopalakrishnan cites several examples from the Tata history to sketch out the kind of culture the group has.

Undoubtedly, the goodwill enjoyed by the group is because of the perception that, as a business house, it has always tried to put into practice the Zoroastrian principles of Humata (Good Thoughts), Hukhta (Good Words) and Hvarshta (Good Deeds).

**Filling the Void within**

Albert Einstein once said:

> Try not to become a man of success, but rather try to become a man of value.

The mistake most of us make in our lives is to equate success with materialistic achievements.

Our scriptures invariably emphasize the need to possess the right values. Spiritual masters always tell us that if we attach too much value to valuables, we end up becoming valueless. 'Successful' CEOs often speak of the inner sense of emptiness they feel, despite all the trappings of an outwardly successful life.

Values are like a fabric which has our ethical and moral strains as the warp and the weft. These form the seeds of our personality, which, if nourished well at the right time, can yield positive results in the long run. The nourishment comes from a pious upbringing and the company of righteous people. Good education does not necessarily nourish our value system, as evidenced by the kind of corporate scams we keep discovering at frequent intervals.

## Towards Inner Resilience and Equipoise

It is one thing to know about the impermanence of things in one's life. But it is quite another to learn to ignore the small stuff and not get swayed by immediate circumstances. Nerves of chilled steel need to be developed. A state of inner calm needs to be cultivated. A habit of calm endurance, both in pleasure and pain, needs to be formed. Inner resilience needs to be deployed.

The *Bhagavad Gita* exhorts one to do precisely this. It goes on to propose that a person who has attained this state of mental equipoise attains immortality.

> यंहिनव्यथयन्त्येतेपुरुषंपुरुषर्षभ।
> समदु:खसुखंधीरंसोऽमृतत्वायकल्पते || 2.15 ||
>
> *The man indeed whom these (contacts with sense objects and the consequent experiences) do not torment, who is even in happiness and sorrow, steadfast, he is eligible for immortality, O best of men.*

## Leading a Vibrant Life

Lord Krishna is not exhorting one to lead a monastic life which would be somewhat monochromatic. He is merely saying not to get swayed by the ups and downs of life. In one's journey towards attaining perfection, one can make the conscious choice of enduring the little joys and pinpricks of life in a light-hearted manner. Instead, one can focus on sticking to one's value systems and one's character, thereby making the journey a vibrant and purposeful one.

Consider the case of a manager who has been given a pep talk by his boss. He is now aware of the bigger picture and is fired with a missionary zeal to achieve his target. At an intellectual level, he is enthused to be participating in a valuable project. He is prepared to make many sacrifices on the way because he has found a deeper purpose behind the task he is entrusted with. If a bouquet is received in the interim, he feels happy but does not slacken his efforts. If some brickbats get flung at him, he takes the feedback in his stride, sifts the wheat from the chaff and chugs along till the target is achieved.

As humanity hurtles forth into a future replete with rapid advances in technology, the need for CEOs to try and remain focused on the core values of their business is only going to become sharper.

*(In chapters 7 and 8, we explore this theme further.)*

# 7

# Values: The Real 'Soul' of Organizations

Vision and mission statements of corporates adorn their walls and can be readily copied. However, the value system of an organization is not something which can be copied very easily. It permeates the entire organization—its hierarchy and its various divisions or departments. It rubs off on most of its employees. Even service providers and supporting manufacturers get tuned to the same frequency. It would perhaps not be wrong to say that values are to an organization what the soul is to a physical body. Businesses which thrive over a long period of time and achieve sustainable commercial success would invariably be found to have sound values at the core of their operations.

Our youth are already reeling under the impact of the latest technologies being unleashed on the unsuspecting workforce with gay abandon, leading to drastic changes in the skills required to thrive in the corporate jungle. However, when they decide to join a new organization, it would be wise on their part to be also aware of the nature of values that such outfits could be following.

## Manifestation of Values

Small things reflect the values being followed—whether nephews and nieces of the top person are getting freely hired to do jobs they are not competent at, whether spaces in the car parking lot are allotted hierarchy-wise or are based on a first-come-first-served basis, whether the corner office has high sound-proof walls all around or is open to all to signify transparency, whether the boss is entitled to charge the company for her spouse accompanying her on a business trip, whether office

"And listen; don't call me 'Aunty' while we are in the office!"

stationery items get whisked off to executives' households for use by their kids, or whether the use of cell phones or social media platforms is viewed with a sense of benign resignation by a hapless human resources honcho.

One striking feature of values is that even if these remain spoken of in hushed tones and get communicated more effectively through grapevines which are embedded deep in any organization, it is the leader who sets the tone. Those down the ladder fall in line. Those who shape up, and have a reasonably good performance on the job, survive and do well. Those who do not, eventually get shipped out. The latter, if they have learnt a lesson or two well, then try to look for other organizations where the values—theirs and those of the organization—happen to be in harmony.

## Looking for Business Heads Who Are Not Only from Mars but Also from Venus!

When head-hunting for a CFO, human resources honchos know well that even though the final three shortlisted aspirants happen to have near-identical qualifications and experience, their personal value systems would set them apart. One might be used to extensive window dressing to please diverse stakeholders, thereby raising the concern for a disaster lurking around the corner in the not-so-distant future. Another might admit to being open to transactions in hard cash, thereby consolidating his own power and pelf in the company, if appointed. Yet another one might take a dim view of any underhand dealings and project the image of someone who believes in transparency with both the internal and statutory auditors, thereby leaving the CEO and the board of directors breathing easier. If the management cares about maintaining high standards of corporate governance, the last one would land the assignment.

Smart organizations on the lookout for leaders and CEOs these days have consciously narrowed down their preference to someone who has the right mix of female and male traits.

Besides good domain knowledge, qualifications and analytical skills, they expect a top honcho to possess such softer skills as empathy, resilience and pain-bearing capacity. It is no longer sufficient for them to be from Mars. It is necessary for them to hail partly from Venus as well. In great demand are those from the tribe of the so-called delicately nurtured ones, albeit with a dash of the traits of someone from the tribe of the so-called sterner sex, or vice versa. In other words, the right combination of *Yin* and *Yang*, much like Arjun a himself!

In their book *Shakti Leadership: Embracing Feminine and Masculine Power in Business*, Nilima Bhat and Raj Sisodia argue that an emphasis on 'masculine' qualities (hierarchical, militaristic, win-at-all-costs, and the like) has led to corruption, environmental degradation, social breakdown, stress, depression, and a host of other serious problems. They show us a more balanced way, an archetype of leadership that is generative, cooperative, creative, inclusive and empathetic, which are traditionally regarded as 'feminine' traits.

CEOs often make the mistake of misunderstanding the trait of empathy. They are focused on achieving goals no matter what the cost to employees. If we treat people only as the means to an end, we will never have their loyalty. Treating our people right is the only way to improve employee engagement and motivation levels. This way, we inspire people, build teams and elicit loyalty.

Great leaders are concerned about getting the job done as well as the well-being of those under their care. It does not mean being overly attentive or soft but demonstrates that one values people. Leaders who possess this trait always make time for people. This is more true in our technology-infested times.

> Nobody cares how much you know, until they know how much you care.
>
> —Theodore Roosevelt

In a recent case in Mumbai in India, an incumbent CEO was picked up by a company car. On the way to the office, owing to incessant rains, the car got stuck in a massive traffic jam. After some time, the aspirant became jittery and unloaded his frustration on the hapless driver. Once they reached the headquarters, the final interview started, but the emotionally hurt driver lost no time in reporting this incident to the human resources department. His feedback was taken seriously. The management wondered if a person who could not even handle with equipoise a simple situation like a traffic jam would be able to make courageous business decisions in tricky and demanding situations. Eventually, a formal offer was never made.

**Values of Organizations**

At the macro level, the values of an organization manifest in the wisdom which underlies their actions. When it comes to achieving the heights of corporate excellence, organizations which have sound long-term values are invariably found to enjoy strong brand equity. Scratch beneath the surface and one is apt to discover the wiser ways in which it conducts its operations. Its initiatives lead to sustainable growth of the business, giving back to society in ways which are imaginative as well as pragmatic.

Speaking to the conglomerate's leadership some time back, Ratan Tata, chairman emeritus of the Tata group, said that the group has been under 'fire' for the past few months due to allegations of mismanagement and 'being in business for reasons other than good corporate governance'. 'The spirit that we had that made us grow to $100-billion revenues has not been through mismanagement and unethical procedures,' he said, adding that it has grown by being a visionary, having a spirit of integrity, unity and doing philanthropy.

In a foreword to the recently published book *Startup Compass*, authored by Ujwal Kalra and Shobhit Shubhankar, N.R. Narayana Murthy, chairman emeritus of Infosys, has shared many lessons learnt by the team of founding members of the IT multinational. Of these, the first and the most important lesson mentioned by him is the importance of articulating values and practising them:

> Values form the backbone of an entrepreneur's determination. The first and the most important tenet of our value system was putting the interest of the company ahead of our personal interest in every decision the founding team took.

## Values Defy Death

Products and organizations have life cycles of their own, just like the human body is prone to many changes—birth, existence, growth, decay, disease, and death. But values outlive these perils of life; somewhat akin to the Self, our inner core, which the *Gita* holds to be eternal and deathless. Values pervade all arms of any organization. In the case of multinationals, these could vary a little in different countries depending upon the respective politico-economic environment of those countries, even though the core would not get tinkered with. These could get tweaked over an extended period but would invariably defy an ignominious death.

> अविनाशितुतद्विद्धियेनसर्वमिदंततम्।
> विनाशमव्ययस्यास्यनकश्चित्कर्तुमर्हति || 2.17 ||
>
> *That which pervades the entire body, know it to be indestructible. No one can cause the destruction of the imperishable soul.*

## A Prescription for Overcoming Fear

Imbibing the contents of this verse could make any CEO diplomatically fearless. Knowing that one's innermost self is indestructible and that no harm can come to one, there is nothing left to fear. One should simply go ahead doing one's job honestly and sincerely, upholding the values of the organization one is working for, without having any apprehensions.

Looking a ferocious director in the eye, or tactfully tackling a bullying colleague, could then become a routine affair!

## The Purpose of an Organization

Why does an organization exist? What is its purpose? Can an organization be run in such a manner as to be long-lived? Can an organization strike a judicial balance between owner enrichment and societal good?

Nikos Mourkiaginnis, in his famous book *Purpose: the Starting Point of Great Companies*, demonstrates that the choice between values and success is no choice at all. He argues that companies must satisfy the need for purpose—a set of values that defines an organization, and inspires and motivates its employees. Rather than organization and structure, *idea*s are what cause companies to go from good to great. Drawing on examples across multiple industries, he demonstrates how a strong purpose is the essential first step towards lasting success.

Businesses face an accelerated pace of change as digitalization, a disruptive business environment, and rapidly changing consumer expectations reshape their world. At the same time, the demands of a new generation of employees for meaning in their work, the declining levels of trust in companies, and a wider debate about the role businesses can or should play in society are reshaping what is expected of organizations.

Over the past few years, a growing number of corporate leaders and experts have spoken out about how a strong shared sense of purpose can help companies meet these new challenges and transform their organizations.

In 2015, to understand why, and more importantly, how, companies are employing purpose to guide and lend impetus to their transformations, Harvard Business Review Analytic Services conducted a survey sponsored by the EY Beacon Institute, called 'The Business Case for Purpose'.

The global survey of 474 executives found that although there is near unanimity in the business community about the value of purpose in driving performance, less than half of the executives surveyed said their company had articulated a strong sense of purpose and used it as a way to make decisions and strengthen motivation. Only a few companies appear to have embedded their purpose to a point where they have reaped their full potential. In those organizations where purpose had become a driver of strategy and decision-making, executives reported a greater ability to deliver revenue growth, and drive successful innovation and ongoing transformation.

This result of the survey suggested that purpose is a powerful, though underutilized, tool—89 per cent of executives surveyed said a strong sense of collective purpose drives employee satisfaction; 84 per cent said it can affect an organization's ability to transform; and 80 per cent said it helps increase customer loyalty.

This is a great insight. An organization's purpose is notmerely to deliver goods and services to its customers. What really matters are the values which determine the choice of these products and services. A purpose which is backed by a sound value system enables the sustainability of a business. Looked at from this perspective, one would not be wrong in concluding that values, which determine the purpose of an organization, indeed constitute its soul.

## Is Following Values a Corporate Luxury?

There is a widespread perception that the larger the business, the broader and deeper is likely to be its adherence to values and ethics. In other words, enterprises which happen to be either in the small scale or in the tiny sector could ill afford a luxury of this kind!

We shall try and find an answer to this aspect of values in some detail in Chapter 8.

# 8

# Values in Some Smaller Outfits

Many CEOs believe values and ethics can wait until a business is financially strong. In other words, the weaker ones, which are in a struggling phase, can't afford the luxury. This approach risks embedding bad habits deeply into the company's culture, making change difficult. Like a tiger's stripes, these habits are hard to shake off. True values stem from the inner conviction of leaders, not from a company's size or profits—and often, strong values lead to better success. Let us relook at the case of Infosys. Since its inception, the founders are known to have resisted the temptation of paying 'speed money' to get things moving faster on the bureaucratic front. Its annual revenue reached US$100 million in 1999, US$1 billion in 2004, US$10 billion in 2017 and US$ 19.3 billion in 2024. The company was formed in 1981, but even as late as 2011, T.V. Mohandas Pai had alleged that his company was asked to pay bribes by government officials to clear projects, which it refused to do.

There are few businesses in the small and medium sector which follow a high standard of values and ethics in their dealings with respective stakeholders. A vast majority of such businesses fight only to ensure survival. All other considerations take a back seat. In any case, their human resources policies, if any, leave much to be desired. They merely beg to be excused for having a rather narrow bandwidth of values, confined only to keeping customers and other stakeholders happy.

## Innovative Practices of Some Smaller Outfits

In owner-driven companies, employees are expected to offer selfless cooperation, often taking pay cuts and leaving their egos at the door. They must be quiet, respectful, and ready for sudden layoffs. As long as their spines are made of cottage cheese, they are tolerated. As and when the cheese starts transforming into mild steel, they need to be prepared to seek greener pastures quickly. Requests for leave are discouraged, and work-life balance is often ignored, as the owner's mood, behaving like the stock market, determines job security and company atmosphere.

Such companies often treat employees like disposable assets, with hiring and firing decisions made arbitrarily, eroding continuity and productivity. Incoming staff never meet outgoing ones, causing valuable experience to be lost and systems to be constantly reinvented. While this lack of structure allows for agility and swift decision-making, it also creates a workplace ruled by unpredictability and fear, keeping everyone on edge.

**How New Business Plans Get Rolled out**

When the Lion King rolls out a new business plan, he simply issues orders: Marketing-Monkeys, Production-Bovines, and Supply-Chain-Goats must dive into their tasks immediately. Human-Resources-Canines handle staffing, Finance-Felines track collections, Research-Pachyderms push innovation, System-Giraffes stretch tight budgets for tech, and Liaison-Fox ensures all permits are secured on time. It is a fast-paced, top-down command where everyone knows their role, no questions asked.

That said, not all small outfits follow this rigid model—some truly respect their people and foster better teamwork. The silver lining is that employees in any such environment, whether tough or supportive, develop stronger resilience and adaptability than those in larger, more system-driven companies. But if you find yourself stuck in a harsh setup, mastering detachment and staying ready to jump the ship for greener pastures becomes the smartest survival skill.

## What Lord Krishna Says

The *Bhagavad Gita* exhorts business owners and CEOs to assign due importance to their values and continue to fight their business wars.

अन्तवन्तइमेदेहानित्यस्योक्ता: शरीरिण: |
अनाशिनोऽप्रमेयस्यतस्माद्युध्यस्वभारत || 2.18 ||

*Only the material body is perishable; the embodied soul within is indestructible, immeasurable and eternal. Therefore, fight, O descendant of Bharata.*

## Values and the Maslow Hierarchy

Different organizations showcase a vibrant spectrum of cultures, with profits—the black of the rainbow—shining brightest, while the dreaded red of losses sends chills down the spines of owners and CEOs. Most businesses evolve following Maslow's Hierarchy of Needs: start-ups first secure funding and talent, then focus on stability and sustainability as key drivers.

As they grow, companies move towards belonging, polishing their corporate image through policies, SOPs, and initiatives to win stakeholder trust. Philanthropy and CSR efforts often mark their path to self-actualization. Throughout this journey, values act as the keel of the ship, as it cruises through the choppy waters of the business environment. However, the bandwidth of its values keeps broadening through all the stages of its growth.

# 9

# Of Reincarnation, Mushrooming and Job Hopping

The *Bhagavad Gita*'s concept of reincarnation finds a corporate parallel in two common phenomena. One is the mushrooming of business entities where the same owners repeatedly create new companies, often to evade taxes and hide behind a 'corporate veil'. This game of hide-and-seek between businesses and tax authorities thrives especially in emerging or stagnant economies with incomplete digitization of records. While governments generally distrust businesses on compliance, some economies see a close, often problematic, relationship between the two, known as crony capitalism. Business owners often view taxes and legal restrictions skeptically, leading to complicated paperwork and higher job security for the accounting and clerical staff.

The second phenomenon is job hopping, which contrasts sharply with past values where long tenure at one company—over five years—was respected. Today, those who stay put too long may be seen as stagnant or unambitious, as frequent moves between jobs have become more common and accepted in the evolving corporate landscape.

वासांसि जीर्णानि यथा विहाय नवानि गृह्णाति नरोऽपराणि |
तथा शरीराणि विहाय जीर्णा न्यन्यानि संयाति नवानि देही || 2.22 ||

*As a person sheds worn-out garments and wears new ones, likewise, at the time of death, the soul casts off its worn-out body and enters a new one.*

Lord Krishna goes on to explain to Arjuna that just as an individual changes her worn-out clothes, so too the soul changes its physical sheath, eventually acquiring a new one by the process of rebirth.

What happens when a CEO has attained her level of incompetence in an organization? Or, when there is a mismatch between her personal values and those of the company she happens to be associated with? In such cases, a separation of ways comes about—either an amicable one or a forced one. Many a time, this happens discreetly. But there are indeed cases when it happens in full public glare, with corporate dirty linen getting washed and paraded in public. The unceremonious ouster of Mr Cyrus Mistry from Tata in 2016 and Mr Vishal Sikka from Infosys in 2017 readily come to one's mind.

Likewise, when the business environment poses fresh challenges, a CEO realizes that having reached her level of incompetence, she could sharpen her saw, refresh her skill set, or start performing under changed circumstances. Or, occasionally, she may press the eject button in her cockpit and glide her way over to greener pastures. A new phase of learning starts. If all goes well, she ends up evolving into a more rounded personality, till the time the next career move becomes either necessary or desirable. This process of evolution can be likened to the journey of a soul through different lives.

Consequent to each shift, as a lioness, she finds ardent followers in the form of deer and monkeys. She also finds obnoxious detractors in the shape of deadly cobras, irrespective of where she works. Only the faces and the names are different.

It dawns upon her that moving on merely owing to a hatred towards the villains in her story does not imply freedom from one of the basic challenges of life—that of handling positives and negatives with equal calmness.

### Hanging the Corporate Boots and Sandals

The professional in question could also discover that she could stick to a single organization for much longer, clawing her way up the corporate ladder. This would indicate that she has built a cocoon around herself in which she finds ample opportunity for learning, personal growth and evolution. She has perhaps reached a level of inner contentment and feels satiated in her comfort zone. She alone is the best judge to chart out her career trajectory. But a day would eventually dawn when she may prefer to hang up her sandals and adjust to a new rhythm in her life and career.

It pays to plan for this new rhythm midway in the career. One of the critical steps which could be taken is to cultivate a hobby which gives one genuine pleasure and relaxation from the hurly-burly of corporate life. Delightful books are at hand. Friends with whom one can share feelings are close by. Learning to play a musical instrument is an option. Drawing, dancing or painting could also be a good antidote to stress. Becoming a member of a different group of people with some common interests comes in handy. So does writing.

**Reasons for Job Hopping**

A rolling stone gathers no moss. The younger lot already takes a jaundiced view of sticking around in an organization beyond a period of one to three years these days. The reasons are many:

1. Unfulfilled need for speedier recognition and advancement.
2. Lack of compatibility with the company culture.
3. Absence of work-life balance, especially when work-from-home is leading to a further blurring of the lines between one's official and personal life.
4. A pink slip, induced by either a pandemic or a change in technology.
5. An obnoxious boss, or a toxic work culture.

There are several advantages of hiring such rolling stones. Their exposure to different operating cultures is better, often resulting in a more flexible approach to things. Their capacity to quickly reset interpersonal relationships is also better. Add to this a richer knowledge of a wider range of markets, and one could have a win-win situation by hiring such professionals.

On the flip side, by hiring such persons, businesses need to remain focused on orienting the new incumbents to their culture. The HR honchos have to keep retraining them.

**Retaining Professionals: A Culture of Trust and Openness**

Paul J. Zak, in his book entitled *Trust Factor: The Science of Creating High-Performance Companies*, highlights the importance of a 'culture of high engagement' in creating great organizations.

He speaks of the 'building blocks of organizational trust' under the acronym OXYTOCIN, which represents Ovation, Expectation, Yield, Transfer, Openness, Caring, Invest and Natural. Simply stated, OXYTOCIN triggers organizational trust, and trust sparks intrinsic motivation, organizational performance and a 'culture of high engagement'.

He shares a touching quote from Bob Chapman, CEO of Barry-Wehmiller, when he shares how Chapman's management team has a 'sacred covenant to treat people well and return them home each day physically and emotionally healthy.' This is a great way to look at a company's responsibility to keep people 'successful and safe', irrespective of their role and location.

**Earning Trust: A Marathon**

Earning trust is not a sprint, but a marathon. A consistent effort is to be made by a leader so others may notice the following traits:

1. A visible streak of genuineness in one's intentions,
2. Capability of providing solutions or doing something worthy, and
3. Dependability for a satisfactory outcome, given the circumstances.

These add to the personal brand equity of a professional.

## Bidding Adieu in Style, Creating Brand Ambassadors!

Let me share a real case where a well-handled separation was used by the company I worked for then, to create a brand ambassador.

A much pampered and popular junior decided to leave the company after a long stint just when he was in fact being considered to take over a key department. Efforts to persuade him to stay put came a cropper. A red-faced bunch of seniors met to discuss what steps could be taken to prevent the person from leaving the company's employment. When all efforts failed, the group decided not to be vindictive. Instead, the exit was facilitated in more ways than one. This gesture left the employee in a highly positive frame of mind. The result is that even today, the channels of communication between the company and the ex-employee remain open and smooth. Whenever the employee needs support in his current assignment, the company is there to back him up. If the company ever gets stuck in tracking down past records, help is just a call away. He even keeps referring any potential employee who he thinks could be hired by the company!

## The Allure of Getting a Brand-new Vehicle!

In his epic poem *Savitri*, Sri Aurobindo, the renowned Indian seer, presents the end of a person's life as a transformative event, a passage, or a door through which one passes towards a greater life. Essentially, the poem recounts the saga of human victory over ignorance and death.

Thus, on the racing tracks of life, death is but a pit stop. One gives up one's creaking old jalopy. In exchange, one gets a shimmering new vehicle. One then zooms off to a newer horizon, the engine firing on all six cylinders. With each pit stop, one evolves further.

The principle of reincarnation mentioned in the *Bhagavad Gita* indirectly captures the way death, a certainty in life—just like the taxes which one must grudgingly bear—can be faced with a smile on one's lips.

# 10

# Bursting the Stress Bubble with Higher Inner Resilience

Managers often get tangled in the complexities of office politics and personal rivalries, much like CEOs carry heavy burdens, but on a more prickly scale. Even small issues like office space or parking allocations can spark envy and gossip, disturbing the fragile harmony among peers. Beneath the calm exterior, feelings of jealousy, ambition and rivalry simmer, making managers fiercely protective of their turf.

Yet, despite their guardedness, managers sometimes let these tensions invade their mental peace, losing sleep over bosses or colleagues who betray their trust. Negative experiences can cloud their judgment and chip away at their confidence. While some may struggle deeply, even contemplating drastic actions, others with stronger resilience shrug off the setbacks, learn from them, and move forward with renewed focus and strength.

Tough bosses routinely rebuke their team members but end up affecting different people differently. Those with a lower self-esteem and a lower inner resilience might even contemplate taking a drastic step under external provocation, in some cases leading even to homicidal thoughts. But those who are wired differently and have a sunnier disposition might just take such occurrences in their stride, shrugging them off, noticing the underlying lessons, and going ahead with the task at hand in a more effective manner.

## Tackling the Virus Called Stress

Pressure is an 'external' stimulus. Stress is what 'we' experience. The level of stress we experience therefore is directly proportional to the pressure we receive. The good news is that stress is inversely proportional to our inner strength and resilience.

A mathematical formulation for stress could qualitatively be along the following lines:

$$S = \frac{[\text{Pressure (External Stimulus)} \times \text{Personality Type} \times \text{Time}]}{[\text{Inner Resilience}]}$$

How does one tackle the hurricane of stress? Building up our inner resilience, practising the 'Art of Creative Dissatisfaction', loosening up and letting go, a habit of forgiveness, a dash of humour, better work-life balance, and meditation can help.

Most of us who have encountered the vagaries of the dreaded coronavirus from 2020 onwards would readily attest to the role inner resilience played in our having survived the pandemic.

## Higher Inner Resilience Is a Stress Buster

A manager with strong inner resilience maintains self-esteem and a balanced view of reality, enabling her to make clear, responsible decisions. She owns her actions without blaming others and approaches failures with honest introspection, avoiding extremes of pride or despair. This mindset helps her respond effectively to challenges and remain objective.

For example, a tech professional facing potential redundancy due to new technologies can either blame circumstances or choose to upskill in areas like AI or blockchain. A resilient manager embraces growth opportunities, adapting to change rather than fearing it, which keeps her career prospects alive and kicking.

Such resilience also reduces stress and anxiety, promoting

better health and happiness. Like a swimmer prepared for rough seas, a resilient manager is ready to face challenges and break through barriers. This inner strength helps her bounce back from setbacks and thrive, driven by positive stress that encourages continual growth.

**The Risk of Sensitivity**

Managers who are sensitive to others' needs do not necessarily make better bosses. Emotions could cloud their judgment, thereby lowering their level of inner resilience. An excess of the milk of human kindness sloshing about in the veins could make them lose their effectiveness as a manager. Stress builds up. Eventually, a burnout gets experienced. Instead, moderation is what the doctor would recommend.

However, when sensitivity gets deployed in tandem with rational thought, as drawn from the company's objectives and policies, they end up being realistically empathic.

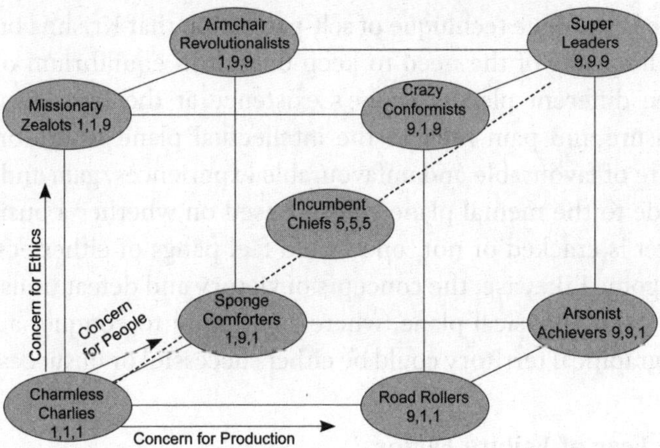


Another way of conveying this delicate balance is by the means of a Blake Mouton Grid, which is built upon two dimensions—Concern for People and Concern for Production. Add to this the third dimension—Concern for Ethics—and one gets somewhat closer to the quality which the *Bhagavad Gita* refers to as *Kshetragya.* In terms of a modified Blake Mouton Grid, the *Gita* is referring here to the 'Super Chiefs', who score high on all three dimensions.

In terms of Maslow's Hierarchy of Needs, one could also call such CEOs and managers as self-actualized ones.

## The *Bhagavad Gita* Offers a Technique of Self-perfection

Lord Krishna explains this beautifully to Arjuna. In Verse 38 of Chapter 2 of the *Bhagavad Gita,* He says:

> सुखदु:खे समे कृत्वा लाभालाभौ जयाजयौ |
> ततो युद्धाय युज्यस्व नैवं पापमवाप्स्यसि || 2.38 ||
>
> *Having attained equanimity in happiness and sorrow, in gain and loss, in victory and defeat, then come out to fight. Thus, you will not incur sin.*

Here is a unique technique of self-perfection that Krishna brings up. It speaks of the need to keep oneself in equilibrium on all three different planes of one's existence at the same time. If pleasure and pain refer to the intellectual plane where one is aware of favourable and unfavourable experiences, gain and loss allude to the mental plane where, based on whether a business target is cracked or not, one would feel pangs of either ecstasy or agony. Likewise, the concepts of victory and defeat transport one to the physical plane, where an attempt to conquer a new geographical territory could be either successful or unsuccessful.

## The Fear of Failure Factor

One of the leading causes of stress is the fear of failure factor. One might have impatient bosses who keep chasing one, forever demanding better and faster results; the kind of souls which are blissfully unaware of what Lord Krishna says here. But those of us who have perfected the art of meeting our boss halfway through would ensure that most of the factors which could lead to a failure are not only highlighted but also acted upon with her support, overt or covert. This way, one ends up making the boss an accomplice to murder, should a failure eventually occur. One may also label this as the 'Art of Reverse Delegation'!

Yet another cause could be the ambition of taking up a voyage to Mars without having the necessary capabilities and resources. In other words, eyeing a lavish buffet spread, allowing greed to dominate prudence, and taking up on one's plate much more than one can chew. This may be resolved by a bout of introspection, which could lead to a better understanding of one's own strengths and weaknesses. Coupled with a realistic leash on one's ambitions and desires, this could lead one to achieve a higher level of excellence.

A good way to burst the stress bubble is surely to develop a higher level of inner resilience. It also helps one to develop an inner connection with one's true Self, as we shall see in Chapter 11.

***(For further thoughts on inner resilience, you may also look up Chapter 16: 'The Attachment-Detachment Conundrum'.)***

# 11

# Resilience and an Inner Connection

## A Composite Lens to View Challenges

A CEO can use a composite lens to analyse challenges from multiple perspectives. The physical lens highlights organizational customs, the intellectual lens weighs outcomes and cost-benefits, the emotional lens considers ethics and humanity, and the spiritual lens focuses on the greater good for society and the environment. When these lenses align, they guide the CEO towards the best possible response to a business challenge.

A powerful example is the 2008 terrorist attack on Mumbai's Taj Mahal Palace Hotel, where employees' quick, empathetic, and well-trained responses reflected harmony across all four lenses—physical, intellectual, emotional and spiritual. This inner balance, or Spiritual Quotient, rooted in resilience, is essential for managers to navigate complex situations effectively and with grace.

In other words, when it comes to understanding the happenings around one, an inner equilibrium is the key facilitator. By attaining this state, a manager can shore up her Spiritual Quotient, of which inner resilience is a critical component.

## Shoring Up Inner Resilience

Sheryl Sandberg, the ex-chief operating officer of Facebook, has this to say about resilience:

> The main thing I learned when I lost my husband was that resilience is not something you're born with, you build

> it. We build it ourselves by knowing we can get through things, and by helping each other get through things we build it in each other. We build it in our companies by having a basic loop where we talk openly about what went wrong. That's one of the things I'm most proud of at Facebook, because for all the challenges we still face, what you don't see is people pointing fingers saying it is someone's fault, and ducking. Instead, we say: 'Ok, how are we going to get better? Why didn't we see [it] coming and what are we not seeing coming now?'

The good news is that it is in our hands to build our resilience. Meditative practices help. The ability and openness to appreciate a deemed adversary's viewpoint also helps. Transcending desires and ego facilitates. Forgiveness assists.

So does a realization that one is acting as per one's own conscience and what one believes to be right. In other words, one is following one's *manav-dharma*, or acting as per one's duty towards humanity and respecting human values. Going a notch higher, if one is always in touch with one's soul, or one's real Self inside, one would be following one's *swa-dharma* or acting as per one's innate sense of righteousness. In a state of that kind, one acquires the attributes of a pure Soul, being the 'knower' of what is happening, and being able to 'see' the same in an objective manner, much as a party of the third part would view the same.

Ignoring people with a negative persona and consciously choosing to remain in the company of some positive thinkers assists.

Wisdom gained from the harsh slings and arrows of life supports us in this endeavour. It follows that introspection helps.

An attitude of 'this too shall pass' helps. In 2020, when coronavirus took *Homo sapiens* by surprise, the initial reaction was a sense of disbelief and shock. Lockdowns of all sizes and shapes made life unimaginably difficult. The livelihoods of millions amongst us got wiped out. Many of us responded by getting into a phase of mental depression. Fear, anxiety, loneliness and helplessness ruled supreme. Quite a few others, aided by benign relatives and friends, were able to take the sweeping changes in their stride by adopting a chin-up attitude.

Gradually, it dawned upon us that the fight against the dreaded virus was never a sprint but a marathon. Reason returned to its throne. Businesses reconfigured their operations suitably. The onset of Industrial Revolution 4.0 picked up pace. Families and individuals learnt to sleep with the enemy, so to say, till the time an apparently effective antidote came up, providing some hope to humanity.

If good times do not last, bad times too have a limited shelf-life!

## Of Micro Resilience

In the field of competitive sports, coaches teach their athletes quick, efficient ways to recover even as they perform on the field. Small adjustments in our daily routines—food, drink, rest, movement and even our thought patterns—can effectively fight the forces that sap our limited resources. By making such micro changes, our brains could quickly get back to firing on all their six cylinders, and our energy levels could see a boost. We can then cope with almost any challenge, pressure or crisis, irrespective of its hue, size or shape. A rhinoceros, ferociously charging at us, could, after noticing the cold and defiant look in our eyes, simply beat a hasty retreat.

## The Technique of Reverse Delegation

Yet another technique advised by Lord Krishna in the *Bhagavad Gita* is that of reverse delegation; in other words, the art of passing the buck to someone higher up!

मयि सर्वाणि कर्माणि संन्यस्याध्यात्मचेतसा |
निराशीर्निर्ममो भूत्वा युध्यस्व विगतज्वर: || 3.30 ||

*Dedicating all actions to Me with a mind fixed in faith on Me, free from expectation and sense of mine (ownership), fight, delivered from fever.*

The technique suggested here is very practical and suited to CEOs and managers of all kinds, irrespective of their state of evolution.

One's desires may still be strong in the mind, attachment to worldly objects may still be strong, the intellect may also not yet be free from confusion and delusion, and the ego may still be governing one's actions. However, surrendering all actions to a superior power with faith and sincerity has several advantages. It calms the mind, intellect and ego, and propels an individual on a natural path of evolution. Perhaps, religion and faith gained popularity owing to this feature of human psychology.

We return to this proposition in Chapter 30, entitled 'The Option of Rewiring Oneself'.

## An Inner Connection to Handle Myriad Challenges with Aplomb

CEOs face constant pressure from customers, employees, shareholders, regulators, and more, making it tough to stay balanced. Only those with nerves of steel and deep inner resilience, often supported by a strong inner connection, can keep performing at their best. Without these qualities, some may even face severe mental health struggles, overwhelmed by debt, business failures or intense life challenges.

For such leaders, having a close, supportive circle and professional counseling can be lifesaving. Positivity, regular breaks with loved ones, a strong team and the belief that tough times will pass help maintain their spirit. Staying connected to one's emotions and maintaining inner awareness is the key to navigating these storms with strength and hope.

In an indirect manner, the *Bhagavad Gita* touches upon the importance of an inner connection for business leaders. It holds that wise are those who enjoy tranquillity and calmness within themselves. Their inner being is in harmony with their outer being. Their decision-making is based on a balanced, well-considered and holistic view of the facts of the case. They do not manage crises in business with knee-jerk reactions. They deal with people according to their respective natures. Impartial they are. Detached they are. Compassionate they happen to be, but never at the cost of their innate wisdom and truth. And never do they compromise on their core values.

# 12

# From an 'I and Me' Approach to a 'We and Us' One

Members of the tribe of managers who believe in the 'I and Me' approach have swollen minds and shallow hearts. Humility is a trait which is sorely missing from their dictionary. They live in a virtual reality, surfing atop the turbulent waves of life believing they remain in total control of things. They think that they punch all the right buttons in their careers. Successes are attributed to their own actions and initiatives. Failures get attributed to external circumstances, to other people, or to the business environment in general.

In terms of an upgraded Blake Mouton Grid (discussed in Chapter 10: 'Bursting the Stress Bubble with Higher Inner Resilience'), they have a propensity to evolve into a leader for whom results alone count. Concern for People gets relegated to the background. Concern for Ethics gets swept under the carpet and conveniently forgotten. In other words, they become CEOs who could be safely classified as road rollers.

## Inclusive Leadership

A 2016 Deloitte study ('The six signature traits of inclusive leadership') indicated that the traits that define Inclusive Leadership are commitment, courage, cognisance of bias, curiosity, cultural intelligence, and collaboration.

Recognizing the contribution of team members is a key factor which helps organizations to scale better heights. It is the starting point of building trust.

To put it simply, leaders who are agile, open-minded in

NEW
MARKETS
NO
ENTRY

embracing change, making choices which balance commercial considerations with the needs of the society at large, and are responsive to the needs of people, are slated to do well. Surely, such leaders can only be working with a 'We and Us' approach to decision-making.

Now think of a bank CEO who has risen through the ranks to break the proverbial glass ceiling. Hard work, an uncanny ability to manage people and resolve conflicts, some tough calls in business, and support from the top have brought her to the helm of affairs. When at the pinnacle of success, she is surrounded by a team of yes-persons, backed by a malleable board of directors, and applauded by the media. Somehow, a sense of invincibility has crept in. She starts believing that she is an all-powerful and accomplished person and has the freedom to do what she wants. What she does not realize is the role destiny has also played in her career and life. On a not-so-fine day, it transpires that sometime in the past, a standard process meant to be strictly followed had been compromized. Eventually, fate sneaks up from the back and strikes her with a lead pipe. A fall from grace comes about. A realization dawns that she had perhaps made the folly of ascribing all her achievements to her personal capabilities alone. In other words, she had been following an 'I and Me' approach, eventually leading to her downfall.

### The Perils of an 'I and Me' Approach: How Intel Came to Be

Eight upcoming scientists, including Robert Noyce, Gordon Moore and Andy Grove, walked out of Shockley Transistor Laboratories, owned by William Shockley, who had previously won the 1956 Nobel Prize in Physics for his work on transistors.

The provocation for 'the traitorous eight'—as referred to by Shockley—to part company with him was the fact that the latter was as brilliant a scientist as he was a poor leader. He is reported to have been pig-headed in many matters, treating his team members with scant regard. He often behaved as if the eight were trying to undermine him. Surely, doping non-electrical conducting materials with germanium and silicon, thus paving the way for the transistor revolution and the chip revolution, was easier for him than keeping his team members charged-up by being a collaborative and humble leader.

When Shockley was ousted from his own company, he joined Stanford as a faculty member. In 1989, he died of prostate cancer, estranged from all his relatives and friends. His children were reported to have learnt of his death through newspapers.

On the other hand, the group of eight who had left him went on to set up Fairchild Conductors and, subsequently, Intel Corporation. Perhaps they made a fortunate transition from an 'I and Me' approach to a 'We and Us' one.

## The 'We and Us' Approach to Decision Making

Life is much like river rafting, where one needs to make quick choices while negotiating the rapids. The team on-board the raft, when working in unison, makes the mission a success.

While following a 'We and Us' approach, one may choose to surrender to a higher power. Externally, the higher power could either be a management senior who is a friend, philosopher and guide, or the values of the organization one happens to be associated with. If one is a believer, one could repose one's trust in a superior power, like one's favourite deity. This aspect has been dealt with in detail in Chapter 12 of the *Bhagavad Gita.*

However, when we surrender in this manner, with faith and sincerity, we do not surrender to any external entity. Essentially, it is one's false self (ego) that surrenders to one's true self—one's innermost reality. This is a sure-shot method of taming the ego.

Essentially, the transformation takes place within oneself. The outcome is that a CEO would then perform her actions without having any petty considerations in mind, like browbeating a colleague, stepping on the toes of someone else or claiming undue credit for work done by others.

In the *Bhagavad Gita*, Lord Krishna exhorts us to do precisely this. He cites three kinds of personality traits, or *gunas*. He asks Arjuna to rise above these and be stationed in the self only.

> त्रैगुण्यविषया वेदा निस्त्रैगुण्यो भवार्जुन |
> निर्द्वन्द्वो नित्यसत्वस्थो निर्योगक्षेम आत्मवान् || 2.45 ||
>
> *The Vedas' concern is with the three gunas. Be without the three gunas, O Arjuna, without the pairs of opposites, ever established in purity, without possessions, possessed of the Self.*

All of us have these three gunas in varying proportions—sattvic (benign goodness), *rajasic* (action-oriented) and *tamasic* (inaction, lethargy, procrastination). In different settings, even the proportions comprising a personality might be somewhat different. A devil in the office could be a loving father at home. Someone who champions the cause of women's empowerment in public could be terrorizing his wife at home.

The bouquets and brickbats hurled at one by life invariably represent opposites that one faces in life—success and failure, joys and sorrows, heat and cold, health and disease, and the like. A manager would typically face many a tough choice to be made in her career—that of chugging along in an assignment which pays well but is not close to her heart, or calling it quits, finding her true calling and pursuing her passion in life; an important meeting at office versus annual day celebrations at her only child's school at the same time; whether or not to show the door to a long-serving cashier who has recently been found having his hand in the till; and the like.

What Lord Krishna is suggesting here is for one to be trans-gunas. This way, one has a constant sense of awareness of one's pure divine nature. The ego becomes pure and free of anxieties which plague one. One attains a balanced and harmonious state in all of one's activities, whether materialistic or spiritual, thereby leading to true happiness within, irrespective of whether one fails or succeeds in one's efforts. He goes on to exhort one to enjoy the bliss of having done a job well, to the best of one's ability.

# 13

# The Perils of Attachment

When owners and founders of businesses hire CEOs, they hope for an attitude of quiet and respectful deference towards themselves, sans dissidence of any kind. Often, their attachment to the business surpasses all other considerations. Thus, fissures between the two power centres soon start popping up. If some of the actions of a CEO are leading to a compromize on the basic values of the business, like in the case of the Tatas and Cyrus Mistry, or Infosys and Vishal Sikka, it is understandable. But if the gaps have arisen due to the way operations are being handled, it just shows that the owner or founder is not willing to let go.

Consider the case of Jet Airways which shut its operations in April 2019 after having been the key player in the Indian airspace for over 25 years. The unwillingness on the part of the promoter family to let go of its control over the business made the airlines eventually crash land. Professionals were hired in top key positions, but the art of delegation was apparently given short shrift.

In family-owned businesses, the younger generation is often raring to go. Many a scion keeps wondering when the elder owner would hang his corporate boots or sandals, so they could have a free hand to nudge the enterprise towards newer markets, adopting the latest technologies sprouting in the era of the Industrial Revolution 4.0. But for most of the elderly owners, it is a tough challenge to give up control. Like the proverbial man who keeps clinging to a tree but blames the tree for not allowing him to let go, they refuse to fade away gracefully into the sunset. During the period of transition, chaos and confusion

"Grandpa, when do you plan to go on that luxury cruise? "

reigns. Hapless employees continue to suffer silently, caught as they are between the divergent thought processes of the two generations.

The war depicted in the epic Mahabharata, of which the *Bhagavad Gita* is an integral part, came about only because King Dhritarashtra could not overcome his attachment to either the throne or his son, Duryodhana. The outcome was the death of all his 100 sons, loss of prestige and kingdom, and of course, social and economic misery of the multitudes who had earlier thrived during his reign.

Those of you who have come across the works of Kahlil Gibran, the Lebanese-American luminary, might recall his poem 'On the Children' which captures the futility of being attached to one's children thus:

> Your children are not your children. They are the sons and daughters of Life's longing for itself. They come through you but not from you, And though they are with you, yet they belong not to you...

**Different Hues of Attachment**

Attachment is an intoxicant which, when taken in excessive doses, leads to perilous outcomes. When consumed without a moderating dose of detachment, it could prove to be a disastrous tissue restorative, a concoction which is surely injurious to the efficiency and effectiveness of a manager.

Attachment with a Lion King could leave a sheep ending up as its prey. If the Lion King himself feels attached to a wily Finance-Fox and ends up promoting him as a CEO, the organization may soon start running only on Standard Operating Procedures, neglecting customer service and employee relationships. A Production-Bovine who is attached to the technology in use on the shop floor would take a jaundiced view of a more efficient technology being planned to be introduced by the management.

A sprightly Operations-Reindeer might start believing that the whole organization would collapse if he were to proceed on leave. A Human-Resources-Canine may start hiring people only from his own ethnic background, resulting in a lack of diversity in the organization. Separations with non-performing employees do not get handled well, impacting down-sizing initiatives of the management.

Often, attachment to a person leads to complications. Those who do not deserve a raise might even end up getting a promotion, impacting employee morale adversely. Those who are competent could get sidelined, increasing the chances of their seeking better prospects elsewhere. Ultimately, the organization suffers. Undue attachment to a senior could gradually transform a junior into a seasoned yes-person. If ever the senior's career graph takes a hit, the one hanging on to his coattails would also suffer.

Likewise, when one gets attached to an experience, whether positive or negative, one's guardian angels go into a state of hibernation. In such cases, disaster often lurks around the corner. A promotion could go to one's head, leading to aberrant behaviour, with negative results quick to follow. Spectacular success in a project could lead to complacency. On the flip side, a sharp public rebuke from someone senior could make one withdraw into an emotional shell, thereby impacting one's performance. One could decide to play the victim card for some time and continue to seek solace from those who are in no way capable of helping. It does not bring about the desired results.

## Attachment and Resistance to Change

In other words, attachment often leads to resistance to change. One's sense of objectivity gets compromised. A tendency to remain in one's comfort zone rules the roost. Innovation takes a back seat. Procrastination kicks in. Delegation gets dumped. Distortions start popping up. Conflicts and dilemmas do not get resolved in an unbiased manner. Relationships with key stakeholders turn sour. Signals of an imminent shift in customer tastes and preferences start getting neglected. Market share starts shrinking. Advances in technology do not get absorbed in the organizational processes. Business takes a hit. Brand equity nosedives. The existence of a business vertical itself may come under a cloud.

Elsewhere, we have already touched upon the way such market leaders as Kodak and Nokia had suffered in the past. Likewise, organizations which resist absorbing the newer technologies coming up in Industrial Revolution 4.0 could face a serious threat of either scaling down or getting completely wiped out in the times to come.

## The Art of Detached Attachment

All this is not to say that attachment is something which can be completely avoided. The concept of attachment is central to organizational life. Attachment is essentially an enduring emotional bond between people, events and belief systems. Experts have studied the nature, development, maintenance and dissolution of this emotional bond through the lens of Attachment Theory, providing an insightful perspective in the understanding of human relationships. The dynamics of leadership are surely impacted by it. So is the concept of trust, mentoring and employer-employee relationships. Employees get motivated and become proactive when under the spell of attachment. It impacts ethical behaviour in a significant manner.

If the Western models of Attachment touch upon its gravitational pull and inevitability, Lord Krishna presents an Eastern template of Detachment. He shows one the possibility of hopping onto a spaceship that is designed to overcome the gravitational pull of the earthly forces of attachment, thereby enabling one to foray into interstellar space and enjoy the captivating beauty of at least a fraction of the vast universe.

कर्मण्येवाधिकारस्ते मा फलेषु कदाचन |
मा कर्मफलहेतुर्भूर्मा ते सङ्गोऽस्त्वकर्मणि || 2.47 ||

*You have a right to perform your prescribed duties, but you are not entitled to the fruits of your actions. Never consider yourself to be the cause of the results of your activities, nor be attached to inaction.*

To put it simply, one is free to do any action (karma), but one does not exercize any power on the resultant fruits, which could be either sweet or bitter, which one may like or dislike. Lord Krishna cautions a professional to never consider herself as the cause or the result of her actions. This way, success does not boost her ego; nor does failure lead her to despondency. He also rules out an attachment to inaction. We explore the cause-and-effect relationship between actions and results in detail in Chapter 32: 'The Operating System of Karma'.

However, can a target be cracked unless the team working on it is truly attached to it? But the sense of attachment need not cloud the team's judgment and make it blind to other options which might result in the target being achieved more effectively and efficiently. Similarly, a leader would do well to give up his likes and dislikes for individual team members and handle all impartially, thereby highlighting the need to remain detached.

'The will to win, the desire to succeed, the urge to reach your full potential...these are the keys that will unlock the door to personal excellence,' said Confucius.

What is desirable is a healthy combination of Attachment and Detachment. Some may allude to it as the 'Art of Detached Attachment'!

We now proceed to examine the concept of detachment in Chapters 14, 15 and 16, which follow.

# 14

# The Perks of Practising Detachment

On a lighter note, one needs to be wary of managements which exhort one to follow the much-misunderstood principle of detachment expounded in the *Bhagavad Gita*. They would have one believe that one should continue to slog all year long but would do well not to expect that elusive overdue promotion. One can then either grin and bear it or take prompt action through proper channels to get oneself detached from the company and move on to greener pastures elsewhere!

**Management by Loftier Objectives**

In real life, is it really possible for one to be detached from the fruits of one's actions? In a business scenario, when a manager is part of an organization, she is expected to deliver results. Efforts put in by her do not count; results alone do. If so, one might well wonder as to how one can remain detached from the outcome. Would it not be going against the philosophy of Management by Objectives?

Moreover, does it not help to be attached to the goal one has set out to achieve? Does success not inspire one to do better? Would a truly detached life not be devoid of its fun and excitement, its ups and downs? Is this approach workable?

These are but some of the dilemmas which the *Bhagavad Gita* solves for a professional. It counsels one not to take actions which are at variance with what is sought to be achieved. It does not necessarily question the objectives. It exhorts us to set our sights higher—to link the goal to the overall good and not merely to quarterly guidelines and such other mundane

"This year, your performance has been excellent. However, the Board of Directors expect you to practice detachment and not keep asking for either a raise or a promotion. Just keep up the good work!"

considerations. In other words, it persuades us to look at the broader picture and act accordingly, suggesting that one should manage by loftier objectives.

A sense of detachment from the immediate goal helps one in different ways. One, as more feedback comes in, there is lesser resistance to tweak the goal a wee bit. Two, by treating the overall good as a pole star, one is bound to navigate the choppy waters of a hostile business environment more effectively. Three, the means come under a sharper focus. Means could be not only material but also psychological, like one's underlying assumptions, prejudices and attitudes. Four, it is easier to align personal goals with those of the organization; likewise, to align the goals of an organization with what works better for society.

When Azim Premji decides to pledge his personal wealth for social causes, or when Tata Trusts start work on distributing iron-fortified salt in a state where women happen to be anaemic, the purpose for which businesses exist gets widened. When the hero of the movie *Swades* (2004, Director: Ashutosh Gowarikar) decides to chuck a promising career with NASA and return to serve his country, he is looking at the bigger picture selflessly.

This is how the *Bhagavad Gita* explains this state of mind:

दूरेण ह्यवरं कर्म बुद्धियोगाद्धनञ्जय |
बुद्धौ शरणमन्विच्छ कृपणा: फलहेतव: || 2.49 ||

*Far inferior to the Yoga of intellect, indeed, is action, O winner of wealth. Take refuge in the intellect. Pitiful are those who live for the fruits.*

Earlier, in Chapter 2, entitled 'Knowledge, Skills, and Attitudes', we had come across verse 2.48 which eulogizes the yoga of the intellect, implying the evenness and equanimity of mind. In the realm of activity, intellect is supreme. However, when one is established in yoga—union with one's true Self—the intellect also attains the divine perspective and the activity carried out by it becomes natural, spontaneous, divine and free from attachment. Lord Krishna takes the argument a little further here, opining that action is inferior to intellect, provided one has achieved an inner unity at that level.

The advice to Arjuna here is to move higher in his internal motivation towards work. Lord Krishna declares that those who work with the motivation of self-enjoyment are miserly. Those who are detached from the fruits and dedicate their work to a higher cause are superior. And those who offer the fruits to God are truly stationed in benign knowledge, backed by a set of healthy attitudes.

As a leader evolves to higher levels of consciousness, she is apt to shed the desire to enjoy the fruits of work and move in the direction of service. In September 2019, on his fifty-fifth birthday, Jack Ma, founder of the e-commerce giant Alibaba, stepped down as executive chairman, to focus on philanthropy and education. Bill Gates, having renounced his position at Microsoft Corporation in 2014, now deploys his energy and time in the service of society.

Similarly, after having had his fill of power and position as the president of the USA, Bill Clinton now preaches the glories of service to humankind and has even written a book on the topic, *Giving: How Each of Us Can Change the World.*

Their engagement with service is praiseworthy, but it might not necessarily measure up to the benchmark of selflessness set by the *Bhagavad Gita.* Philanthropists may take such actions to build their networks globally and to acquire some more fame.

One of the popular Hindi adages raises a pertinent question:

पूत कपूत तो का धन संचय,
पूत सपूत तो का धन संचय?

*Why accumulate wealth for an unworthy son; why accumulate wealth for a worthy son? An unworthy son would soon fritter it away, whereas a worthy one would create the wealth of his own.*

In India, Living-My-Promise (LMP), a small community of

like-minded Good Samaritans, is already spreading the cause of philanthropy. It aims to get upper-middle-class Indians with a net worth of more than INR one crore to promise to donate a minimum 50 per cent of their wealth to charity. The group is driven to bring to the mainstream the practice of sharing wealth, not just giving leftovers.

## The False Notion that One Is the 'Actor' or the 'Doer'

The risk here is that one may start entertaining a false notion that one is the 'actor' or the 'doer'. Thereby arises one's anxiety for success and a burning attachment to the result of one's actions. The 'doer', when he fails at something and does not find a hapless scapegoat upon whom the blame can be off-loaded, may go on to lose self-confidence and even start hating himself.

Managers could readily be held to be of three kinds. There are those who happen to be politicians at heart and who believe in the 'would' scenario. They could go on to make great marketing honchos. Then there are those who are philosophers at heart who repose their faith in a 'should' scenario. They are cut out for a great career in accounting, auditing and systems design. And then there are those who do their best, given the circumstances and constraints they face while executing a decision. These are the 'could' kind, who come closest to the concept of detachment. Success does not buoy their spirits unnecessarily. Failure does not depress them easily. Seldom would they be seen in a state of intellectual impotency.

## Of Detachment, Creativity and Innovation

What fuels mighty achievements and the unique creations of artists like Vincent van Gogh or Michelangelo? Could they have produced their masterpieces if they were worried about market value or recognition? Newton, too, wasn't distracted by past or future when the apple fell—otherwise, he might have missed discovering gravity. Similarly, a Silicon Valley innovator's best ideas come from a focused, present-minded state conducive to creativity.

Beneath every inspired work lies the soul's quest for bliss through doing something unique with effort and detachment. Living fully in the present moment helps one embrace an inspired life. Creativity flows like a form of meditation, where the creator, universe and surroundings align in harmony—a state of 'Inspired Self-forgetfulness' or 'Detached Attachment'. Beyond boosting creativity, detachment brings many other benefits, which we shall explore in the following chapters.

*(For the role of detachment in (i) anger management, please see Chapter 24,and (ii) managing office politics, please see Chapter 26.)*

# 15

# Detachment: The Art of Living in the Present

The *Bhagavad Gita* teaches that a CEO should avoid worrying about the rewards of her actions or obsessing over past events, as both distract from the present moment. Instead, she should focus on doing her best now, keeping stakeholders informed, and acting with virtuous righteousness. This mindset frees her from mental burdens, allowing her to find joy in the work itself, which becomes its own reward. Even amid chaos, this detached perspective helps maintain calm, treating challenges like passing clouds rather than sources of stress.

Who is this witness? It is not the mind. The mind is incapable of witnessing. Lord Krishna says that one's soul is *the* witness. If the CEO assumes a witness-like stance—witnessing her own thoughts, likes, dislikes, actions and intentions—she is in resonance with her inner Self. This has the potential to bring about harmony between her thoughts, her words, and her actions, thereby making her an inwardly happier and outwardly successful professional.

## Management: The Art of the Possible

When striving to achieve a goal, a manager who practises detachment works effectively regardless of favourable or adverse circumstances. She does not get swayed by short-term pressures, personal biases, or setbacks, nor does she succumb to self-pity. This balanced approach helps her keep the organization's overall good in focus, making sound decisions without being clouded by emotions.

In situations like organizational downsizing, the CEO and human resources head must handle transitions with fairness and transparency. Competent employees may be reassigned, while others receive assistance or severance packages. A detached approach, free from personal emotions or prejudices, ensures the process is handled smoothly, enhancing the company's brand and creating goodwill even among those who are compelled to leave.

Likewise, detachment is crucial for leaders across functions—whether a chief marketing officer launching a new brand, a chief finance officer recommending audit changes, or a production manager adopting new technology. It enables them to embrace change without clinging to old ways. Even in delegation and conflict resolution, detachment helps managers avoid micromanagement, remain impartial, and maintain harmony, ultimately benefiting both their teams and the organization.

*(We delve into this aspect in further detail in Chapter 25, 'Being a Gallant Knight When Conflicts Abound', and in Chapter 26, 'Stem Cell Therapy for Office Politics'.)*

## Achieving Excellence in Execution and Living a Free Life!

The *Bhagavad Gita* tells us that by practising the art of detachment, one learns to live in the present moment, neither fuming about what one did in the past nor anxious about what the morrow might bring. It is this skill which is alluded to as yoga.

बुद्धियुक्तो जहातीह उभे सुकृतदुष्कृते |
तस्माद्योगाय युज्यस्व योग: कर्मसु कौशलम् || 2.50 ||

*He whose intellect is united casts off both good and bad actions here. Therefore, take recourse to Yoga. Yoga is skill in actions.*

It is not difficult to appreciate that a sense of detachment helps professionals in many ways—to remain objective, to retain a sense of balance, to resolve conflicts in a bipartisan manner, to embrace change with lesser resistance, to handle adverse situations better and to remain committed to the overall good of the organization and the society.

At a personal level, a sense of detachment assists one in not only achieving better excellence in execution but also in keeping oneself out of any comfort zone. To keep learning newer skills. To look for exciting assignments even when one is happy with the present job because the change would enable one to grow faster professionally. By overcoming desires and winning over anger, one can forgive oneself as well as others and lead a more peaceful existence.

***(We return to the virtues of living in the present in the following chapters as well: 17, 22 and 30.)***

# 16

# The Attachment-Detachment Conundrum

Much like a proficient swimmer participating in a competition, a smart CEO needs to operate in two diametrically opposite styles at the same time—one of attachment and another of detachment. She needs to be an enthusiastic participant in the operations and swim along with the current. Often, she also needs to sit back on the banks of the river, keenly observe the direction in which she is headed and make a detached and objective assessment of the situation. There is thus an inherent duality embedded in her role. Her role as a passionate participant must always embrace that of the intellectual spectator. The 'who' and 'why' of her concerns should constantly enfold the 'what' and 'how' of her methods.

With maturity, a person gains the ability to detach from passionate participation in the operations and also do a pitiless analysis of the overall contours and working of the system. Successful CEOs know that after all the analysis is done, they will still need to throw themselves back into the mix. One may call this art a hybrid style of functioning.

## Detachment in Action

A sense of detachment, as taught in the *Bhagavad Gita*, doesn't mean losing focus on goals or adopting a defeatist mindset. Instead, it is about maintaining balance in the face of both success and failure. Wise leaders stay humble after victories, remembering key success factors for future use, and when failures strike, they take responsibility, learn from feedback, and bounce back stronger. This balanced detachment not only sharpens objectivity but also boosts productivity, enabling leaders to keep moving forward with renewed energy.

Peter Drucker exemplified this approach through his critical yet fair guidance to top CEOs, maintaining a professional distance that allowed him to offer timeless wisdom without attachment. Similarly, NASA's Apollo astronauts demonstrated remarkable resilience and calm despite tragic setbacks, driven by an unwavering commitment to their mission. The fact that they lost several of their colleagues in space mishaps does not deter them from continuing to participate in our space explorations, providing invaluable inputs to our scientists and technocrats. Their tenacity continues to inspire humanity's ongoing exploration of space, proving that detachment fuels perseverance and progress even in the face of adversity.

## Trusteeship: Yet Another Facet of Detachment

When business owners willingly cede control over the enterprises set up and nurtured by them for decades, they reveal a streak of detachment lurking within their bosoms. Likewise, when they form charitable trusts which get a major share of the profits earned from operations, they not only do so due to tax avoidance considerations. They then also endorse the concept of trusteeship, yet another manifestation of the spirit of detachment.

## Inner Resilience and Equanimity

Professionals need to know not only what is to be done, but also how it must be done. Lord Krishna does not fail them. He recommends an 'evenness of mind', the tranquillity of inner composure in handling all the pairs of opposites in their careers and lives—success and failure, praise and reprimand, hiring and firing, sprees of expansion and down-sizing, products and services which are at opposite ends of their life cycles, mergers and demergers, favourable and unfavourable circumstances, and the like. A jaunty sangfroid, so to say. This, indeed, is held to be the real yoga.

In the process, we need to give up our false expectations, wrong imaginations, daydreams about the fruits of our actions, anxieties for results, resistance to change and fears about future events which are still in the womb of the universal force called Time.

## Of Impulse and Intuition

The trick lies in getting rid of unnecessary desires and in controlling our egos. Most of us who do not realize this fact end up being driven by our impulses. We could end up splurging our hard-earned money on things which we do not really need. Those of us who happen to be hot-tempered find it difficult to resist an impulse to get angry.

However, intuition is a quiet knowing from the silent mind. Unlike sudden hunches which sound like very bright ideas one day and fade away over time, intuition has a much longer shelf-life. It arises from a deeper awareness of pure consciousness and not from the relatively shallow level of our active thinking mind. Meditation is a good route for developing insight and intuition.

## The Traits of a Super Leader

Hers is a balanced personality, free of unreasonable desires which pose the danger of her losing sight of her sense of righteousness. She does not have a binding attachment to her emotions. Nor does she have a jealous preference for her pet ideas or her pet people. She scoffs at any signs of nepotism. She encourages her team members to be nay-sayers, so voices of dissent can be heard and judiciously dealt with. She radiates positivity all around her. She is committed to the organization's goals and looks after her team members much like a lioness would protect her cubs.

Such a person of steady wisdom is described in the *Bhagavad Gita* as a *Sthita-Prajna*. Consider the following:

दु:खेष्वनुद्विग्नमना: सुखेषु विगतस्पृह: |
वीतरागभयक्रोध: स्थितधीर्मुनिरुच्यते || 2.56 ||

*He whose mind is unperturbed amid sorrows; who among pleasures is free from longing; from whom attachment, fear and anger have departed; he is said to be a sage of steady intellect.*

Two concerns may arise here. One, could there really be persons who could be held to have all these qualities? Two, in real life, is it possible for one to be free of one's basket of desires and one's ego?

In his book *Beyond the Last Blue Mountain*, R.M. Lala quotes the case of Jamsetji Tata, the founder of the Tata group. It was he who gave the group a unique position in India. In his later years, he did not ask 'What enterprise is the most profitable?' but, 'What does the nation need?' Since the answer in his times was steel, hydroelectric power or an institute of science, he made his best efforts to fulfil that need.

He is reported to have once said something very basic:

> We do not claim to be more unselfish, more generous, or more philanthropic than other people. But we think we started on sound and straightforward business principles, considering the interests of the shareholders our own, and the health and welfare of the employees the sure foundation of our prosperity.

Alfred Sloan is reported to have once remarked, 'What is good for General Motors is good for America.' J.R.D. Tata always thought the other way around. 'What is good for India is good for Tatas.'

Theirs is only one example of a business house which is clear in its goals and in its priorities. Godrej is yet another business house which uses a spiritual paradigm to govern its operations. Ardeshir Godrej started his career as a lawyer but left it after realizing that a client's success in a case is often linked to a twisting of the truth. His next endeavour was to make surgical instruments. But when the customer insisted on marketing these under a 'foreign' brand name, he did not pursue the idea further.

Despite these reverses, he maintained his equipoise. Around the year 1897, he ventured into locks without springs. The company gradually made a name for itself in the world-class security gadgets market. He also succeeded in producing stable toilet soaps from vegetable oils instead of animal fats. The rest, as one would say, is history.

Both groups keep following a people-centric approach to their business decisions. Like Asian Paints, Hindustan Unilever, Infosys, Johnson & Johnson, Mahindra, Eicher, and many others, they keep shielding their staff from major business upheavals, like the coronavirus which surfaced during 2020. Such organizations surely earn brownie points in respect of enjoying employee goodwill.

### Fine-tuning Desires and Egos

Getting rid of desires and ego is no cakewalk. A CEO may introspect and fine-tune her desires, so they are aligned with the values of the organization she works for. In the process, her personal desires take a back seat. Likewise, getting rid of one's ego completely has a flip side. One could end up becoming a doormat and getting taken advantage of by all and sundry. Arguably, her wisdom and intuition can help her retain her individuality even while letting go of her ego. Ask any CEO who has ever worked in a single-owner-driven company, and she would attest to the basic principle of leaving the ego at the office gate itself!

Professionals who remain undistracted by transient

entrapments can be rational and calm. They are steadfast in reaching their goals and go on to make successful business leaders.

*(For inner resilience, please see Chapter 10: 'Bursting the Stress Bubble with Higher Inner Resilience'; for ego, please see Chapter 21: 'Ego: A Serpent or a Saviour?'; for role of detachment in profit-sharing, please see Chapter 28: 'Profit Is Not a Dirty Word!'.)*

## 17

# Some Secrets of Happiness

The *Bhagavad Gita* is of the view that the way to happiness is through detachment. This, when practised, leads to freedom from desires, enabling one to control one's anger. In turn, one avoids delusion and the resultant loss of memory. This way, one avoids loss in discrimination and eventual ruination.

ध्यायतो विषयान्पुंस: सङ्गस्तेषूपजायते |
सङ्गात्सञ्जायते काम: कामात्क्रोधोऽभिजायते || 2.62 ||

क्रोधाद्भवति सम्मोह: सम्मोहात्स्मृतिविभ्रम: |
स्मृतिभ्रंशाद् बुद्धिनाशो बुद्धिनाशात्प्रणश्यति || 2.63 ||

*Pondering on the objects (of the senses) a man develops attachment for them; from attachment springs up desire; desire gives rise to anger. From anger arises delusion, from delusion distortion of memory; from distortion of memory, destruction of intellect; through destruction of intellect, he perishes.*

Nothing succeeds like a success, and nothing fails like a failure. Analysing the underlying causes of a business failure often leads one to conclude that the proposition above is not a hypothetical one.

Consider the case of Uber, the San Francisco-based company which has been trying to rehabilitate its image after a torrent of scandals in 2017 turned customers away. The turmoil resulted in the ouster of founder and then-Chief Executive Travis Kalanick and the acknowledgement that the company had developed a culture of harassment. When in its expansionist mode, the company met its competitors head-on, did not prioritize regulatory compliance and even made light of harassment of clueless passengers at the hands of undisciplined drivers, including a case of rape in India. The company also faced a severe dent in its reputation and revenues due to an investigation into a software tool and a data security breach affecting the information of millions of users which it chose not to declare for more than a year.

Finances and company culture were not the only problems Uber faced then. The company also needed to manage its relationships with drivers and customers. When Dara Khosrowshahi took over as the CEO in 2017, his main task was to clean up the image of a company that had become one of the most despised in the country, in part due to revelations about Uber's corporate culture. He redefined the core values of the company to focus on 'customer obsession'. His key message has been: 'We do the right thing. Period.' Under his stewardship, the company's gross revenue had shot up to USD 37.281 billion in 2023.

**Looking the Problem in the Eye**

When the *Bhagavad Gita* alludes to anger, it covers this emotion in all its negative hues, be it frustration, resentment, aversion, despondency, feelings of revenge, and so on. Essentially, anger deludes the mind by distorting one's perspective.

One way to overcome anger and be happy is to look one's opponent in the eye and make the party of the other part blink first. A charging hippopotamus, when looked in the eye by a white hunter in the wild forest, often decides to beat a hasty retreat, having decided not to risk facing the wrath of the high-bore rifle it notices in the hunter's hands.

A case in point is that of Nirma which took on the might of Hindustan Unilever in the Indian detergent market in the 1980s. Surf, a popular high-class branded detergent from the latter had a monopoly in the market till the year 1987, when a low-cost detergent Nirma came about. Targeted at the lower-income group, it soon started eating into the market share of Surf. The multinational responded by launching a new brand Wheel at a competitive price point. The new brand slowly grabbed a healthy market share. Eventually, the customers benefited.

This is how His Highness the Dalai Lama explains the underlying logic in his book *The Art of Happiness*:

> In our daily lives problems are bound to arise. The biggest problems in our lives are the ones that we inevitably have to face, like old age, illness, and death. Trying to avoid our problems or simply not thinking about them may provide temporary relief, but I think that there is a better approach.
>
> If you directly confront your suffering, you will be in a better position to appreciate the depth and nature of the problem. If you are in a battle, as long as you remain ignorant of the status and combat capability of your enemy, you will be totally unprepared and paralyzed by fear.
>
> However, if you know the fighting capability of your opponents, what sort of weapons they have and so on, then you're in a much better position when you engage in war. In the same way, if you confront your problems rather than avoid them, you will be in a better position to deal with them.

In Robin S. Sharma's famous book *The Monk Who Sold His Ferrari*, Julian says that goals and dreams for the future are very essential elements in every truly successful life. But he advises never to put off happiness for the sake of achievement; never to put off the things that are important for your well-being and satisfaction to a later time. 'Today is the day to live fully...never put off living!' he says. In other words, control your senses and enjoy a peaceful life.

The *Bhagavad Gita* reinforces this message as follows:

रागद्वेषवियुक्तैस्तु विषयानिन्द्रियैश्चरन् |
आत्मवश्यैर्विधेयात्मा प्रसादमधिगच्छति ||2.64 ||

*But one who controls the mind, and is free from attachment and aversion, even while using the objects of the senses, attains peace.*

यदा हि नेन्द्रियार्थेषु न कर्मस्वनुषज्जते |
सर्वसङ्कल्पसंन्यासी योगारूढस्तदोच्यते || 6.4 ||

*When a man does not cling to the objects of the senses or to actions, when he has relinquished all incentives of desire, he is said to have ascended to Yoga.*

A CEO who exercises self-control would eventually experience a sense of inner peace. She would patiently hear out a voice of dissent and use the feedback judiciously. She would see something positive happening and share it with others, without getting attached to it. She would smell a coup in the making and take appropriate steps to defuse the situation objectively. She would praise in public but reprimand in private. She would taste either the sweetness of a resounding success or the sourness of a colossal failure but would neither become complacent nor reach a stage of despondency thereafter. She would sit back and redraw her business plans and put them in motion.

Regular meditation leads one to better self-control and inner peace. The *Bhagavad Gita* even prescribes the method to practise meditation. Anyone interested here can look up verses from 14 and 18 of its Chapter 6.

Suffice it to capture here the following:

यदा विनियतं चित्तमात्मन्येवावतिष्ठते |
नि:स्पृह: सर्वकामेभ्यो युक्त इत्युच्यते तदा || 6.18 ||

*With thorough discipline, they learn to withdraw the mind from selfish cravings and rivet it on the unsurpassable*

> *good of the Self. Such persons are said to be in Yog and are free from all yearning of the senses.*

**Some Manifestations of Self-control**

A true sign of self-control in the workplace is treating women with fairness and respect—something still too often ignored. Just as a cashier caught stealing faces consequences, powerful men abusing their positions harm vulnerable female colleagues, fuelling movements like #MeToo. When management turns a blind eye or handles these issues secretly, it damages the company's reputation. Real leadership demands transparency and courage to create a safe, equitable environment.

While politics often defends flawed leaders and confuses voters, business groups like the Tatas, owned by philanthropic trusts, set an example by managing wealth with detachment and social responsibility. True happiness comes from letting go of ego and unchecked desires, controlling anger, nurturing inner peace, and helping those in need.

*(For detachment, you may like to revisit the previous few chapters. Living in the present is a theme which we had touched upon in Chapter 15; we return to it in Chapter 22: 'Ego, Negativity and the Power of Now'. For happiness through control of desires, please see Chapter 23.)*

# 18

# Don't Worry, Be Happy

Which issues plague the mind of an outwardly successful and apparently happy CEO?

Perhaps due recognition, more power and pelf, special privileges, a fat expense account, rapid growth, stock options, a loyal and committed team comprising persons who happen to be competent in areas where she herself may be weaker, executing her business plans more effectively and efficiently, and the like.

## The Incessant Ripples of Desire

In general, the Happiness Quotient of any professional could be defined as follows:

$$\mathbf{HQ} = \frac{\mathbf{[FD\,(t)]}}{\mathbf{[AD\,(t)]}} \times \mathbf{f\,(IR,IG)}$$

Where **HQ** is **H**appiness **Q**uotient, **FD (t)** is the number of **F**ulfilled **D**esires at a given point in time, **AD (t)** represents the grand total of **A**ll her **D**esires at the same point in time. The notation **f (IR, IG)** suggests that **HQ** is directly proportional to her **I**nner **R**esilience and to the **I**nner **G**low of satisfaction she feels when a job is well done. A happier CEO could often be spotted in the recreation room, perfecting her aim at throwing darts!

However, the equation above needs to be considered with a pinch of salt. Because there is an end to one's needs, but not to one's desires. Much like mighty waves which keep hitting the shore of an ocean, desires keep relentlessly pounding one. But

it does indicate that one's level of happiness could be improved upon merely by enlarging the scope of **F**ulfilled **D**esires, or, by reducing the spread of **A**ll of our **D**esires.

The former, enlarging the scope of **FD**, is a Western proposition, leading to crass commercialism. A heavy dose of advertising and public relations keeps the inner fires of desires burning brighter with each passing year, prompting the hapless customers to keep chasing their own elusive rainbows and mirages in the Sahara Desert. Corporates keep stoking these embers of desire and customers keep falling prey to the same at regular intervals.

The latter proposition, of reducing the spread of **AD**, happens to be an Eastern construct. By keeping a check on one's desires, one can attain a state of happiness. This calls for an inner awakening and a realization that one needs to outgrow one's sensual gratification and consciously shepherd oneself to use one's intellect to restrict the spread of one's desires. Or, to focus on desires which are either aligned with the values of the organization or which happen to be our needs.

Western experts had originally recommended a Command-and-Control model to generate wealth and had gone on to imply that stark materialism is the way to seek peace and happiness. However, the Eastern approach is based on an inward blossoming, an inner growth and development which holds an inner glow of success superior to sensual gratification of an external nature. By proactively adopting a Conscious-and-Compassionate approach, several businesses have already recognized the truth that they have a greater purpose, much beyond merely delivering value to their shareholders.

Conscious businesses have trusting, authentic, innovative and caring cultures that make working there a source of both personal growth and professional fulfilment. They endeavour to create financial, intellectual, social, cultural, emotional, spiritual, physical and ecological wealth for all their stakeholders.

There are many labels for an approach of this kind.

Compassionate Capitalism, Humane Capitalism and Inclusive Capitalism are some. Socially Responsible Investing and Impact Investing are others. Nilima Bhat and Raj Sisodia label this as 'Shakti Leadership', highlighting the need for balancing masculine and feminine aspects in decision-making. R. Edward Freeman refers to it as 'Stakeholder Capitalism'. According to him, profit and purpose, humanity and economics, business and ethics can go '*and*-in-hand'!

## Of Gallant Knights

Knights in shining armour play an important role not only in our fairy tales but also in the business world!

Dr Ian Marshall and Danah Zohar, in their 2001 book *SQ: Connecting With Our Spiritual Intelligence* speak of knights, the leaders who choose to embark on a spiritual path. Having sensed something fundamentally sacred underlying human life, they embed this reality in their actions and their life's work.

According to them, in both life and work, the knight abides by five principles:

- There is something sacred, some deeper, shared consciousness, unfolding in this universe and providing a baseline for every aspect of life.
- Life and all its enterprises are interconnected.
- All human endeavour, including business, is part of the larger and richer fabric of the whole universe.
- The relationship of the healthy individual to the world is one of engagement and responsibility.
- Service conveys a deep sense of humility and gratitude.

## An Inward Blossoming

The *Bhagavad Gita* gives us a clue to be happy and to create happier working places. Consider this verse:

यदा संहरते चायं कूर्मोऽङ्गानीव सर्वशः |
इन्द्रियाणीन्द्रियार्थेभ्यस्तस्य प्रज्ञा प्रतिष्ठिता ||2.58 ||

*And when he withdraws his senses from their objects, as a tortoise draws in his limbs from all sides, his intellect is established.*

The senses, like the limbs of a tortoise, are necessary for mundane activities of life but happen to be vulnerable. They must be protected from danger at times and for this, they must be fully under the control of the mind/intellect and must withdraw at its command.

*Thirukkural,* a poetic composition of great antiquity in Tamil literature, quotes the same example. One of its verses can be interpreted as follows:

> If a man lives a life of self-control and withdraws the five senses from tempting pleasures as a tortoise, when it senses danger, draws its head and limbs into its shell, he shall have insured himself against evil in seven births thereafter.
>
> (verse 126)

What is being recommended here is not a suppression of desires but a voluntary renunciation of those desires which take us on a path of sensuous gratification, sans a higher purpose in our life and career.

This takes us back to the idea of living in the present. It also reminds us of the desirability of adopting a 'We and Us' approach to problem-solving rather than an 'I and Me' one.

## Creating Happier Working Places

With the advent of Industrial Revolution 4.0, many CEOs and human resource honchos these days can be found worried trying to figure out how to create happier working places even while maintaining a sense of discipline, decorum and decency. Happier people make organizations thrive and prosper.

Dr Noelle Nelson, in her book *Make More Money by Making Your Employees Happy*, explains how progressive employers try to understand the pain points of their employees and then try to address the same. One of the several examples she quotes is that of Paul O'Neil who took over the reins of ALCOA in 1987, the world's leading producer of aluminium; O'Neil announced that his sole priority was to increase worker safety. This came as a shock to the company's directors. O'Neil understood, however, that safety was a major concern for his workers. Over the next 13 years, employee productivity soared as accident rates decreased from roughly one per week per plant to some plants going years without an accident. When O'Neil stepped away just over a decade later, ALCOA's annual income had grown 500 per cent!

True happiness comes from inner peace and harmony with others, which management must nurture by providing the right support and tools. Employees value recognition, meaningful work, and positive relationships, seeking fulfillment beyond just monetary rewards.

*(For happiness through control of desires, please see Chapter 23.)*

# 19

# Detachment, Forgiveness and Inner Peace

There are many fringe benefits of practising detachment. Being able to forgive and moving on with our lives is one such perk. This is one of the most effective ways to attain inner peace.

A lion which is on a hunting spree in Masai Mara is blissfully unaware of regression analysis, but its mind is sharp enough to figure out how to outmanoeuvre its prey. It is fully focused on getting a fresh dose of vitamins.

However, *Homo sapiens* are blessed with higher mental faculties. The human mind uses its analytical approach to bring up opposites in any given situation. So, we have good-bad, like-dislike, love-hate, positive-negative, and the like.

On the other hand, our heart nudges us in another direction. We put ourselves in the shoes of the party of the other part. We realize that his viewpoint is as important and correct to him as is ours to us. The sense of balance inherent in a confrontational situation gets appreciated better. We experience a sense of inner peace.

Albert Einstein is reported to have said as follows:

> Weak people revenge. Strong people forgive. Intelligent people ignore.

It is not that 'bad' things which happen to us become 'good'. Rather, it is our viewpoint that changes. We cannot wish away the slippage of an overdue promotion out of our hands. Nor can we change our aggressive lion bosses into amiable swans, or slippery chameleon subordinates into docile ducks. Likewise, an accident, an illness, or death cannot be avoided. But by 'allowing it to be' and by 'accepting it as it is', we take our thought processes beyond the mind which is forever throwing polarizing positive-negative darts at us. Forgiving becomes easier. Forgiving others. Forgiving life. Even forgiving ourselves.

### A Close Encounter with Death: Forgiving Oneself

When my wife passed away at a relatively younger age, the whole family was devastated. My whole world turned upside down. I could not forgive myself for not having done enough to save her from the clutches of death. Taking her to the nearest hospital on that fateful day could have saved her life. Being with her but not being able to surmise that Death was silently enfolding her in its steely arms was another regret which kept gnawing at my inner peace for quite some time.

Eventually, however, wisdom dawned. By thinking that I could have saved her from the long-term consequences of the multiple illnesses she suffered from, I was perhaps ascribing to myself some superpowers which I just do not possess. When enveloped in the searing hot pain of separation, even messages of *Bhagavad Gita* about human mortality failed to provide relief initially.

She supported me throughout our marriage of close to four decades. She left behind two wonderful kids with a sound value system. Grief within has slowly turned into sweet memories of our happier times spent together. Painful memories still trouble me occassionally, but the amplitude as well as the frequency of the same has come down over time. A sort of reconciliation with reality has taken place.

### Of Aggressive Bosses and Public Reprimands

Some of the lion-like bosses I have had to work with in my long career were not easy to tolerate at times. Often, they made unreasonable demands on me. They had a penchant for unduly burdening me with work when they felt that I was already delivering well on the targets assigned to me. Their rebukes and reprimands would often get dished out in full public view, making me lose control over my team members.

As long as I kept fuming internally and continued to nurse grudges against them, I was miserable. It was *my* peace of mind which was adversely affected, not *theirs*. After some initial hiccups, I found inner peace in giving it back to them occasionally in the same coin. In some cases, when the right opportunity presented itself, I sat down to have peaceful chats with them, understanding their frustration and anger, and explaining my limitations. Gradually, a sense of balance was obtained.

One cannot expect tigers to change their stripes. But by understanding their viewpoint better, one could forgive them easily. Thereafter, their unreasonable show of temper does not touch one's inner core. In fact, with each such episode, one could learn more and grow as a seasoned professional. Looking back at my experience, I even feel grateful to such terror bosses for having enriched my life.

## Forgiving Team Members

There are several areas where one may forgive a colleague or a team member. Incompetence can be tolerated, and steps taken to address the same. Ignorance is understandable and can be handled. A sense of insecurity need not be taken a jaundiced view of. Even bad manners could be tolerated to some extent.

But what one feels strongly about is a lack of integrity. In a commercial enterprise, the focus can never be on shaping one's character. Yes, the top can set the tone by the kind of value system it espouses. However, an absence of the same does not justify an employee exceeding the limits of integrity. Forgiving such team members would only weaken the foundations of the enterprise in the long run. On the other hand, one would advocate that an example be made of such cases, so others get a clear message as to what goes and what does not.

Also, forgiveness does not mean that one allows others to treat one badly. The annual package one receives helps one to discharge one's duties, not to be bullied by someone else and eventually becoming a doormat. The key message is to take the right action without either love or hatred playing spoilsport. It helps to cultivate an attitude of understanding the nature of the other person and acting accordingly.

Forgiving someone is not a mark of weak character; rather, it is a mark of one's strong character. It is a position of strength.

## Letting Go of Vengeful Thoughts

In Chapter 32, 'The Karma Operating System', we shall see that it is not easy for one to crawl out of the cause-effect relationship that one's actions and reactions have. One would be surely reminded of the Third Law of Motion dished out by Isaac Newton. By carrying vengeful thoughts within, we allow the villain of our story to keep sapping our energies for a much longer duration. We end up giving a fresh lease of life to negativity within, thereby risking our own mental health.

However, by putting oneself in another person's shoes, one can perhaps surmise what drove the party of the other part to do what is being deeply resented. One may question oneself as to why one should let go of one's own value system and stoop down to the level of the other person, who is bound to suffer the same ignominy at the hands of a party of the third part at some point of time in future. Whereas that person carries the burden of his actions on his shoulders, our destiny is in our own hands. By exercising the choice of showing grace and forgiving, one is merely shepherding one's future in a more positive direction.

This is indeed a sign of inner resilience and maturity. Yes, appropriate steps must be taken to use one's softer skills to convey one's resentment, lest this gesture be taken as a sign of weakness by the party of the other part.

## Going with the Flow

Please note that one does not refer to happiness here. One could be excused for not having been happy in many situations of the kind mentioned above. But by giving up resistance, underneath the pall of gloom, one may experience a deep serenity within, and a kind of stillness.

A sense of detachment indeed helps. So does a subconscious drive to overcome a desire to always come out a winner in any situation. Avoiding the momentary pleasure of having unleashed my raw anger over those who appeared to be the villains in my story at that point in time, rather than handling them tactfully with a calm mind, has supported me through many tricky situations.

One does not imply here that one has attained the exalted status of strictly following what the *Bhagavad Gita* prescribes.

विहाय कामान्य: सर्वान्पुमांश्चरति नि:स्पृह: |
निर्ममो निरहङ्कार: स शान्तिमधिगच्छति || 2.71 ||

When a man acts without longings, having relinquished all desires, free from the sense of I and 'mine'; he attains peace.

शक्नोतीहैव य: सोढुं प्राक्शरीरविमोक्षणात् |
कामक्रोधोद्भवं वेगं स युक्त: स सुखी नर: || 5.23 ||

*He who is able, even here, before liberation from the body, to resist the force born out of desire and anger, is united. He is a happy man.*

One does what is to be done. One accepts what is. One utilizes one's energies more efficiently. Eventually, the flow of life envelops one back in its rapids.

*(For happiness through control of desires, please see Chapter 23.)*

# 20

# Different Hues of Happiness

Quite a few CEOs, when they wake up the day after having closed a crucial business deal, experience a sense of calm happiness within. The flowers are in full bloom, the sun shines with due benevolence, the birds and the bees hop around doing what Mother Nature has ordained them to do, God is in heaven, and all appears to be fine with the world.

The *Bhagavad Gita* speaks of three kinds of happiness—the sattvic (pure) kind, the rajasic (passionate) kind, and the tamasic (dull) kind.

## Sattvic: The Unalloyed Bliss of Happiness

The happiness that a CEO experiences when she has firmed up a plan to downsize the business, having meticulously planned the forced separation with all kinds of employees—whether the drivers or the passengers—and has even convinced the board of directors to go ahead with the same, would be that of the pure kind. A path-breaking approach has been taken. Her vision, courage and conviction are easily visible. Much hard work and effort has gone into planning the work to be done. Details have been examined with a fine-tooth comb. While working on such plans, the proverbial midnight oil has been burnt. Some personal sacrifices have been made. Initial pain and difficulties have been suffered and overcome. Above all, the interests of all stakeholders have been factored in. A combination of the hard work put in, the self-control exercised in the process, the resultant sense of self-perfection and the inner glow of satisfaction at having planned to spread sweetness and light at a challenging time for the organization, is bound to result in a state of happiness of this kind.

When we use the term 'peace', this is indeed the kind of happiness we refer to.

> यत्तदग्रे विषमिव परिणामेऽमृतोपमम् |
> तत्सुखं सात्विकं प्रोक्तमात्मबुद्धिप्रसादजम् || 18.37 ||
>
> *That which seems like poison at first, but tastes like nectar in the end, is said to be happiness in the sattvic mode. It is generated by the pure intellect that is situated in self-knowledge.*

Dr Verghese Kurien, the person responsible for the White Revolution of India, lived a life which did not involve giving up worldly pleasures; yet, he practised a philosophy of 'living for others.' In his biography, he states that:

> ...but if you work for others, there is a deeper sense of fulfilment, and if things are handled well, the money too is more than adequate.

The *Bhagavad Gita* touches upon this facet of our professional and personal lives as follows:

> कर्मणैव हि संसिद्धिमास्थिता जनकादय: |
> लोकसंग्रहमेवापि सम्पश्यन्कर्तुमर्हसि || 3.20 ||
>
> *By action only, indeed, Janaka and others gained perfection. Moreover, even looking to the welfare of the world, you should perform action.*

We could interpret the term 'welfare of the world' in different ways. Sustainability and care for the environment and for local communities is one way. Running operations without being prejudiced about caste, colour, sex or creed could be another way. Ensuring that the package disparity between different levels in the organization is kept in check is yet another way. Living by setting good examples for others is one more way. As stated by

Dr Kurien, actions which benefit others lead to happiness within.

For those of you who have come across the movie *Invictus* (2009, Director: Clint Eastwood), the visionary leadership of Nelson Mandela comes across very clearly. He blunts the edge of apartheid by using the game of rugby to unite his populace. Eventually, the people cheered Springboks, the team of the South African Rugby Union, to a victory in the 1995 Rugby World Cup.

One can well imagine the kind of unalloyed happiness experienced by those at the helm of affairs who manage to attain a superordinate goal in a challenging situation.

Many CEOs have a sedentary lifestyle. They keep fighting the battle of the abdominal bulge. When they take their doctor's advice seriously and start jogging or brisk walking, the initial pain and resistance from within acts as a deterrent. However, once a habit is formed, the body starts craving physical activity. They end up enjoying better health and happiness.

### Rajasic: The Mundane Shade of Happiness

A passionate kind of happiness gets experienced when the CEO's ambition of occupying a C-suite is fulfilled. Or, when she gets a reserved parking slot earmarked for her vehicle. Or, even when the security guard and the liftman salute her upon entry to her fiefdom. Power, pelf and prestige present a package which gives rise to a fleeting sense of happiness in her bosom. But beneath the happiness is a layer of anxiety because none of these can be taken for granted. In fact, the risk of her developing a queen-size ego and believing that she is omnipotent is rather high. A major setback in her career could just be around the corner, sneaking up and striking her with the stuffed eel-skin of business life.

विषयेन्द्रियसंयोगाद्यत्तदग्रेऽमृतोपमम् |
परिणामे विषमिव तत्सुखं राजसं स्मृतम् || 18.38 ||

*The happiness, arising out of the contact of senses and their objects which is like nectar in the beginning but like poison in the end, is said to be rajasic.*

Indira Nooyi, ex-president of PepsiCo, says:

> Just because you are CEO, don't think you have landed. You must continually increase your learning, the way you think, and the way you approach the organization.

## Tamasic: Happiness which Leads to a Fall from Grace

A dull kind of happiness is one which is based entirely on the gratification of the senses. Lord Krishna points out three specific causes which result in happiness of this kind:

1. When emotional and mental sleep leads to one not being able to understand reality, or one trudges through life without a clear goal.
2. A state of inertia of the intellect when one decides to let others govern one's life or allows one's impulses to govern her decisions and approach to problem-solving.
3. Ignoring the 'inner voice', one perfects the art of heedlessness and often gets into an adventurous mode, indulging in sensory gratification, eventually leading to a spectacular downfall.

> यदग्रे चानुबन्धे च सुखं मोहनमात्मन: |
> निद्रालस्यप्रमादोत्थं तत्तामसमुदाहृतम् || 18.39 ||
>
> *That happiness arising out of sleep, laziness, and inadvertence, which is self-delusive both in the beginning and in the end, is said to be tamàsic.*

Happiness arising out of laziness and procrastination would fall in this category. If one decides to outsource one's intellect and refuses to read between the lines, so to say, one is bound to end up in a disastrous situation. Even when the writing on the wall is clear and one continues to sleep-walk through a situation, one is eventually bound to run into a much bigger problem. At a broader level, corporate scandals arising out of a temptation to look for shortcuts and deviations from a set of ethics and public safety standards would also fall in this category.

Ask Martin Winterkorn, the former chairman of the board of directors of Volkswagen AG, who put in his papers in September 2015, several days after the infamous emissions cheating scandal came up. Winterkorn had then apologized for Volkswagen AG having installed software in its diesel cars to allow the vehicles to pass emissions tests by showing lesser emissions when the vehicle was undergoing testing but otherwise polluting the environment at amounts well beyond legal limits.

He also resigned as chairman of Audi on 11 November 2015, after further information associated with the scandal was revealed about VW's gasoline-powered engines. He was criminally indicted over the emissions cheating scandal in the USA on the 3 May 2018 on charges of fraud and conspiracy. In April 2019, he was criminally indicted on charges of fraud in Germany. He is currently a fugitive of justice in the United States of America and is wanted by the Environmental Protection Agency for Conspiracy to Defraud the United States, Conspiracy to Commit Wire Fraud, Conspiracy to Violate the Clean Air Act, and three counts of Wire Fraud.

His is a clear case for the kind of transient happiness CEOs should not aim for.

A wise CEO who happens to be aware of different hues of happiness would manage the wild horses of her desires, her egoistic tendencies and her anger and resentments in such a manner as to truly aim for the sattvic variety of happiness. In other words, do a great job and experience the inner glow of contentment.

However, Peter Drucker is of the opinion that happiness is irrelevant in the management context: 'Never mind your happiness; do your duty.'

Sure enough, he made a comment of this kind with an

outdated concept of business, most likely run on a Command-and-Control model. In today's world, people's happiness governs the performance of duties in any organization. Employers ignore this at their own long-term risk and peril.

In the chapters which follow, we look at different aspects of desires, egoistic tendencies and anger.

*(In Chapter 33, 'Punching the Right Buttons', we discuss the three kinds of actions—sattvic, rajasic and tamasic.*

*In Chapter 34, 'Inertia, Procrastination and Corporate Scams', we cover the perils of a lack of agility in decision-making.*

*In Chapters 44–46, 'Gita and Industrial Revolution 4.0', we discuss quite a few corporate scandals, mostly arising out of deviations from values and ethics.)*

# 21

# Ego: A Serpent or a Saviour?

Ego is often held to be a supreme villain, just like the serpent in the Garden of Eden. It is a deceptive creature which promotes as good what has been forbidden by a higher power. It shows cunning in its deception. All religious scriptures exhort one to sublimate one's ego.

Broadly speaking, desire, lust and anger would also fall in the same category—negative instincts which need to be summarily shunned by smart managers. We shall take these up later and here only try to look at some of the nuances of ego in the life and career of leaders.

Hapless CEOs and business leaders often wonder if giving up their ego would not create more problems than it might solve. Pull the skeleton of ego out and what one gets is merely a spineless lump of skin, muscles and tissues, duly backed by an analytical apparatus which keeps buzzing with a bevy of grey cells. The risk of being treated like a fly on the wall makes them shudder inwardly. So does the prospect of having to make unethical choices under the unsavoury influence of either a board member or a partner.

## Ego and Its Constituents

One's ego has two constituents—the core and the peripheral.

The core ego acts like a spinal cord of the mental make-up of a person during her lifetime. It is the key to survival. It supports one's physical frame as long as the same happens to be alive and kicking. It ensures that CEOs can articulate and assert themselves and do not end up becoming a doormat. It

"What she needs badly is a dash of humility!"

fuels the growth and evolution of the personality over time. In terms of the modified Blake Mouton Grid discussed earlier, those who behave like road rollers, implying a high concern for results and low concern for people and ethics, often mellow down with age. Over time, they could start behaving like Super Chiefs, scoring high on all the three concerns mentioned above.

The peripheral ego projects our individuality arising out of our relationships with people and objects in the materialistic world. It propels a CEO's urge towards the C-suite and exclusive perks and privileges. It makes a manager crave bouquets and detest brickbats coming her way. It makes a person puffed up with pride, just like a balloon with a lot of hot air inside. When the sharp needle of either a disaster or a reprimand punctures it, the person could simply collapse like a pack of cards.

In spiritual terms, the core ego is one's innermost reality. The peripheral ego creates a false individuality, leading to an equally illusory centre of desires. It would not be wrong to liken this to the experience of watching a movie, involving a willing suspension of disbelief on one's part. One laughs or cries in sync with those on the screen. Even though one knows that incidents unfolding on the screen are unreal, one temporarily lives through the same. One lives in a virtual world of one's own, judging people and incidents through the virtual glasses which offer a simulated view which may or may not match with the real world. The risk here is that the desires of a CEO emanating from her peripheral ego could often work against the desired objectives of a business enterprise.

If the core ego acts like a high-powered rocket which overcomes the drag of gravity (read: our challenges) and keeps propelling us through the corporate universe, the peripheral ego acts like a group of booster engines which help us to out-manoeuvre the asteroids and other space debris which life keeps flinging at us. Our worldview is defined by how we may imagine these slings and arrows of fate to be—positive or negative.

By no stretch of imagination can the author be considered

knowledgeable in the field of either psychology or theology. However, it is his considered belief that perhaps all our scriptures advise us to keep the core component under check *and* to get rid of the peripheral ego.

## Ego: The Perks and the Perils

The ego is intricately linked to our sense of self-worth, or self-assurance. It leads us to where we want to be in our careers. But having arrived, it needs to be kept on a tight leash to ensure that one becomes a successful leader.

In the book *Leadership Without Ego*, Isaac Getz, Robert Davids and Brian Carney argue that leaders must abandon their egos and be truly authentic to be most effective. The book stresses the importance of leaders empowering staff to think and make decisions for themselves and the importance of renouncing their egos to do this.

Ego plays an important role in creating the image of a CEO. But if this results in her becoming smug and over-confident, she runs the risk of surrounding herself with yes-persons, thereby shutting out and neglecting dissenting voices. She may then become a control freak and could eventually get relegated to a relatively inconsequential corner of the organization.

In the book *'I Am Something': A New Leader Mindset*, Prof. G.P. Rao speaks of three kinds of leader mindsets: 'I Am Everything', 'I Am Nothing' and 'I Am Something'. In an empirical study done by him and presented in the book, it was found that as many as 75.55 per cent of those who participated were following an 'I Am Something' mindset. Surely, this mindset indicates that the concerned respondents have managed to keep their respective egos on a tight leash.

Elsewhere, in Chapter 12, we have already touched upon the transition of a manager from an 'I and Me' approach to a 'We and Us' one. Getting rid of our peripheral egos plays a crucial role in the same.

## What the *Bhagavad Gita* Recommends

Lord Krishna tells us that knowledge alone can help one out of the intricate maze of ego.

> ज्ञानेन तु तदज्ञानं येषां नाशितमात्मनः |
> तेषामादित्यवज्ज्ञानं प्रकाशयति तत्परम् || 5.16 ||
>
> *Those who have destroyed this ignorance by the knowledge of Self, for them that knowledge, shining like sun, reveals the Supreme.*

When one is ignorant of the Self within oneself, identifies oneself with the body, and considers oneself to be the doer as well as the enjoyer of one's actions, one lives in the realm of darkness. But when the bright sunlight of knowledge caresses one, the illusion beats a hasty retreat, much like a deadly cobra which suddenly senses some unwelcome vibrations in the ground it treads on, and slithers away to its comfort zone. The soul then wakes up to its true spiritual identity, enabling the CEO to realize her full potential.

## The Mount Everest Phenomenon, Jackals and Giraffes

Howsoever proficient and righteous a CEO might be in delivering results, she is likely to have many distracters. These could be people who are vile, malicious, cruel, belligerent and insolent. Although they do not possess righteous qualities themselves, they simply love finding fault in everyone else. They consider themselves all-important and view others with their supercilious lenses. They behave as if they happen to inhabit Mount Everest, whereas all others operate from such low-lying mountains as K-2 or Nanda Devi. They are envious of others' success. Upon facing opposition, they become enraged and cause agony to others as well as to their own selves. They disregard and disrespect the Supreme Soul which is seated within their own hearts and the hearts of others.

They may greet another person with a '*namaste*', the non-contact manner of respectfully greeting and honouring a person. But they are blissfully unaware of the fact that, literally speaking, the term means 'I bow to thee.' The gesture is an acknowledgement of the soul in one by the soul in another.

One handles such persons with wisdom, patience, a cool temperament, and a dash of some fleet-footed diplomacy.

अहङ्कारं बलं दर्पं कामं क्रोधं च संश्रिताः |
मामात्मपरदेहेषु प्रद्विषन्तोऽभ्यसूयकाः || 16.18 ||

*Subject to ego, power, insolence, desire and anger, these fault-finding people hate Me situated in their own and others' bodies.*

Marshal B. Rosenberg, a proponent of nonviolent communication, chooses two animals to convey his ideas with power and clarity. The jackal within us is result-oriented, judgmental and authoritarian. The giraffe is both gentle and strong, regarding whatever comes up with kindness, communicating from its heart, and seeking connection and clarity.

In her book *The Giraffe and Jackal Within*, Justine Moi says that it is possible to give space to the jackal, while at the same time, out of a deep desire to contribute to happiness and peace for all, being able to be a giraffe.

One's ego is a potent tool provided to us by nature. Its wise use could lead one to a state of sattvic happiness.

**Of Humility**

Here is yet another trait which has an inbuilt element of duplicity. When it serves as a safeguard against one's pride and vanity, it becomes an asset. But when it leads one to underrate one's own talents and inner capacity, it ends up being a liability. One loses one's self-confidence and even tends to behave like a doormat, permitting others to trample over one with gay abandon.

## From Being Essential to Being Highly Desirable!

Keeping one's ego in check is easier said than done. It is something that the CEOs need to do themselves. It is an inner realization which leads to a trigger. A high degree of self-confidence, conviction and trust reposed in others act as catalysts, facilitating this inner transformation.

If done, the effort would not be to make oneself indispensable. Instead, one evolves from being essential to being highly desirable and respected by the top management! That is why it is said that one of the signs of one being a good boss is when the supporting team works well, irrespective of whether one is physically absent or present at the place of work.

If successes keep rolling in irrespective of her physical presence, progress for her and the whole team cannot be far behind.

*(The role of ego in resolving conflicts has been discussed in Chapter 25.)*

# 22

# Ego, Negativity and the Power of Now

It is no secret that negativity is injurious to one's health. When a manager's nerves start sticking out of her body, twisting themselves about like snakes and getting all knotted at the ends, she is surely taking a grave view of the matter. She might look like a female gorilla of testy and impatient habit, someone from whom the villain called Life has just decided to withhold a banana which is otherwise within striking distance.

What do wise CEOs do when they are feeling very low? Some could resort to gulping down an extra dose of their favourite tissue restorative, whereas others may curl up in bed with a humorous book, with a kettle of steaming hot tea by their side. Some may decide to wallow in self-pity and continue to remain low and despondent, while others may just decide to take a stroll around the lake nearby and simply look at the ducks flapping about their wings on its placid waters.

One of the ways in which negativity manifests is in one resisting whatever may be on offer. It would not be wrong to say that all negativity is resistance. Negativity could range from irritation or impatience to fierce anger, or from a depressed mood or sullen resentment to suicidal despair. Somctimes, when inner resilience is down in the dumps, even a minor situation may produce intense negativity, such as anger, depression, or deep grief.

In Chapter 17, 'Secrets of Happiness', we had touched upon verses 2.62 and 2.63 of the *Bhagavad Gita,* which lay bare the consequences of living in a virtual world under the influence of one's peripheral ego. To recapitulate, non-fulfilment of desires leads one to anger. Anger leads to clouding of judgment, which results in bewilderment of the memory. When the memory is bewildered, the intellect gets destroyed. When the intellect is destroyed, one is ruined.

## The Bonding between Negativity and Ego

Believe it or not, there is an intimate connection between ego and negativity. For the ego believes that negativity is a tool which it can effectively use to manipulate reality and work things out in its favour. It carries the mistaken notion that, through it, it can either attract a desirable condition or dissolve an undesirable one.

If one observes one's negative thoughts as an impartial observer, it will become apparent that one believes in remaining cocooned in a state of unhappiness so one may secure what one wants. But nothing could be farther from the truth. Negativity may work for electrons when they keep zipping around within the confines of an atom. On the plane inhabited by *Homo sapiens*, it does not work. It is not capable of attracting a positive condition. On the contrary, negativity hinders the coming about of a desirable situation. Nor is it capable of dissolving an undesirable one. In fact, by imparting to it the power inherent in one's thoughts, it simply perpetuates itself. Often, the universe could then manifest it on the physical plane, making life tougher. The only purpose it serves is that it strengthens the ego. The ego simply loves it. Secretly, it relishes the pampering it gets from those who care for us.

Our media moguls know this fact only too well. That is how the stuff they peddle is mostly negative. Give them disasters like wars, genocides, murders and rapes any day. Animated recreations of the event soon flood your grey cells. This also explains why negative news tends to travel much faster than positive news. Very subtly, negative news pampers our ego, leaving its peddlers laughing all the way to their banks.

## The Perils of Mental Evolution

Negativity is unnatural. Look at any other life form on our planet. It is not easy for one to come across an unhappy flower or a stressed oak tree. A depressed dolphin is pretty nigh impossible to locate. So are reindeer which have a problem with their self-esteem, elephants that cannot relax, or a peacock that carries hatred and resentment. These creatures, with brains far simpler than ours, teach us a vital lesson: to accept what *is* and live fully in the present moment. Their primal instinct for survival shows us the power of authenticity and being connected to our true selves.

Watch swans on a lake, peacefully floating and splashing, fully at ease in the Now. If a conflict with another swan comes about, it is brief and forgotten almost instantly—no anger, no grudges, no desire for revenge. They simply move on, embodying a natural grace and inner peace that many despondent CEOs could learn from.

Such are the perils *Homo sapiens* face for having an evolved mind!

## The Veil of Ignorance

According to the *Bhagavad Gita*, one suffers at the hands of negativity due to three factors: ignorance, faithlessness and self-doubt. It takes one away from the goal of absolute happiness, which applies to all the living beings on this planet. Lord Krishna exhorts Arjuna to pick up the sword of knowledge, cut through the doubts that have arisen in his heart, stand up, and perform his duty.

> अज्ञश्चाश्रद्दधानश्च संशयात्मा विनश्यति |
> नायं लोकोऽस्ति न परो न सुखं संशयात्मन: || 4.40 ||
>
> *The one who is without knowledge, without faith and is of a doubting nature, perishes. For the doubting mind there is no happiness, either in this world or the other world.*

तस्मादज्ञानसम्भूतं हृत्स्थं ज्ञानासिनात्मनः |
छित्त्वैनं संशयं योगमातिष्ठोत्तिष्ठ भारत || 4.42 ||

*Therefore, having cut asunder with the sword of knowledge this doubt of yours, born of ignorance and rooted in the heart, resort to yoga, arise, stand up and take action, O Bharata.*

Ignorance is suffered by those who do not have the requisite knowledge. Knowledge recommended here is that of the Self—at least a clear intellectual understanding of the same. The 'Doubting Thomases' come in for a harsh criticism here, because they are incapable of enjoying any situation, however perfect and just it might be, given the overall circumstances.

**A 'No Vacancy' Sign for Negativity!**

Lifestyle diseases often sneak into our bodies uninvited, settling in and forcing us into uneasy coexistence. Similarly, negative thoughts quietly invade the mind, leading to delusions and psychological disorders. When these two join forces, they feed off each other, causing psychosomatic illnesses. Though not a medical expert, I believe suppressed negative emotions often open the door for lifestyle diseases to take hold.

Our thoughts, like parasites, gain power from us—whether positive or negative. Fighting them means fighting our own energy, so the best approach is to simply ignore negative thoughts and deny them entry. Picture a hungry street dog that, finding no food, quickly moves on to seek sustenance elsewhere. In the same way, when negative thoughts meet resistance, they vanish, conserving a CEO's energy to focus on what truly matters—separating actionable ideas from distractions and acting on them with focus and passion.

Lord Krishna declares that we can never win in a direct fight against our own senses. Ultimately, the senses overpower the mind.

यततो ह्यपि कौन्तेय पुरुषस्य विपश्चितः |
इन्द्रियाणि प्रमाथीनि हरन्ति प्रसभं मनः || 2.60 ||

*The turbulent senses, O son of Kunti, forcibly carry away the mind even of a striving intelligent man.*

Not to fret, though. He goes on to offer an olive branch in the very next verse. The suggestion is to follow a three-step do-it-yourself technique. All senses need to be disciplined first. Sitting in a calm state, sans agitation of any kind, is the second step. Surrender to Him is the last step.

तानि सर्वाणि संयम्य युक्त आसीत मत्परः |
वशे हि यस्येन्द्रियाणि तस्य प्रज्ञा प्रतिष्ठिता || 2.61 ||

*Having disciplined them all, let him sit united surrendering to Me; for his intellect is established whose senses are under control.*

It is obvious that one needs to observe one's thoughts with due concern and alacrity. These are like fluffy clouds passing by in a wind-swept sky of pristine azure shade. Ceaseless vigilance is the way out. By conscious effort, one can observe thoughts and make them go away. As soon as these try to enter our abode—like unbidden guests—they need to be immediately pushed out, not being allowed to find a foothold in the mind. Sheer neglect is what these deserve, thereby leading one to experience true happiness and peace. The Mother of Sri Aurobindo Ashram endorses an approach of this kind.

## The Slingshot of Negative Emotions

There are indeed occasions when an insult hurled at one acts like a wake-up call. The scales fall from one's eyes, prompting one to introspect. A pitiless self-analysis could follow. An action plan gets worked on to overcome one's weaknesses which had been identified. One ends up becoming a better professional.

In other words, the slingshot of negative emotions nudges one to take positive steps.

Those of you who have seen the movie *Inside Out* (2015, Director: Pete Docter) would have surely admired the way it captured an essential fact of life—that human emotions not only affect our worldview and interpersonal relations but also significantly moderate the same. The five emotions depicted in the movie were Joy, Sadness, Fear, Disgust and Anger. Towards the end of the narrative, Joy finally understands the purpose of Sadness: to induce empathy in others. By preventing Riley, the kid heroine, from feeling sad, Joy was also keeping her from feeling true happiness. Joy eventually hands over the controls to Sadness, which then prompts Riley to return home, ending up with a willing acceptance of her new life in San Francisco, California.

Hence, negativity could also be made to lead one to positive outcomes, provided one uses it as a tool to attain a state of perfection.

*(The theme of living in the present has also been discussed in chapters 15 and 17.)*

# 23

# Being under the Spell of Desires

Some might agree that chief marketing officers could easily be dubbed *chief desire officers*—clever strategists who fuel consumer craving while fattening brand revenues. With an eye on both desire and the dollar, they craft seductive campaigns that keep customers hooked and profits soaring. Armed with Philip Kotler's 4 Ps—Product, Price, Place and Promotion—they now wield a fifth: Password, symbolizing the digital tools and AI-driven tactics reshaping the marketing game. Backed by ad agencies and market researchers, they fan the flames of desire, turning wants into pseudo needs, and then the latter into must-haves.

This relentless push gives rise to *planned obsolescence*, where every new gadget is barely unboxed before its shinier successor hits the shelves, endorsed by a beloved celebrity. Consumers, ever hopeful, stay stuck on a treadmill of desire, chasing the mirage of fulfilment. Yet, this cycle drives the engine of commerce—creating jobs, satisfying investors, and filling coffers across industries. So while marketers may stir the pot of endless craving, they also grease the wheels of the economy, keeping the system buzzing and stakeholders smiling.

## The Relentless Pounding of Desires on Our Mental Shores

Can one really indulge in any action in the absence of a carrot named desire dangling in front of one's nose? Desires are like the waves of the sea. They keep lashing at the seashore without enjoying any commercial break. Even as one is slogging to fulfil a desire, a few more pile up.

The positive side of desires is that they keep one going.

Take the example of any business. Its desire for profit is central to its endeavours. For a professional, desire for recognition and reward keeps prompting her efforts.

But the flip side is that desires often spin out of control and obfuscate one's real needs. One gets exhausted even while trying to fulfil some simple desires. Even as many on one's bucket list get ticked off as having been met, the ego is forever pouring in fresh ones into the bucket.

Mirza Ghalib, the prominent Urdu and Persian poet, has beautifully captured this fact of life in one of his compositions.

*Hazāroñ khvāhisheñ aisī ki har khvāhish pe dam nikle*
*Bahut nikle mire armān lekin phir bhī kam nikle...*

*I have a thousand yearnings, each one afflicts me so,*
*Many were fulfilled for sure, not enough although...*

Consider the example of a food chain, where each species playing a customer thrives on another species which dons the garb of a reluctant product. In a Swedish lake, for example, Osprey feed on northern pike, which in turn feed on perch, which eat bleak, which feed on mountain shrimp. Neither of these species experience grief. Once the basic need for nourishment is fulfilled, the attention towards diet goes off the radar.

**The Bucket List**

A CEO's bucket list might include goals like completing a successful project, reaching the C-suite, enjoying perks like reserved parking, or being celebrated at high-profile events. While the first is reasonable, the others can quietly fuel ego and lead to inappropriate behavior.

When desires are met, the CEO may feel energized and confident, but this boost can quickly turn into arrogance and impatience, causing frequent outbursts and a 'my way or the highway' attitude. Her humility fades, and she may start believing she controls everything, risking her own downfall.

If desires go unfulfilled, frustration and resentment can cloud her judgment, leading to misplaced blame, harsh actions, and poor decisions that harm both herself and the organization.

## The Three Enemies of Inner Peace and Happiness

The *Bhagavad Gita* is of the view that lust, anger and greed are the three gateways to hell.

त्रिविधं नरकस्येदं द्वारं नाशनमात्मन: |
काम: क्रोधस्तथा लोभस्तस्मादेतत्त्रयं त्यजेत् || 16.21 ||

*Threefold is the gate to hell destructive of the self; desire, anger and greed; therefore, one should renounce these three.*

When desires get throttled, anger sprouts, often creating a tsunami of destructive thoughts. However, if some desires get fulfilled, new ones keep pounding the shore repeatedly. Eventually, the rocks of one's mental strength get pulverized into the sand of greed, walking through which is not much fun. Greed generates a perennial sense of dissatisfaction with what *is* and does not permit one to restrict oneself to fulfilling one's needs alone. One's consciousness is forever caught in the triumvirate of lust, desire and anger.

काम एष क्रोध एष रजोगुणसमुद्भव: ||
महाशनो महापाप्मा विद्ध्येनमिह वैरिणम् || 3.37 ||

*It is desire, it is anger, born of Rajo-Guna, all-consuming and most evil. Know this to be the enemy here (on earth).*

The Vedas use the word *kām*, or lust, not only for sexual desires but also to include all desires for material enjoyment based on the bodily concept of the self. Thus, lust shows itself in many ways—the urge for money, physical cravings, craving for prestige, the drive for power, amorous intentions, and the like.

Lord Krishna identifies this 'lust' for worldly enjoyment as the cause of sin, as the malignant tumour attacking us from within, eating us from within. The mode of passion deludes the soul into believing that worldly objects will give satisfaction, and so one creates desires to acquire them. When desire is satisfied, it gives birth to greed; when it is not satisfied, it gives rise to anger. One commits sins under the influence of all three—lust, greed and anger. Greed is nothing but intensified desire, while anger is frustrated desire. Thus, lust, or desire, is held to be the root of all evil.

**A Monochromatic Life?**

Can we truly act without the lure of desire? Living fully in the present—free from past regrets or future cravings—might sound ideal, but a life without desire risks becoming dull, fit only for a monk renouncing the world. The balance lies in distinguishing real needs from mistaken desires, which is why many spiritual paths encourage living normally while staying connected to the true Self.

Another way to manage desire is by focusing it on others' welfare instead of just personal gratification. Philanthropic business owners show how this is possible, unlike nature's food chains where each species feeds the next without excess or grief. Humans, however, want more as they get more, making giving—like offering food—the highest form of generosity.

Desires often push us to chase goals obsessively, delaying what truly matters—time with loved ones, hobbies, and inner peace. In this rush, we lose sight of the bigger picture and forget that true happiness comes from nurturing ourselves and those we care about, not from fulfilling every want.

*(For additional perspectives on happiness and inner peace, you may like to revisit chapters 17–20.)*

# 24

# The Angry Birds in Management

Life often feels like a roller-coaster, tossing us around with forces beyond our control. In the process, we sometimes vent our frustrations on unsuspecting targets—at home, it might be a spouse; at work, we might either be the recipient or the source of someone else's misplaced anger. When this happens, we instinctively seek out a scapegoat to absorb our emotional spillover, continuing a cycle that never really resolves anything.

Anger trickles down the corporate hierarchy like a toxic relay race. The CEO snaps at the VP, who vents at the GM, who then lashes out at the manager, and so on—until even the office boy kicks the dog, and the dog goes after the cat. Each person offloads their irritation onto someone else, leaving behind a workplace full of gloomy faces, hunched shoulders, and whispered complaints. By midday, productivity takes a nosedive, and the only ones smiling are the tea vendors observing the circus with quiet amusement.

**When Anger Becomes Predictable and Routine**

Many bosses have honed their skills of managing and controlling affairs by using what they consider to be the deadliest weapon they have at their disposal—anger. A public display of anger leaves those around them shaking and shivering. This gives them a feeling of having overpowered their hapless subjects. However, when this becomes a predictable and routine affair, several things happen.

One, the blame game starts. I did not do it, sir. It was she who forgot to ship the material on time, sir. Thus, the power of human ingenuity gets dissipated in inventing new excuses, bringing down productivity.

Two, the quick-fix approach comes into play. People get used to seeking look-good short-term fixes. The long-term implications are conveniently forgotten.

Three, some people develop resistance to it. Next bout of shouting and one could see them merely shuffling their feet and trying to put on a melancholy mask to hide their chuckles. In other words, there is no attempt at a genuine improvement in one's work.

Four, occasionally, the boss might willy-nilly acquire the habit of apportioning blame on a poor junior without a fair hearing being given to all the parties concerned. All employees detest this disservice to the principles of natural justice. The respect for a senior is no longer real, it is feigned. A culture of hypocrisy gets perpetuated. Eventually, operational efficiency nosedives.

In such outfits, when the boss enters the workplace, a frenzy of activity starts. Electrified at the boss's presence, the employees run around like headless chickens. Physical presence and activity get interpreted as a sign of efficiency. Those who can think quickly on their feet suddenly remember a very crucial issue for which they need to seek invaluable guidance from the boss. Or a file which has been gathering dust for a long time suddenly gets pulled out for an intensive scrutiny.

Five, seniors who support the boss end up having to spend a great deal of time on simply mollifying the hurt juniors. Invariably, they have an extra box of tissue papers readily available, just in case the tormented souls need to wipe off their tears. No senior is comfortable having to work with a sulking manager who might otherwise be a star performer. Many of them end up donning the extra hat of being *chief listening officer*s of the company. Seniors' contribution towards company's goals faces a real risk of getting diluted.

Six, efforts towards team building and brainstorming invariably suffer, since being shouted at and being ridiculed in public is not people's idea of fun in life.

## A Case of Pavlovian Conditioning

Admittedly, there are juniors who feel they have been wronged and do not hesitate to register a protest. They have the guts to look the boss in the eye and make him/her beat a hasty retreat, much like a hunter with a shotgun who, while taking a stroll in the corporate jungle, suddenly encounters a lioness who has just had a fight with her soul mate.

In such organizations, one could often run into morose executives. When prodded as to the reasons for their despondency, they are quite likely to come up with the explanation that they were yet to get the daily 'quota' of shouting from the boss! Pavlov would have been delighted to include this form of conditioning as well in his research work.

## Tackling Someone Who Is Angry

Leaders who are at peace with themselves and are not intoxicated with their own power and pelf happen to be inherently good at understanding the psychology of those around them. Patience, listening ability, a calm disposition and a friendly banter can help evaporate the anger simmering within a team member.

## Of Oceans and Immersed Volcanoes

Eleanor Roosevelt is reported to have once said that 'anger is one letter short of danger.' Anger is highly contagious, much like negative news.

Mankind can perhaps be divided into two kinds. There are the 'ocean' types—those who are turbulent on the surface but calm deeper inside. One really admires CEOs who can feign anger and use it as a tool to set things right.

Then there are the 'immersed volcano' types—the vast lake may look very placid on the surface but could be seething with anger within. It is this kind which causes maximum damage to one's own well-being.

## Some Antibiotics against Bacterium Anger Spirilla

There are no easy solutions to controlling one's anger. One must first learn to accept oneself, and feel happy and contented inside. One also needs to empathize with others and accept them as they are. Then alone does one stand a chance of nudging others towards rectifying the mistake and in ensuring that it does not recur. The basic quality one needs to have is the capacity of always observing oneself and following a strict self-discipline as to when a display of anger is done and when it is not.

Equanimity helps. Detachment helps. Above all, a tight leash on one's desires helps. Accepting that things would not always be perfect helps. At times, allowing team members to make mistakes in execution of plans helps.

Austerity of speech helps; so does self-control in so many ways. Steaming off and sharing one's feelings with someone who is trusted and would lend an empathic ear assists. Deep breathing helps. Soothing music also helps. A dash of humour helps. A 'laughter break' with a colleague who has a sunny outlook towards life could bring some relief. Exercising or a bout of brisk walking could help.

Getting busy with another challenge for the day is yet another antidote to anger. Trying to change one's own perspective on things helps. Agitated nerves can also get calmed down by a spot of meditation.

## A Spot of Meditation

The *Bhagavad Gita,* in its Chapter 6, goes into great detail as far as meditation is concerned. It describes the purpose of meditation, where and how it can be done, and the benefits accruing to one who follows the instructions contained in verses 6.11–6.15.

Sample this verse:

> शुचौ देशे प्रतिष्ठाप्य स्थिरमासनमात्मन: |
> नात्युच्छ्रितं नातिनीचं चैलाजिनकुशोत्तरम् || 6.11 ||

> *In a clean place, having set his seat firm, neither very high nor very low, having placed sacred grass (Kusha), deerskin and cloth one upon the other.*

The cleanliness of the place is prescribed as the very first pre-condition, so the physical being is at ease, can concentrate well and turn its gaze inwards.

Tranquillity of mind is a precondition. The reward is an inner calm, accompanied by the evaporation of one's anger.

Rudolph Tanzi, professor of neurology at Harvard University, opines as follows:

> Meditation is one of the ways to engage in restorative activities that may provide relief for our immune systems, easing the day-to-day stress of a body constantly trying to protect itself. This could then lead to healthier ageing.

It appears that in the long run, meditation somehow realigns our molecular networks in such a way as to boost our capacity to handle stress and improve the body's immune function. The results of a 2016 study ('Meditation and vacation effects impact disease-associated molecular phenotypes') conducted by Mt Sinai's Icahn School of Medicine along with Harvard Medical School and the University of California confirm this.

## The Heartfulness Way

What this way offers is a chance for us to get transformed from inside out, enabling us to see the world in a new way, without the filters of our limitations. The technique comprises three practices—meditation, cleaning and prayer.

The basic nature of the mind is to analyse, to compartmentalize, and to divide. This method advises us to focus on our heart and listen to its subtle 'signals', neglecting the 'noise' being made by our restless mind. Gradually, the mind realizes that it is no longer welcome when we are in that state and starts becoming restful and quiet. Over time, our intuitive and inspirational capabilities improve.

Having practised this method myself for over 25 years now, I can attest to its efficacy.

## Desires on a Tight Leash

Our dream merchants have already perfected the art of marketing anger as a potent tool for seeking revenge. Think of such movie franchises like *Kill Bill* or *Ocean's Eleven* and countless others from Hollywood, the 1970s angry-young-man whodunits from Bollywood which catapulted Amitabh Bachchan to stardom, or much of the kind of stuff which we love lapping up on OTT channels these days, and one would realize the necessity of a separate book on revenge-based themes which eulogize anger, showcasing it as a virtue of sorts. Our politicians routinely invoke such passions amongst the gullible citizens, thereby retaining their hold on to power.

Albert Einstein had said:

> To dwell on the things that depress or anger us does not help in overcoming them. One must knock them down alone.

As discussed in Chapter 18, 'Some Secrets to Happiness', we have seen that the *Bhagavad Gita,* in verses 2.62 and 2.63, captures the root cause of all shades of anger: desires. If one were to try and control the root itself, much of one's energies could then be ploughed into nurturing trees which yield juicier fruits in one's career and life.

***(For inner resilience and equanimity, please look up Chapter 10; for detachment, chapters 13–16; for desires, Chapter 23;and for austerity of speech, Chapter 37.)***

# 25

# Being a Gallant Knight when Conflicts Abound

One of the harsh slings and arrows of life CEOs necessarily face is that of managing conflicts of different hues, sizes and shapes which keep popping up regularly between their team members.

The most critical of these arise when their values do not match with those of the organization. There are also cases where dealing with an obdurate superior proves to be a challenge. Conflicts also arise when CEOs need to take such unpopular decisions as winding up, retrenchments, disciplinary actions and dealing with unions. These also come up in the realm of customer servicing and managing service providers. Then there are instances of inter-department rivalry, turf wars and company politics.

There is about any conflict a wild, gusty fury—latent or otherwise—which affects the average mortal with something of the helplessness induced by a vast clashing of the elements. It may initially seem to be outside a CEO's jurisdiction, inducing a sense of futility of intervention, but could soon come knocking vigorously at the cabin door of the CEO.

## A Parallel with Dogfights

Corporate conflicts often resemble chaotic dogfights, where every participant is fiercely guarding their territory while onlookers from across the company watch with keen interest. Some merely bark from the sidelines, but many jump into the fray on general principle, eager to be seen in action without understanding the root cause.

PRODUCTION
SALES

These battles don't last forever, thanks to the timely arrival of a sharp, commanding figure—a top dog with a gift for crisis management and influence. This leader, often a CEO, may not radiate peace, but their authority and presence quickly calm the chaos, prompting both spectators and fighters to shift their loyalty towards the one who restores order.

## Managing King-size Egos

Consider the case of Mr Ratan Tata, who was entrusted with the task of steering the group through turbulent waters in 1991 by Mr J.R.D. Tata. He took over the reins of the group at a time when it was an empire made up of several independent fiefdoms, run by stalwarts like Mr Darbari Seth, Mr Russi Mody, Mr Ajit Kerkar and Mr Nani Palkhivala. A gradual purge followed, leading to amicable separations, save and except for the case of Mr Russi Mody. He got ousted in 1993 as the chairman and managing director of what was then TISCO and is now Tata Steel Ltd. It was an unceremonious dethroning for the head of the country's biggest private steelmaker. However, a friendly handshake did follow a few years later.

One has no clue how such conflicts in the uppermost hierarchy of the prestigious group were resolved. However, one may surmise that the tools used would have involved the following initiatives: (a) suitable policy changes, (b) separations handled without ruffling feathers but after a series of polite feelers had been sent out, (c) post-retirement needs addressed in advance, (d) a tight leash on the egos, and (e) a definite dash of detachment, equipoise and positivity in handling the whole process.

## Conflict in Case of a Value Mismatch

When there's a clear mismatch between an individual's values and those of the organization, it is often wiser for both to part ways. This prevents long-term friction and protects the brand equity of both the employee and the company. A respectful exit is better than a prolonged misalignment that benefits no one.

### Managing an Obdurate Senior

When faced with a difficult boss, the best approach is to remain polite yet firm, present facts clearly, and highlight potential risks without letting ego get in the way. Taking a professional, emotion-free stance builds credibility over time. Eventually, even a biased superior begins to recognize the value of balanced, objective input—and in the process, you grow as a leader by learning to master your own ego.

### Winding Up a Business

In a business wind-up, traditional roles often flip: marketing teams focus on protecting the brand's image while sales teams help distributors liquidate inventory. Purchase departments turn into marketers to offload stock, and operations staff shift focus to prepping machines and facilities for disposal. Finance reviews outstanding obligations, while HR works to support affected employees through job placements and counselling.

Effective business closure demands thoughtful planning and a human touch—caring equally for star performers and silent contributors alike. Legal advice and a savvy read of internal grapevines can smoothen the process. Smart CEOs manage team egos skilfully, safeguarding harmony while protecting stakeholder interests.

### Handling Sensitive Separations

Tact, diplomacy, fairness and equipoise help in these cases.

In one of the organizations I worked for, we had a

cashier who had spent close to 25 years with the company. Being a cashier, he had access to skeletons in the proverbial corporate cupboard. He was found by auditors to be having his own hand in the till. A carefully planned separation, backed by legal advice, was put in motion. Over a 10-month period, all the funds siphoned off by him in the past were recovered.

The same was the case in another company where the human resources chief was himself found having a romantic liaison with one of his junior team members. While a thorough enquiry was being conducted, the chief was asked to proceed on leave without pay. Eventually, his services were summarily terminated, and he left in disgrace.

In both the cases cited above, the management was driven by a value system which had at its core the basic principle of righteous conduct.

### What Lord Krishna Says

He exhorts CEOs to have a purified intellect and thus be ruthless in cases where an example is to be made, and a clear message is to be conveyed across the organization.

> यस्य नाहङ् कृतो भावो बुद्धिर्यस्य न लिप्यते |
> हत्वाऽपि स इमाँल्लोकान्न हन्ति न निबध्यते || 18.17 ||

> *He who has no egoistic disposition and whose attitude is not contaminated, even killing the entire universe, he neither kills nor gets bound.*

Having an intellect which is free of false values of possession, acquisition and ownership of one's actions comes in handy when handling conflicts of all kinds.

### Peace Is the Way

Deepak Chopra is of the following view:

> A peaceful way of resolving a conflict is by showing respect for your opponent. The mistake often made is to demonstrate power rather than respect... I have often heard from professional negotiators that seemingly insurmountable obstacles can disappear as snow before the sun when the parties concerned really get the idea that they are being treated equally.

*(Chapter 21, 'Ego: A Serpent or a Saviour?', speaks of the role of ego.)*

# 26

# Stem Cell Therapy for Office Politics

How does one remove the stems from the leaves that keep popping up in the poison ivy of office politics? Ask a manager who has benefited from such politics, and he or she would be unwilling to even accept it exists. Prod someone who has lost out on that coveted promotion to the corner office, and he (or she) would be spouting venom and making out a strong case for an imagined degradation in company values, how nepotism rules the roost, the toxicity in the work culture, and how unfair life in general is.

## Nipping It in the Bud

Smart leaders would nip office politics in the bud. This is how they go about doing it.

### *Minimizing One-to-one Interactions*

A smart leader knows that solving a team problem means getting everyone around the table and encouraging open, honest dialogue. They listen patiently to the outspoken voices while gently drawing out the quieter ones, making sure every perspective is heard. By fostering a transparent culture, the team stays focused, hits goals more effectively—and avoids the gossip and confusion that come from secretive side meetings.

### *Prompt and Open Redressal*

It is wiser to confront issues early and expose troublemakers, rather than let problems simmer and grow. In large bureaucratic organizations, unchecked rumours often turn into perceived truths, hurting both morale and momentum.

Delays kill the element of surprise and fuel cliques based on assumed favouritism, ultimately damaging the workplace culture.

*Selective Use of Underground Cable Connections*

Informal structures and groups are invariably more effective than formal ones. Smart leaders take advantage of such informal groupings and communication channels to clean up the political mess. Team members who try to earn brownie points from the boss by reporting juicy gossip at frequent intervals get discouraged, whereas those who have solid data and clinching evidence to share in an open forum get all the encouragement they deserve.

*Transparent Policies Help*

Organizations which keep tweaking policies to suit specific individuals or groups end up suffering in the long run. Employees loathe the absence of a level playing field and eventually seek brighter horizons elsewhere. Even after parting company, they tend to become negative ambassadors of the organization, thereby holding back potential employees from showing up at the HR outpost.

*Being Fair and Lovely*

A leader who maintains equipoise and is widely perceived to be fair enables a cleaner work culture. He or she does not discriminate between team members based on their race, caste, creed or sex, and ends up creating a strong meritocracy-based set-up. Such attributes and behavioural norms cascade down the hierarchy, thereby improving the overall performance of the organization.

Such leaders cannot please all the people at all times, but people just end up loving them.

## Action Laced with Detachment

The *Bhagavad Gita* enjoins one to act in the 'sattvic' mode, free of individual prejudices, being just and fair, and in the overall good of the organization.

> नियतं सङ्गरहितमरागद्वेषत: कृतम् |
> अफलप्रेप्सुना कर्म यतत्सात्विकमुच्यते || 18.23 ||
>
> *The assigned action, which is done without attachment, attraction (or) repulsion and without clinging to (its) fruit, that is declared to be sattvic (pure).*

Such actions would produce peace within and harmony without in the realm of activity. It is an obligatory action on the part of a CEO to defuse situations arising out of petty politics in his domain of control. It is a work which is done for work's own sake, in an attitude that work itself is worship.

Seniors who are like a wily fox and indulge in playing politics often end up being victims of the web of deceit spun by them over time. Operations eventually suffer. Their pious intentions of optimal time management go for a toss, what with political affairs eating disproportionately more into their productive hours.

## Being a Relaxed and Gentle CEO

Most executives still expect their bosses to be aggressive taskmasters, barking orders and charging ahead. But that old-school style faded with the first Industrial Revolution. In today's age of Industry 4.0, the most effective leaders are those with calm confidence—steel at their core, but duly upholstered by a diplomatic and empathic approach to problem solving. They know that real power lies in quiet strength, not in loud commands.

Unfortunately, many managers still operate in panic mode, afraid that appearing calm means losing their edge or missing out on promotions. This anxious hustle drains their energy, stifles creativity, and clouds decision-making. In contrast, the most successful leaders today are composed, focused, and driven by inner peace rather than fear. They radiate clarity, inspire trust, and consistently deliver results—without the chaos. And while no workplace is entirely free from politics, smart leaders know how to manage it calmly, keeping the environment healthy and productive.

All said and done, only the foolhardy would chase the utopia of an organization totally devoid of any kind of politics. However, timely doses of stem cell therapy are necessary to keep the ambient political temperature at a healthier level, thereby keeping an organization running smoothly.

*(In chapters 13–16, we had examined various facets of attachment and detachment.)*

# 27

# A Jaundiced View of Procrastination and Hypocrisy

Procrastination is a virtue,
Where one saves energy—it is true,
Only to spend it more efficiently later,
Sleeping over a problem and shutting an overnight door
Till the time the answer comes from one's divine core,
Wasting time to brood over a problem,
Till a solution automatically pops up in
one's conscious mind,
Buying time in one's quest for perfection,
Lot of merit in snoozing amidst life's
mundane humdrum,
Oh, the virtues of being a lazy bum!

For those among us who do not wish to live the life of an early worm which gets caught by an early bird, the *Bhagavad Gita* does not provide any solace. It takes a jaundiced view of procrastination and scoffs at the kind of sentiments expressed in the composition above. Instead, it encourages us to put our best foot forward and act promptly and effectively on issues at hand, with a sense of detachment, devoid of our bloated ego and our sensory likes and dislikes. It does not even take a lenient view of our relishing the luxury of attaining a state of inaction!

न हि कश्चित्क्षणमपि जातु तिष्ठत्यकर्मकृत् |
कार्यते ह्यवशः कर्म सर्वः प्रकृतिजैर्गुणैः || 3.5 ||

*No one, indeed, can remain even for a moment without performing action; for everyone is helplessly driven to activity by gunas born of nature (nature-born qualities).*

"Sorry, Maa'm, I have no time to read these at home.
You know that I take work home."

We are forever under the influence of the triple tendencies of benign activity (*sattva*), activity (*rajas*) and inactivity (*tamas*) inherent in us. Remaining inactive is not an option. We are advised to act vigorously with the right attitude, utilizing the knowledge, the skill sets and the resources at our command. This way, we can avoid internal waste of energy and enjoy growth within.

When tamas prevails, one becomes inactive, dull and lazy; when rajas prevails, one is active, passionate about cracking targets and full of energy; and when one is sattvic, one is calm, sweet and gentle, simply because of the balancing of both action and inaction.

> नियतं कुरु कर्म त्वं कर्म ज्यायो ह्यकर्मण: |
> शरीरयात्रापि च ते न प्रसिद्ध्येदकर्मण: || 3.8 ||
>
> *Perform the prescribed action. Action is indeed superior to inaction. Even the journey of your body will not be possible without action.*

Here, body, in a general sense, would include mind, intellect as well as ego.

Both these propositions apply to individuals as well as to corporates.

## Procrastination versus Agility

Several examples can be quoted when it comes to corporates who are caught napping when their products reach the end of their life cycles, and the dark clouds of newer technologies start appearing over the horizon. Despite adverse headwinds and the wolves of newer and more innovative products snapping at their heels, their responses are plagued by the virus of tamas. A deep attachment to the existing product range and business model perhaps gives such businesses a misplaced sense of invincibility. The results are catastrophic for all stakeholders.

## Kodak: The Rise and Fall of an Organization

Take the example of Kodak, a company founded in 1888, which dominated the traditional photography market to the extent that recording a moment for posterity came to be known as a 'Kodak moment'. As late as in 1976, it commanded 90 per cent of film sales and 85 per cent of camera sales in the USA. Kodak's rivalry with Fuji eventually took it to the World Trade Organization, which was not held to be valid in 1995. Observers suggested that Kodak was slow to react to changes and underestimated its rivals. This impression further gained ground when it recognized the upcoming threat of digital photography but failed to meet the challenge head-on. Kodak failed to anticipate how fast digital cameras would become easily affordable and more convenient to use.

Soon, Sony took over the leadership, followed by other competitors who could offer similar products at much cheaper prices. By 2010, its share in the US digital camera market had fallen to seven per cent, placing it behind Canon, Sony, Nikon, and others. Also, the photography market started gradually shifting to smartphones and tablets.

By 2012, Kodak had filed for bankruptcy protection under Chapter 11. In 2013, it announced having emerged from bankruptcy as a technology company focused on imaging for business.

Nowhere does the *Bhagavad Gita* recommend hapless endurance of the setbacks experienced in one's career or business. That would indicate an attitude which has its origins in the dark recesses of the mind, harbouring such tendencies as procrastination. Instead, the reader is persuaded to appreciate the sunlit valleys of life through which flow the rivulets of agile and proactive action, duly laced with wisdom and joy.

## Of Ethics, Morality and Hypocrisy

Hypocrisy of the kind displayed by Arjuna, when he questions the utility of killing his kinsmen on the battlefield, is something which is derided by Krishna.

> कर्मेन्द्रियाणि संयम्य य आस्ते मनसा स्मरन् |
> इन्द्रियार्थान्विमूढात्मा मिथ्याचार: स उच्यते || 3.6 ||
>
> *He who sits, restraining the organs of action, (but)*
> *dwelling in his mind on the objects of senses, self-deluded,*
> *he is said to be a hypocrite.*

Many businesses have perfected the art of making a grand show of morality and ethics in the facets they reveal to their customers, internal auditors and concerned regulatory agencies, while internally running their operations in a dubious manner. Non-payment of provident fund dues, including the contribution already made by employees, is one such practice. Splitting up businesses artificially to avoid paying rightful dues to the government of the day is another method resorted to. So is the tendency to short-change employees in respect of wages actually paid and reported in the books of accounts. Manipulating stock valuation figures and artificially beefing up sales receivables is another clever device by which shareholders and financiers are kept in a benign frame of mind. Greenwashing happens to be a buzzword these days.

This also begs the question as to how does one handle hypocrites in one's team? Exposing them, if necessary, in public, could drive home a powerful message. Handling them with tact and resource could be an option. Yes-men could also do much damage to the spirit of transparency and openness in a CEO's dream team.

Business owners and CEOs who continue to live in a state of self-denial, delusion and hypocrisy end up eroding their brand equities over time.

# 28

# Profit Is Not a Dirty Word!

Inside the glitzy world in which business honchos hang around, there are two popular misconceptions about spirituality. One, the latter may make them softer leaders, thereby giving rise to insubordination and lack of control. Two, that earning profits and the creation of wealth happen to be taboos.

Abandon the thought. The way Krishna goes about motivating Arjuna to do his duty and fight his kinsmen on the battlefield of Kurukshetra demonstrates that going soft is never recommended. His method may be soft, but his message is as tough as nails. Krishna is empathetic and answers all queries raised by Arjuna across the narrative in a patient manner. His is the kid-skin glove which hides a hand of chilled steel.

Likewise, it is wrong to surmise that our scriptures take a dim view of either profits being generated, or wealth being amassed. Instead, a spirit of give and take prevails. *Quid pro quo* is the name of the game. Transactions are gleefully entered into. To offer something that one possesses and to expect something in return that one desires to possess is an idea which is at the core of the term 'karma'. It is not a sin to market a product or a service for which customers are willing to pay. Business moves that result in a surplus—which could either be ploughed back into the business or even shared with society at large—offer a model which comes highly recommended.

**The Vedic Viewpoint**

According to instructions imparted in the Vedas, karma implies sacrificial offerings made to celestials to seek boons and prosperity. The Vedas inspire all to be associated with the increase of wealth. These advise one not to reject or condemn wealth. These urge one to be prosperous.

*Rig Veda Samhita* clearly speaks of soliciting fortune, wealth, treasures, and riches from celestials. (verses 55.10, 54.15, 15.3, and so on.)

*Taittiriya Upanishad* exhorts one to live by the vow that wealth shall be multiplied. Maximizing wealth is to be encouraged. One shall not reject wealth. (Part 3, 'Bhrigu Valli', verses 8, 9 and 10).

Vedic wisdom, especially in the *Isha Upanishad*, says that one should see one's wealth as a consequence of many things: one's entrepreneurial success, a gift of one's past activities, an opportunity to share it with others through benevolent and intelligent charity, and the like.

A text from the *Atharva Veda* says: 'May you earn as by a hundred hands and disburse by a thousand.' Obviously, it puts a premium on charity, Corporate Social Responsibility (CSR) and other initiatives which support sustainability.

Thus, generating profits and creating wealth is something which is not scoffed at by Indian scriptures of yore.

A 2017 study by Deloitte ('2030 Purpose: Good business and a better purpose') indicated that a commitment to sustainable development is compatible with enduring commercial success.

## What the Bhagavad Gita Says

सहयज्ञा: प्रजा: सृष्ट्वा पुरोवाच प्रजापति: |
अनेन प्रसविष्यध्वमेष वोऽस्त्विष्टकामधुक || 3.10 ||

*In the beginning, having created mankind along with Yajnya, the lord of creation (Brahma) said, 'By this (Yajnya) you shall prosper; may this yield the fulfilment of your wishes.'*

The term '*yajnya*' used here essentially means the prescribed duty, whether of an individual or that of an organization.

Lord Krishna advises one to do one's duty. An industrialist, a businessman or a trader must make enough money to expand business, create more jobs and embark on more welfare activities. Prosperity is not shunned but wholeheartedly embraced.

> देवान्भावयतानेन ते देवा भावयन्तु वः ।
> परस्परं भावयन्तः श्रेयः परमवाप्स्यथ || 3.11 ||
>
> *Through Yajnya (sacrifices) you sustain the gods and let those gods sustain you. By mutually sustaining one another you will attain the highest good.*

If business owners and company directors are considered to be the equivalent of celestial gods and humans to be employees, a prospect at which the former might be too pleased, but the latter might not be amused, this verse could bring into focus the key challenge of collective bargaining. Often, one finds that job security and a year-on-year increase in pay packets are the key concerns for the latter. What gets regrettably ignored is a matching desire of the latter to improve their productivity, irrespective of the colour of the collar—blue, grey or white. Prosperity comes about when a business and its employees work together to make this happen.

## The Gap between the Haves and the Have-nots

The *Bhagavad Gita* takes a rather dim view of not sharing wealth and profits with others.

> इष्टान्भोगान्हि वो देवा दास्यन्ते यज्ञभाविताः ।
> तैर्दत्तानप्रदायैभ्यो यो भुङ्क्ते स्तेन एव सः || 3.12 ||
>
> *Fostered by the Yajnya (sacrifices), the gods will certainly bestow the enjoyments you desire. But he who enjoys their gifts without offering to them is merely a thief.*

Lord Krishna suggests that the reward one gets after performing one's duty, should not be considered as one's sole claim; but rather as the gift of gods and should be enjoyed after expressing one's gratitude to them. Whoever enjoys such gifts without thus thanking gods is a thief.

A report released by OXFAM in January 2023, 'Survival of the Richest', pointed out that in the last few years after the pandemic, wealth inequalities have risen even more sharply:

> Billionaires have seen extraordinary increases in their wealth. During the pandemic and cost-of-living crisis years since 2020, $26 trillion (63 per cent) of all new wealth was captured by the richest 1 per cent, while $16 trillion (37 per cent) went to the rest of the world put together. A billionaire gained roughly $1.7 million for every $1 of new global wealth earned by a person in the bottom 90 per cent. Billionaire fortunes have increased by $2.7 billion a day. This comes on top of a decade of historic gains—the number and wealth of billionaires having doubled over the last ten years.

All these lead to social friction. Whereas macroeconomic policies are formulated by the government of the day, individual organizations can also pitch in and do their bit to address this issue.

Some time back, Infosys management had been advised to do some introspection on this front by N.R. Narayana Murthy, one of its co-founders. At a talk delivered towards the end of 2017, he advised the top management at the company to make 'sacrifices' to maintain the common man's faith in capitalism. He is reported to have said:

> If we believe in capitalism, if we believe that is the best solution for the country to move forward, then the leaders of capitalism will have to demonstrate self-restraints in apportioning to themselves the part of the benefits that come out of running companies.

The issue of wage disparity between their highest and lowest rungs is something that vigilant and responsible managements can ignore only at their own peril.

## Of Personal Time and Philanthropy

Krishna also clarifies that surpluses can only be generated through sacrificial action; also, a part of the surplus thus generated could be offered to address societal ills.

> यज्ञशिष्टामृतभुजो यान्ति ब्रह्म सनातनम् |
> नायं लोकोऽस्त्ययज्ञस्य कुतोऽन्य: कुरुसत्तम || 4.31 ||
>
> *Those who know the secret of sacrifice, and engaging in it, partake of its remnants that are like nectar, advance towards the Absolute Truth. O best of the Kurus, those who perform no sacrifice find no happiness either in this world or the next.*

Business owners and CEOs often achieve results based on sacrifices of several kinds. Quality time with loved ones could go for a toss. Work-life balance could get disturbed. Long-term stress could jeopardize personal well-being. The development of children does not get as much attention as it truly deserves.

After Indira Nooyi, PepsiCo's first female CEO, stepped down from her role in 2018, she said there were times she wished she had prioritized family:

> I've been blessed with an amazing career, but if I'm being honest, there have been moments I wish I'd spent more time with my children and family.

During her tenure, she followed the adage of 'Performance with Purpose' and initiated several schemes which brought in healthier products for the customers, without losing sight of sustainability concerns.

> दातव्यमिति यद्दानं दीयतेऽनुपकारिणे |
> देशे काले च पात्रे च तद्दानं सात्विकं स्मृतम् || 17.20 ||

> *A gift given with (the thought or conviction), 'It is to be given' to the proper person who will not reciprocate it, at the proper place and time, is known as sattvic.*

This is where the role of Corporate Social Responsibility and philanthropy gets highlighted yet again. According to 'India Philanthropy Report 2024' by Bain & Company:

> Private philanthropy grew 10 per cent in FY 2023, to INR 1.2 lakh crore ($15 billion). This faster growth (vs. FY 2018–2023's 5 per cent annual growth) was driven by growth in family philanthropy (15 per cent) and retail (12 per cent). However, segments like corporate social responsibility (CSR) and high-net-worth individual (HNI)/affluent donations grew moderately at 7 per cent, despite an expanding donor base.

> Working for profits with a sense of detachment and renunciation reflects one's inner power of self-control. It often enables one to produce results which help to build stronger brand equity for a business.

Ratan Tata, in one of his media interactions in 2020, is reported to have remarked as under:

> Chasing profits is not a bad thing—the question is what do you do to get there, how much value you're adding to your customers and shareholders, and how ethical that journey has been.

# 29

# Different Facets of Karma Yoga

P.G. Wodehouse, the renowned British humourist, in one of his narratives (*Ring for Jeeves*), speaks of A.B. Spottsworth, an American hunter who, while pottering about in a Kenyan forest, shoots at a lion. He thinks the ferocious animal is dead, but the latter thinks it is not. The animal takes a jaundiced view of the proceedings and is deeply offended at being disturbed in what it thinks is its own territory. The outcome of the melee that ensues is that only the mangled mortal remains of the hunter leave the forest. Mrs Spottsworth, though shell-shocked, is secretly delighted at having inherited sacksful of the green stuff.

Both the hunter and the lion acted as per their innate nature and performed their respective karma. The lady in question ended up adding resources to her kitty, possibly owing to some past accumulated karma carried over from her previous lives. Such are the mysterious ways in which Karma Yoga manifests itself. No doubt, lesser mortals keep twiddling their thumbs trying to figure out a mathematical model which might enable them to exactly forecast the results of all their actions!

While the Vedas use the term karma to represent sacrificial offerings (yajnya) and rituals to propitiate higher powers and seek boons and benefits, the *Bhagavad Gita* uses the term in a much wider sense. Here are some of the facets of karma which are captured therein.

**Teamwork**

All people in a CEO's team happen to be different. The duty of the CEO is toinvolve everyone in her struggle to live up to her own ideal and strive at the same time to make the ideal as near as possible to the truth.

An overall picture of the importance of the team's contribution to a target being cracked surely helps. Members then take justifiable pride in punching the right buttons. When a pack of wolves starts chasing a herd of sheep, each wolf tries its best to corner a hapless sheep and add to the bounty of the pack.

The *Bhagavad Gita* cautions one to avoid the temptation of taking the entire credit for success. Such acts of selfishness vitiate the working relationships and often lead to either the team drifting apart or some members resorting to hypocrisy in the days to come.

> यज्ञशिष्टाशिन: सन्तो मुच्यन्ते सर्वकिल्बिषै: |
> भुञ्जते ते त्वघं पापा ये पचन्त्यात्मकारणात् || 3.13 ||
>
> *The righteous who eat the remains of the Yajnya are freed from all sins. But the unrighteous who cook for themselves alone, truly they eat sin.*

Managers put their best foot forward and make personal sacrifices in the process. A senior who recognizes this openly and shares the credit with all team members is bound to be more effective in delivering results to the organization.

### Of Satisfaction and Contentment

When satisfaction and contentment become the two wheels of the bicycle of life, the fork in the road to endless desires automatically gets avoided.

> यस्त्वात्मरतिरेव स्यादात्मतृप्तश्च मानव: |
> आत्मन्येव च सन्तुष्टस्तस्य कार्यं न विद्यते || 3.17 ||
>
> *But the man whose delight is in the Self alone, who is gratified with the Self and is contented in the Self; for him there is no duty.*

The term 'duty' often has a negative connotation attached to it, primarily because it is taken as a burden. But when one does work which is one's passion, performance of duty becomes a delight. Work then becomes a journey to achieve perfection.

The central message of the movie *3 Idiots* (2009, Director: Rajkumar Hirani) was precisely this: follow your passion. Attain excellence in whatever you do. Money will follow. Be happy.

Yet another aspect which one may consider is that a dash of Creative Dissatisfaction can help one to attain a state of perfection faster. Likewise, contentment can often lead to an absence of adequate motivation to do work. The trick here is to ensure that the fire in one's belly is never allowed to die down completely but kept aglow.

### Responsible Leadership

The responsibility on the shoulders of a leader is rather heavy. She must walk the talk and set an example for others to follow. If she herself is prone to using her expense account to accommodate outings for her loved ones, others will lose no time to sniff it out and follow in her footsteps.

> यद्यदाचरति श्रेष्ठस्तत्तदेवेतरो जनः |
> स यत्प्रमाणं कुरुते लोकस्तदनुवर्तते || 3.21 ||
>
> *Whatsoever a noble man does, the very same is also done by other men. Whatever standard he sets, the world follows it.*

Unless the leader keeps acting diligently, the followers would not be motivated to do so. The viruses of corruption and procrastination are highly communicable and would gradually spread across the organization.

**Kinds of Actions**

कर्मणो ह्यपि बोद्धव्यं बोद्धव्यं च विकर्मण: |
अकर्मणश्च बोद्धव्यं गहना कर्मणो गति: || 4.17 ||

*You must understand the nature of all three:*
*recommended action, wrong action and inaction. The*
*truth about these is profound and difficult to understand.*

It is the underlying motive of an action which determines the category it falls into. The *Bhagavad Gita* classifies actions into two—the desirable kind and the undesirable kind. The former kind is the one which contributes towards one's evolution and is alluded to as karma. The latter results in one's degeneration and is referred to as '*vi-karma*'. As to the third one—inaction ('*a-karma*')—it stands totally rejected because one's life itself cannot be sustained by it.

**Of 'Eureka!' Moments and Contemplative Downtime**

A common foundation of all 'Eureka' moments is a phase of idleness; in other words, the capability of a wannabe innovator to live in the present moment. Some scientists in California now say that even lesser mortals can benefit from a spot of daydreaming. This goes on to prove—if proof was ever needed—that sitting idle is not wasteful, as many whip-cracking CEOs would have us believe. A vast majority of managers, workers and students would heartily attest to the fact that difficult assignments are handled much better if only preceded by a spot of contemplative downtime. This way, they are likely to envision a more productive approach to the issue at hand, resulting in substantial savings for the organization they serve.

As Tom Hodgkinson says, 'The art of living is the art of bringing dreams and reality together.'

This is how the *Bhagavad Gita* captures this thought.

कर्मण्यकर्म य: पश्येदकर्मणि च कर्म य: |
स बुद्धिमान्मनुष्येषु स युक्त: कृत्स्नकर्मकृत् || 4.18 ||

*He who sees inaction in action and action in inaction, is wise among men. He is united. He has accomplished all action.*

A manager who is seen quietly sitting on her desk is not necessarily to be viewed as being inactive. It is very likely that her grey cells are working feverishly to find a solution to a staggering problem at hand. Such physical moments of cessation of activity are merely external symbols of the kind of quietude, repose and serenity she is experiencing. Or, perhaps, she is experiencing a 'Eureka!' moment. Programmers, code-writers and innovators of all sizes, shapes and hues go through such phases; in fact, their output depends on it. This is the same state in which artists, authors and musicians find themselves when coming up with their best compositions.

The ideal CEO would be one who, amid the greatest silence and solitude, finds intense activity, and during intense activity, finds the silence and solitude of the desert. This is truly the secret of work.

**Of Start-ups and Entrepreneurship**

The mindset of entrepreneurs is not too difficult to understand. They dream big and aspire to offer a novel service or product to their target segment. They are prepared to take risks. They have a belief in their capabilities, irrespective of the business environment. They are not shy when it comes to seeking support. They are always willing to learn and leverage their networking abilities to the hilt. They are good in developing and executing a business strategy.

In the context of the *Bhagavad Gita*, Lord Krishna's message to Arjuna is clear. He is born a prince, trained in the art of war, and has always displayed his love for heroism and adventure.

Acting as per his innate nature, even if it is imperfect, is far superior to the option of suppressing his own personality and copying the activities of someone else, even though it leads to his leading a nobler and diviner life.

श्रेयान्स्वधर्मो विगुण: परधर्मात्स्वनुष्ठितात् |
स्वधर्मे निधनं श्रेय: परधर्मो भयावह: || 3.35 ||

*Because one can perform it, one's own dharma, (though) lesser in merit, is better than the dharma of another. Death in one's own dharma is good; the dharma of another is dreadful.*

One's own dharma (the path of righteousness) is determined by three factors: one's nature, circumstances, and the stage of evolution. It is better to follow it.

Though the context is different, there is an indirect message to managers here to become job creators and not job seekers. It can also be interpreted to mean that it is better to do something in accordance with one's own nature, even if it is done imperfectly, rather than doing something perfectly as per someone else's nature.

The patriotic song '*Ekla Chalo Re*', composed by Nobel Prize -winner Rabindranath Tagore in 1905, goes a step further and exhorts one to act as per one's own convictions, even when there is no support forthcoming from any other quarter!

# 30

# The Option of Re-wiring Oneself

For anyone who is interested in rewiring oneself to lead a happier and more fulfilling life is apt to find in the *Bhagavad Gita* clear tips as to how a goal of this kind could be accomplished.

### Reverse Delegation: The Technique of Working Right

Smart managers invariably meet their bosses halfway through. Before the boss starts worrying about the status of a crucial task, the manager has already kept her in the loop by conveying the ongoing situation. There are two distinct advantages of an approach of this kind. One, the boss's blood pressure is always under control, earning the manager a requisite number of brownie points. Two, the boss willy-nilly becomes a partner in crime, so to say, were things to go wrong somehow. Call it Reverse Delegation, if you will!

Some of you may recall our having touched upon this topic briefly in Chapter 11, 'Resilience and an Inner Connection', earlier.

By no stretch of imagination can bosses really be compared to Lord Krishna! However, if the manager has reposed his faith in the boss, navigating the choppy waters of a corporate career becomes a tad easier.

The *Bhagavad Gita* captures the art of Reverse Delegation as follows:

मयि सर्वाणि कर्माणि संन्यस्याध्यात्मचेतसा |
निराशीर्निर्ममो भूत्वा युध्यस्व विगतज्वर: || 3.30 ||

> *Dedicating all actions to Me with a mind fixed in faith on Me, free from expectation and sense of mine (ownership), fight, delivered from fever.*

Actions tend to leave behind impressions on one's psyche. These impressions then go on to generate impulses to act more vigorously. Good action will eventually bring about a good effect, whereas bad action would have a bad outcome. The way to neutralize the effect of this bondage is to be detached from the results.

It is not easy for one to cultivate a sense of detachment from the results of one's actions. But the technique proposed here has the potential to catapult one out of this vicious cycle.

By siphoning off the elements of ego, desire and selfishness out of one's motives to act, the latter could be held to be renounced. Renouncing an action surely does not imply an insipid life of inactivity. It merely means giving up wrong motives behind one's actions.

Hope is indeed the high-octane fuel that keeps a vast majority of us going. But according to the *Bhagavad Gita*, hope is something which belongs to the future. The ego is an entity which is partially made up of one's past impressions. A feverish anxiety about one's circumstances in the present is also held to be undesirable. Thus, one is egged on to fight, living fully in the present moment.

In the movie *Kung Fu Panda* (2008, Directors: John Stevenson and Mark Osborne), Grand Master Oogway, an old Galapagos tortoise, motivates a demoralized Po Ping, the giant panda, as follows:

> You are too concerned with what was and what will be. There is a saying: yesterday is history, tomorrow is a mystery, but today is a gift. That is why it is called the present.

Po's morale gets boosted, and he goes on to achieve the goal he has set for himself.

*The Power of Now: A Guide to Spiritual Enlightenment,* a book by Eckhart Tolle, conveys a similar message—that what counts is living in the present moment and avoiding thoughts of either the past or the future.

## Reorientation, Not Repression

However, knowing a technique for rewiring oneself and acting on it are two entirely different things, simply because of one's preoccupation with one's own thought processes, as determined by the composition of one's own nature and personal disposition.

> सदृशं चेष्टते स्वस्याः प्रकृतेर्ज्ञानवानपि |
> प्रकृतिं यान्ति भूतानि निग्रहः किं करिष्यति || 3.33 ||
>
> *All beings follow their own nature. Even the enlightened ones act according to their own nature. What will restraint do?*

Repression of one's innate nature could prove to be counterproductive. The only way out is to reorient one's thoughts and actions to a loftier goal in life which, when achieved, would benefit a wider set of persons. Enlightened trade unionists know this fact only too well.

## Senses on a Tight Leash

When one comes across a wonderful advertisement, whether on television or social media, one's mind subconsciously registers it as a 'good' experience. When one reads about a pathetic event in the press, the mind registers it as a 'bad' experience.

Stimuli of all kinds are thus segregated by the mind as either good or bad. Gradually, one develops a liking for the good ones and an aversion to the bad ones.

इन्द्रियस्येन्द्रियस्यार्थे रागद्वेषौ व्यवस्थितौ |
तयोर्न वशमागच्छेत्तौ ह्यस्य परिपन्थिनौ || 3.34 ||

*The senses naturally experience attachment and aversion to the sense objects, but do not be controlled by them, for they are waylayers and foes.*

The proposal here is not to run away from the harsh slings and arrows of fate. Instead, one is being encouraged to face these upfront, with a mastery over oneself.

## A Check on Desires

The *Bhagavad Gita* goes on to describe how one's basket of wishes makes it difficult for one to be discriminatory in handling people, events and circumstances. When one wears the spectacles of desires, one tends to take a subjective and a jaundiced view of things around one.

धूमेनाव्रियते वह्निर्यथादर्शो मलेन च |
यथोल्बेनावृतो गर्भस्तथा तेनेदमावृतम् || 3.38 ||

*As fire is covered by smoke, as a mirror by dust, as an embryo is covered by the womb, similarly one's knowledge gets shrouded by desire.*

Krishna enjoins one to slay this enemy within and not get swayed by it.

तस्मात्त्वमिन्द्रियाण्यादौ नियम्य भरतर्षभ |
पाप्मानं प्रजहि ह्येनं ज्ञानविज्ञाननाशनम् || 3.41 ||

*Therefore, having first regulated the senses, O best of Bharatas, shake off this evil (of desire), the destroyer of knowledge and realization.*

Admittedly, desires happen to be one's driving force within, propelling one towards the fulfilment of needs and even self-actualization. But left without check, devoid of wisdom and one's discriminatory powers or knowledge, these could lead one to ruin.

Quite a few of the steps mentioned here also lead to one achieving a better work-life balance in one's life. We discuss this further in the following chapter.

Regular meditation offers the possibility of a conscious withdrawal of one's identification with one's body, mind and intellect. A state of objective awareness can be attained, thereby facilitating decision-making.

The onus of rewiring oneself is entirely upon one alone!

# 31

# Karma Yoga and Work-life Balance

Some of us may wonder as to what precisely is meant by the term Karma Yoga. Well, for ordinary folks like us who continue our trek in the corporate jungle facing a Lion King boss here and a hissing cobra there, the answer is perhaps this: to keep on with our trek through the dense foliage of our career and life based on what one may allude to as a spiritual compass. Some such steps towards self-help we covered in the previous chapter.

## Work sans a Burnout

The Manual of Motivation we refer to as the *Bhagavad Gita* recommends a constructive reorganization of our life and career. It nudges us to give our attitudes and desires a positive spin. It does not advise us to either destroy or reject the expansive rainbow of possibilities that life offers to us. Rather, it motivates us to go out for an invigorating jog and return with our batteries duly charged up. Or, to go on a trek to the higher levels of the mountain nearest us, so we may soak in the pristine beauty of a rainbow and breathe in the fresh, unpolluted air there. The basic idea is to hand over to an aspirant a balm for her bruised soul.

Nowhere does this unique scripture from India recommend one to work so much as to suffer from burnout and distress. All things in moderation is its key message—whether diligent work or relaxation.

नात्यश्नतस्तु योगोऽस्ति न चैकान्तमनश्नतः ।
न चाति स्वप्नशीलस्य जाग्रतो नैव चार्जुन ॥ 6.16 ॥

OFFICE
HOME

> *Yoga, indeed, is not for him who eats too much nor for him who does not eat at all, O Arjuna; it is not for him who is too much given to sleep nor indeed for him who keeps awake (too much).*

An imperative requisite which can facilitate an aspirant's search for the Self within is that of moderation, whether in one's diet or in one's rest and relaxation. Keeping our bodies in good shape requires us to develop an inner sensitive ear, listening to the gentle murmurs of our fragile physical frames. We neglect these only at our own risk and peril.

At one stage in my own career, I faced a highly stressful situation for over 15 months. My body was quick to register a protest. A cardiac surgery soon became necessary. Post-surgery, when the effect of general anaesthesia wore out, I woke up surrounded by all kinds of tubes connected to my body, an oxygen mask covering my mouth and nose, and a wide array of medical gadgets which merrily kept on trilling and twittering at their own whims and fancy, carolling much like a bunch of linnets in springtime.

Gradually, realization dawned upon my negligible grey cells and frayed nerves that in the pursuit of career goals and a misplaced sense of loyalty to the organization I happened to be associated with then had led me to neglect the gentle murmuring emanating from under the bonnet of the vehicle assigned to me during this lifetime. For the latter part of the stressful time, my family tried its best to convince me to hit the eject button in the cockpit, but, much like the obstinate Balam's ass, I chugged along. I alone was responsible for the kind of surgical trauma I had inflicted upon myself!

## A Balance between Life and Career

> युक्ताहारविहारस्य युक्तचेष्टस्य कर्मसु ।
> युक्तस्वप्नावबोधस्य योगो भवति दुःखहा ॥ 6.17 ॥

> *For him who is moderate in food and recreation, moderate of effort in actions, moderate in sleep and waking, for him is the yoga, the destroyer of sorrow.*

It is natural for CEOs to get deeply involved with the work they do. However, in an era of 24x7 connectivity, if career concerns start regularly interfering with one's personal life, and if domestic challenges tend to gain supremacy while one is trying to grapple with business challenges, a highly stressful situation gets created.

By striking a judicious balance between the two, one improves one's delivery of results, sleeps easy and leads a happier life.

## The OECD Report on Work-life Balance

Those who are on the business treadmill not only enjoy the perks but also suffer the perils of achieving results. The equanimity with which a CEO successfully combines work, family commitments and personal life is important for the well-being of all members in a household. Managements can create a favourable ecosystem to support this with flexible working practices, making it easier for career-oriented parents to strike a better balance between work and home life. Thanks to a raging pandemic during 2019–23, many companies had already veered around to this viewpoint.

A report published by the Organization of Economic Cooperation and Development in 2020 covered 22 countries and used an analytical approach. One factor which the report considers is the amount of time a person spends at work. It is widely known that long hours spent at work end up impairing personal health, lower safety and increase stress. They define 'long hours' to mean a week exceeding 50 hours.

Mexico is the country with the highest proportion of people working very long hours in paid work, with 27 per cent, followed by Turkey with nearly 25 per cent and Colombia with almost 24 per cent of employees. The comparable figure for the Netherlands happens to be 0.3 per cent and Sweden 0.9 per cent. When it came to work-life balance, Italy registered the best score, followed by Norway.

Time happens to be a one-sided and finite commodity. A Workmonitor report published by Randstad in early 2025 reported that for the first time in the report's 22-year history, work-life balance surpassed pay as the leading motivator for employees all over the world.

- The research, which surveyed over 26,000 workers in 35 markets across Europe, Asia Pacific and the Americas, found that despite the challenging economic landscape, geopolitical shifts and technological advances, talent continues to have multifaceted expectations, reshaping the future of the workplace.
- For the first time in Workmonitor's history, work-life balance is deemed more important than pay (83 per cent vs 82 per cent). The report shows that talent prioritizes personalization, community and future-ready skilling, and employers need to be ready to respond.
- Talent are taking action if their expectations are not met, as almost half (45 per cent) say they have campaigned for better conditions at work. This is further evidenced by 44 per cent reporting they have quit a job because they thought their workplace was toxic, a relative increase of over 33 per cent compared to last year.

## Life: A Prepaid Card with Limited Validity!

Some time back, Ratan Tata, chairman emeritus of the Tata group from India, while addressing management students passing out of one of the institutes in India, is reported to have advised them thus:

> Don't just have career or academic goals. Set goals to give you a balanced, successful life. Balanced means ensuring

your health, relationships, mental peace are all in good order. There is no point in getting a promotion on the day of your breakup. There is no fun in driving a car if your back hurts. Shopping is not enjoyable if your mind is full of tensions. Don't take life seriously. Life is not meant to be taken seriously, as we are really temporary here. We are like a prepaid card with limited validity.

## 32

# The Karma Operating System

The proposition of reincarnation contained in the *Bhagavad Gita* leads one to an interesting corollary—that of accumulation of the effect of one's actions over several lives. It is as if one has a ledger of one's karmas, showing a credit as well as a debit balance.

The good news is that if one's present is based on one's past actions and thoughts, one can use one's free will to shape one's own future by punching the right buttons in the present.

### A Do-it-yourself Approach

In other words, what is on offer here is a do-it-yourself approach. This is how Lord Krishna explains it:

उद्धरेदात्मनात्मानं नात्मानमवसादयेत् ।
आत्मैव ह्यात्मनो बन्धुरात्मैव रिपुरात्मनः ॥ 6.5 ॥

*One should elevate the Self by the Self. Self should not be degraded. Self alone is the friend of Self; Self alone is the enemy of Self.*

Ultimately, it is up to an aspirant alone to accept the responsibility for either blessing or damning herself. Each life of ours presents an opportunity for Self-growth and the strength to break free from one's bubble of misconceptions and prejudices. How we make use of these is up to ourselves.

The Divine is not a chief administrative officer who keeps an account of all of one's thoughts and actions of endless lifetimes. If that had been the case, our guardian angels would have had to undertake a massive work of this nature with the help of blockchain technology using supercomputers, managing huge, distributed ledgers. A system of that kind would have had to be backed by an elaborate system of codes, an impenetrable information security firewall, and a sharp operating system which would have given our colleagues in the Silicon Valley a run for their money.

> नादत्ते कस्यचित्पापं न चैव सुकृतं विभुः ।
> अज्ञानेनावृतं ज्ञानं तेन मुह्यन्ति जन्तवः ॥ 5.15 ॥
>
> *The omnipresent God does not involve Himself in the sinful or virtuous deeds of anyone. The living entities are deluded because their inner knowledge is covered by ignorance.*

## Starting Afresh, with a Not-so-clean Slate

But one's personal system is designed such that when one is reborn, the operating system of karma gets freshly installed. Past files containing memories get quarantined in the deep recesses of the subconscious, only to be partially retrieved if one decides to undergo professional regression therapy of some kind. Evidence of this kind has been reported by Dr Brian Leslie Weiss in a series of books, like the one entitled *Many Lives, Many Masters*. But there is no dearth of sceptics who take a dim view of an approach of this kind.

As to our memories of a life getting wiped off the slate upon our death, an analogy can perhaps be drawn from what are known as the Zeigarnik Effect and the Ovsiankina Effect. According to these, when a task gets completed, if the perception we have is that it is indeed over, our mind hits the delete button. But our memory cells carry forward the tasks of which we carry a perception that the same remain incomplete. This shapes the baggage of our tendencies, or *samskaras*.

Likewise, we have the unique concept of what the *Bhagavad Gita* alludes to as *sanchita karma* or accumulated actions. This balance sheet of one's actions, stored in the celestial cloud at the time of death, is not unlike a listing of current assets and liabilities which could get utilized, albeit with a time gap, in the following lives. Good deeds assume the character of an asset, whereas bad ones tend to become a liability.

A fraction of the sanchita karmas gets carried forward from the past life and gets referred to as destiny (*praarabdha*), which determines the contours of our present life. The core karma application computes the result from one's actions in the present life, keeping in view one's brought forward sanchita karmas, and keeps updating the ledger, which shows the credit as well as the debit balance to be carried forward to the succeeding lives.

**The Theory of Karma**

In accordance with the theory of karma, the spiritual earnings of an unsuccessful aspirant in the previous lives eventually bear fruit. While the praarabdha decides the results of the actions of present life, the personality is shaped by the tendencies developed during past lives along with unfinished agenda.

Ones who had not made much progress in their past lives on the spiritual front are kept waiting in the stack of celestial abodes, whereas those who had traversed quite a distance and developed dispassion are not sent to the celestial abodes. They are born in a spiritually evolved family, to facilitate the continuance of their journey, albeit through a newly installed operating system, along with the updated ledger in the cloud. Such a birth is a great fortune because the parents inculcate divine wisdom in the child from the very beginning, thereby putting the new-born soul on a faster track of evolution.

Lord Krishna explains this concept as follows:

प्राप्य पुण्यकृतां लोकानुषित्वा शाश्वती: समा: |
शुचीनां श्रीमतां गेहे योगभ्रष्टोऽभिजायते || 6.41 ||

*Having attained the worlds of the righteous and having dwelt there for countless years, he who strays from yoga is born in the house of the pure and illustrious.*

अथवा योगिनामेव कुले भवति धीमताम् ।
एतद्धि दुर्लभतरं लोके जन्म यदीदृशम् ॥ 6.42 ॥

*Or he is newly born in a family of Yogis endowed with wisdom, though such a birth as this on earth is more difficult to attain.*

If Charles Darwin had ever ventured to touch upon the process of further evolution of human consciousness, *Homo sapiens* would perhaps have been enlightened on the subject. However, here we are given a proposition which provides us a ready template for the spiritual ascension of an individual. It also provides us with a tacit assurance that all our benign motivations are likely to get fulfilled sooner or later, provided these are strong enough and are accompanied by intense activities appropriate for their fulfilment.

तत्र तं बुद्धिसंयोगं लभते पौर्वदेहिकम् ।
यतते च ततो भूयः संसिद्धौ कुरुनन्दन ॥ 6.43 ॥

*Thus, he regains that level of union reached by the intellect in his former body, and by virtue of this, O joy of the Kurus, he strives yet more for perfection.*

Stalwarts like Buddha, Christ, Adi Shankaracharya, Swami Vivekananda and Mother Teresa, who continue to inspire lesser mortals the world over, were surely purer souls who had attained a much higher level of perfection in their previous lives, thereby leading by example in their lives that we happen to know of. All such people obviously hailed from a rare breed.

When one considers the prospect of a soul having many lives, the importance of perseverance takes on a deeper meaning. Whereas many of us pursue several things with a single-minded devotion in our lives and produce significant results for ourselves and for those around us, here we find an overarching endeavour of perseverance, spread over many lives. The project of attaining liberation is managed throughout the life cycle of one's journey. With each life, one's brand equity may get a brighter sheen.

प्रयत्नाद्यतमानस्तु योगी संशुद्धकिल्बिषः |
अनेकजन्मसंसिद्धस्ततो याति परां गतिम् || 6.45 ||

*But the yogi who strives with zeal, purified of all sin and perfected through many births, becomes purified from material desires and attains perfection.*

A CEO who has aligned herself to the practice of self-control and detachment is bound to be as close to perfection as possible. This does not permit her to avoid acting as an intra-preneur, though. Taking a proprietary interest in the scheme of things is essential to her personal growth and evolution in the realm of management.

**Easing the Iron Grip of Karma**

If what one is now is the result of our past actions, it follows that whatever one wishes to be in the future can be produced by one's present actions, though one can never be sure if the result would accrue in the present life or in a subsequent life. Thus, one is enabled to create the contours of one's own future, as it manifests, whether in this life, or in a succeeding life.

Though the *Bhagavad Gita* waxes eloquent on Karma Yoga, it does not necessarily showcase the theory of karma. Instead, the enticement on offer here is that it shows one a way to transcend the cycle of one's actions, by overcoming one's pride, by practising the art of detachment, by being aware of one's true Self within, by controlling one's desires and by freeing oneself from the duality of happiness and sorrow.

निर्मानमोहा जितसङ्गदोषा अध्यात्मनित्या विनिवृत्तकामाः |
द्वन्द्वैर्विमुक्ताः सुखदुःखसंज्ञै गच्छन्त्यमूढाः पदमव्ययं तत् || 15.5 ||

*Free from the delusion of pride, overcoming the evil of attachment, ever established in Self-knowledge, rid of desires, free from the duality of happiness and sorrow, such liberated persons attain My eternal abode.*

Note the sequence in which the operating system gets reconfigured thus. The delusion of pride must go first before a beginning can be made. The duality of happiness and sorrow is the last to go.

It is a well-recognized fact that in any given hierarchy, rules governing the conduct of employees vary depending upon one's level in the corporate ladder. Take the mundane example of punching clocks or gadgets which help administrators keep a track of late comers or early leavers from a factory. The rules which govern, say, shop-floor level employees, cannot be the same as those applied to CEOs, simply because the latter's roles are far wider. The hapless souls must maintain their sangfroid in an era of 24x7 connectivity. Hence, their time-bound physical availability on the campus need not be as strict as that of a shop-floor employee. However, most of them who happen to be heading manufacturing activities, set a healthy example by being on their desk some 30-odd minutes before the workday starts. This way, they not only avoid traffic blues of a rush hour but also enjoy a quiet time which helps them to organize their work better for the day.

The theory of karma espoused in Indian scriptures applies only to those who operate at the material level of things. As they start growing out of the operational level and give up attachment, as well as aversion, altogether and perform all actions with a sense of duty, maintaining their equipoise in success and failure, they get released from the bondage of their own actions. With such a balance in the account, the application rewards them with higher privileges. Such souls end up easing the iron grip of karma on their lives. Unless they start abusing their privileges, they end up experiencing the bliss of true freedom.

The sanchita karmas of such realized souls could be declared to be inoperative in nature. Their personal karma operating system and the core karma application would get deactivated.

Indeed, the proposition of enabling one to transcend the cycle of karma is a unique selling proposition of the *Bhagavad Gita*.

*(Related chapters: 40 and 41, 'Free Will and Destiny'.)*

# 33

# Punching the Right Buttons

What happens when a business ends up facing an existential threat, either due to a sudden change in government policy, or owing to advances in technology, or simply owing to a global pandemic like COVID-19 which pulls the rug from under its feet?

The owners and CEOs could then feel like a trapped herd of cows which faces a ferocious lioness who has not had her daily quota of vitamins for some time. If the leader of the herd decides to act in a detached manner and firmly locks its eyes with those of the lioness, all ready to defend the younger lot in the startled and petrified pack, there is a remote possibility that the lioness may lose its firm resolve, change her mind, and go off chasing the deer herd nearby instead.

In other words, engaging with the enemy could bring about satisfactory results. CEOs can get busy interacting with the mandarins who could influence the government policy in a way which would be beneficial to the business. If the threat emanates from newer technologies being unleashed, the possibility of an expert getting consulted and some timely steps taken might stave off the dreaded prospect of an imminent closure. This could involve automation, upgradation of a customer grievance redressal system with the aid of blockchain technology, or a massive retraining of the workforce, so the proportion of those likely to be handed pink slips could be kept under check.

If the existential threat comes up due to a global health challenge which leaves the business model in tatters and disrupts the supply chains, the top priority turns out to be that of servicing the critical requirements of customers while shielding the employees to the extent possible.

### Punching a Series of Buttons

I distinctly remember the late evening two decades back when the permission to build a three-star hotel on the promenade in the coastal city I lived and worked in was suddenly withdrawn, purely due to political considerations. The permission had taken three years to be obtained, though its withdrawal happened within a span of a few hours. A false claim was laid at the promoter's doorstep—that owing to a basement construction activity undertaken at the hotel site, seawater had entered the city!

Prompt legal steps were taken. 36 hours later, we could obtain a stay from the relevant court, on the grounds that the action taken by the authorities was unilateral. We were never given an opportunity to offer an explanation on the allegations, thereby violating the principles of natural justice.

The authorities were obviously in no hurry to conclude the matter. As time rolled by, losses began to mount. Wisdom dawned that a confrontation with the government of the day was not going to bring home the bacon. Two parallel tracks of engagement were laid. The owner started an informal dialogue with the then chief minister of the state, whereas yours truly started interacting with senior bureaucrats, explaining the facts of the case.

11 months later, the permission to build the hotel was restored. As a precondition, the legal case against the government had by then already been withdrawn by us. The hotel today occupies a place of pride on the main promenade of the city.

As the crisis kept unfolding, we kept learning newer lessons. Of acting in harmony. Of working with a detached attachment to ensure that the project was completed. A series of buttons had to be punched to get the desired results.

## Kinds of Buttons

The *Bhagavad Gita* posits that not acting is *not* an option. It goes on to categorize all actions into three kinds: sattvic, rajasic and tamasic.

### *Sattvic Action*

A 'sattvic' action is held to be the best. It is work which is taken up for work's own sake, in an attitude that work itself is worship. Actions performed in a spirit of inspiration and with a sense of attachment would fall in this category. So would actions which are propelled neither by love nor by hate. These are acts of grace which are not acts of obligation. These are not actions arising out of one's likes and dislikes.

When Rohan Narayana Murty initiated Murty Classics Library, a project to translate and publish ancient Indian manuscripts from other languages into English, he did so not because it benefited the Infosys business in any way. Likewise, some successful business magnates pledge their wealth to solve social problems, though, being publicity-shy, they do so quietly, away from the glare of media highlights.

Business leaders who follow a 'We and Us' approach would fall in this category. They punch buttons based on teamwork. They give credit where it is due. They respect human values. They balance their concern for production, concern for people and concern for ethics while taking decisions. They possess an 'I Am Something' mindset, as against either an 'I Am Everything' or an 'I Am Nothing' mindset. Their people are highly motivated, and willing to put their best foot forward.

नियतं सङ्गरहितमरागद्वेषत: कृतम् |
अफलप्रेप्सुना कर्म यतत्सात्त्विकमुच्यते || 18.23 ||

*The assigned action, which is done without attachment, attraction (or) repulsion and without clinging to (its) fruit that is called 'sattvic'.*

*Rajasic Action*

An action which is driven by passion is held to be 'rajasic' in nature. These are CEOs who have an 'I Am Everything' mindset. They are compelled to act under the influence of their arrogant ego sense. Their belief is that if they do not nano-manage affairs, nothing will move. Tension and strain are a part of their lives. Exhaustion due to anxiety and a fear of failure is a part of their body-mind-soul composition. When calculated risks taken by them backfire, they run a much higher risk of being shattered and attaining a state of hibernation.

A vast majority of business leaders and CEOs yours truly has come across in his long career fall in this category. Power and pelf constitute the oxygen which keeps them ticking. Relentless chasing of quarterly goals ensures that they keep sprinting on the business treadmill. Unfortunately, in the process, they forget that running a business is more of a marathon. Fly-by-night operations do not last long. A myopic vision eases out a strategic approach. Often, this compromises the sustainability of operations.

यत्तुकामेप्सुना कर्म साहङ्कारेण वा पुन: |
क्रियते बहुलायासं तद्राजसमुदाहृतम् || 18.24 ||

*But that action which is done by the one clinging to desire*
*or with ego and with lot of trouble is declared to be rajasic.*

Here is something which would interest CEOs who are keen on adding shine to their organization's brand equity.

When Stephen Cannon became president and CEO of Mercedes-Benz USA, he recognized that success was about more than just his vehicles. It was about how much the people who sold and serviced the cars cared and how generously they behaved. 'Every encounter with the brand,' he declared, 'must be as extraordinary as the machine itself.'

'There is no scientific process, no algorithm, to inspire a salesperson or a service person to do something extraordinary,'

Cannon is reported to have said. 'The only way you get there is to educate people, excite them, *incite* them. Give them permission to rise to the occasion when the occasion to do something arises. This is not about following instructions. It is about taking a leap of faith.'

Over the last few years, this leap of faith unleashed all sorts of everyday acts of kindness. A customer coming in to pick up his car was surprised by a birthday celebration at the dealership; another with a flat tyre pulling into a dealership and being sent off on her errand with a tyre taken off a new car on display.

A crucial step taken was to build genuine pride in the brand among the sales and service staff. A programme was created through which all 23,000 dealership employees got to drive a new Mercedes-Benz for 48 hours. The company put close to 800 cars in the field, at a cost of millions of dollars. Employees often timed their turns behind the wheel to correspond with important events—picking up grandma on her ninetieth birthday, driving a daughter and her friends to a Sweet 16, and even bringing a newborn baby home from the hospital. The participants took photos, made videos and, in one case, even wrote a rap song, to chronicle their 48 hours.

This bottom-up, peer-to-peer commitment to customers at Mercedes-Benz USA is an illuminating example of service transformation. It is also a reminder for leaders in all sorts of fields: management cannot order people to be kind, but it can enable the spread of the virus of kindness at the front-end level, thereby building and retaining customer loyalty.

## An Assurance

Lord Krishna offers an assurance to the effect that those who act with benign motives shall never come to harm.

पार्थ नैवेह नामुत्र विनाशस्तस्य विद्यते ।
न हि कल्याणकृत्कश्चिद्दुर्गतिं तात गच्छति ॥ 6.40 ॥

*O Partha, there is no destruction for him in this world*
*or hereafter, for no one who acts righteously, (my) child,*
*comes to misfortune.*

Here is a principle which holds that if one's efforts are benign, purposeful, and happen to be rooted in one's value system, no harm can come one's way. That is how we often find that hard work which appears to have led one nowhere in a project handled in the past suddenly becomes very useful in another project even after a lapse of time.

In other words, no work which is done with a benign motive ever goes to waste. Sooner or later, it bears fruit.

Irrespective of whether the actions are of a sattvic or rajasic kind, the assurance holds good. Even if there are mistakes and lapses on one's part, the guarantee stands.

## Three Kinds of Actions

Actions of a 'sattvic' kind would win a hearty approval of those with a saintly disposition; though the same would be looked askance by worldly people like us. Actions of a 'rajasic' kind surely win accolades from worldly people like us.

Yet another kind of action the *Bhagavad Gita* mentions is the 'tamasic' kind. These are hailed only by cynics who take a jaundiced view of life in general. We now proceed to explore the realm of such actions in the chapter which follows.

*(We had discussed the three kinds of happiness in Chapter 20: 'Different Hues of Happiness.')*

# 34

# Of Inertia, Procrastination and Corporate Scams

Other than actions of either a 'sattvic' kind or a 'rajasic' kind, the *Bhagavad Gita* also speaks of a third kind of action: the 'tamasic' kind.

This category covers the dull kind of actions performed without any regard to the consequences thereof or the injury and grief caused to others by their action. CEOs and business owners who believe in shortcuts and compromises take such actions. By doing so, they surrender their dignity and status. All they demand is transient gratification and the fulfilment of a business goal, even if the means are of a dubious kind.

## The State of Inertia

In the realm of physics, Newton's First Law of Motion captures the state of inertia rather well. When applied to the context we discuss here, it would read somewhat along the following lines:

> A task which has been put on hold will remain undone till the time an external force is applied.

Those who repose their trust in Theory X dished out by Douglas McGregor would heartily approve of this sentiment.

The force, however, could come either from one's boss or from a peer or a subordinate. A boss may not allow one to breathe easy till the time the results get delivered. A peer may excel in such a way as to nudge one to get one's act right.

PUBLIC RELATIONS
DIWALI SWEETS
HAPPY DIWALI
SWEETS
To MR
SWEETS
Happy Diwali
SWEETS

Relatively brilliant (or exceedingly dull) subordinates could likewise prompt one to jump into the fray and start punching the right buttons.

In matters of domestic chores, reluctant husbands succumb to the pressure applied by a nagging wife all the time.

Those who push one might sound being a villain at the time. In retrospect, one would realize that they deserve to be treated with respect. Often, one's harshest critics and detractors turn out to be the catalysts of one's rapid growth—materially, psychologically and spiritually.

There could be several reasons as to why such actions get resorted to.

1. The inertia of remaining in one's comfort zone.
2. A work culture which is aggressive, and which suppresses constructive dissent.
3. A myopic approach on part of the top management which prohibits independent decision making.
4. Greed, avarice, and an attachment to business goals.
5. Taking risks which, if detected, could be 'managed'.
6. An ostrich-like attitude based on a belief that issues, when slept over long enough, would not get followed up by those affected and will soon melt away.
7. The excuse that the regulatory culture is such as to encourage corrupt practices.

Yours truly has had the opportunity of working at the opposite ends of the corruption spectrum—with a large conglomerate where a senior manager got fired due to his having promised a meagre amount to a government official to secure a critical approval, and another one wherein the image of the outfit was that of a 'briefcase company', implying that its owner believed that most of the problems could be solved by paying 'speed money'. The main challenge faced in the latter case was that, eventually, no wheels would move until a monetary lubricant was made available!

## The Viruses of Procrastination and Complacency

One manifestation of a tendency of the 'tamasic' kind is procrastination.

Many executives believe in the adage that it is the early worm which gets caught. So, why hurry? Some bosses have an agricultural mindset. They have perfected the art of throwing proposals in the dustbin with an unerring aim, till the time a crisis comes up on the same issue. If so, all the juniors take the rap. The seed of the proposal now becomes the boss's idea and things get moving. The Yes-men, the Senior Nodders and the Junior Nodders heartily applaud when the boss corners the entire credit for the pirated idea.

Complacency is yet another manifestation of a thinking of the 'tamasic' kind. A sure sign of this is the singular absence of a sparkle in the eye of the person suffering from this virus.

An antidote package could well comprise a sustained programme of employee engagement, empathic mentorship, job rotation, re-skilling initiatives and compulsory recreational breaks. Human resources honchos need to act like sharp-eyed eagles, spot their prey roaming aimlessly in the Nevada desert, swoop down upon them with agility and take corrective steps without delay.

## What Lord Krishna Says

The *Bhagavad Gita* is succinct in its classification of the 'tamasic' kind of actions as under:

> अनुबन्धं क्षयं हिंसामनपेक्ष्य च पौरुषम् |
> मोहादारभ्यते कर्म यत्तत्तामसमुच्यते || 18.25 ||
>
> *The action, which is initiated by delusion, without regard to consequence, loss, violence, and capability is called tamasic.*

Management is about knowledge, skills and attitudes. Ignorance comes about when a manager's knowledge becomes a victim of selective amnesia. To satisfy the ego, even tasks which exceed one's own skills and abilities get taken up. An attitude of neglecting the consequences of one's actions clouds the judgment.

Actions and decisions of this kind are a sure recipe for disaster.

## 35

# The Perks and the Perils of Perfection

Smart managers always aim for perfection in whatever they work upon. It is said that Mr R.M. Lala, an editor, writer and publisher of repute, once commented to Mr J.R.D. Tata that the latter believed in excellence. The great man is said to have retorted thus:

> Not excellence. Perfection. You aim for perfection, you will attain excellence. If you aim for excellence, you will go lower.

### Attaining Perfection

As customers, we expect perfection in whatever we buy, whether products or services. From the supply side, the higher the level of perfection, the higher the costs involved. Thus, a pragmatic approach is often taken, so the offering remains not only attractive to a customer but can also look competition in the eye.

Perfection involves many things; shunning an attitude of compromise on basic product or service characteristics; a strong belief in the utility-cost ratio of the offering; attention to details; an unquenchable thirst for excellence; constant endeavour towards innovation; close monitoring of customer expectations; constant supervision coupled with delegation; and ceaseless vigilance. Employees play a crucial role in this drive and managements need to ensure that they get operational freedom at all levels, duly balanced with a sense of collective responsibility. It helps if mistakes in execution are permitted and corrected.

One of the critical factors which could facilitate all this to happen is a culture which celebrates a high degree of inner resilience and equanimity. People do not leave companies; they often leave toxic work cultures. Creating the right operating culture which enables an organization to keep growing is a collective responsibility of the senior management.

The *Bhagavad Gita* recommends that to excel in our careers, we need to keep driving our sleighs through knee-deep snow without a sense of attachment while keeping the reindeer of our senses on a tight leash.

> यस्त्विन्द्रियाणि मनसा नियम्यारभतेऽर्जुन ।
> कर्मेन्द्रियैः कर्मयोगमसक्तः स विशिष्यते ॥ 3.7 ॥
>
> *But he who, controlling the senses with the mind, without attachment engages the organs of action in the yoga of action, he excels, O Arjuna.*

There is not much merit in trying to control the senses by force, while the mind continues to dwell in the sense objects. The intellect should first convince the mind and then the mind should control the senses. Then only can detachment be stable, and one can reap the real benefits of a balanced and detached approach.

Often, one's attachment to products and people results in one being in a comfort zone, something one loathes to venture out of. This leads to spectacular downfalls, whether in business or in career. Conversely, it shows one how to excel in whatever one undertakes to do.

Elsewhere, Lord Krishna also points out that one would do well to appreciate one's innate nature—arising out of the interplay of one's own gunas—and act in accordance with the same, performing actions which are worthy of being performed. Work backed by an attitude of this kind is worship indeed and leads one to a state of perfection. No work is either ugly or impure; it is only the consciousness in which we do it that determines its true worth.

यतः प्रवृत्तिर्भूतानां येन सर्वमिदं ततम् |
स्वकर्मणा तमभ्यर्च्य सिद्धिं विन्दति मानवः || 18.46 ||

*From whom is all the tendencies of the beings and by whom all this is pervading—worshipping Him through one's own action, a man attains perfection.*

This is one of the key messages of the *Bhagavad Gita*.

## When Bouquets and Brickbats Make a Difference to Us

One can never please all the people all the time. But it is not easy to accept this reality. One of the lessons our guardian angels teach us while we live our lives is the unavoidable need to deal with the disapproval of others. Our friends, relatives, colleagues and others have their own ideas of evaluating life, and our ideas may not always match with theirs.

This affects us in two ways. One, we chug along our lives, trying to win the approval of others. We constantly worry about what others would think or say. This creates a baseline stress which takes its own toll over an extended period. Two, we end up mortgaging our happiness to others whom we either need in our lives or we respect. An encouraging pat from them makes our day. A scowl from them ruins it. Three, when we receive bricks and not bouquets, such negative sentiments as anger, resentment, hurt and frustration pollute our thought processes.

Yes, we all prefer to have bouquets but not brickbats. However, if we deal with them with a sense of equanimity, bouquets merely become pleasant surprises and brickbats merely serve as a reminder of what we need to do better the next time around. If taken seriously and received in gay abundance, bouquets could lead to complacency. Brickbats have the potential to hasten our journey towards perfection.

## Perfection Is a Relative Term

Perfection is not an absolute term!

Yours truly has had a rich experience in the leather goods and footwear industry. If the leather goods manufacturing could afford a deviation of, say, up to five mm, the footwear manufacturing process could not tolerate even a two mm deviation. The toe, the quarter and the vamp of a shoe have all to be taken care of. Otherwise, sizes would all go topsy turvy, leaving the manufacturer saddled with loads of non-moving stuff!

Moreover, when a deadline of delivery is looming large, the quality hawks relax their standards and start behaving like doves instead, 'passing' items which may otherwise be in the 'failure' category at normal times.

## Making Peace with Imperfection

Somehow, inner peace and an overdrive for perfection are inversely correlated. Our need to attain perfection, when moderated and kept under check, leads us to excel in whatever we do. In turn, this leads to an inner glow of satisfaction. But when it becomes an uncontrolled obsession, stress becomes our companion. An absolute perfectionist could never relish a sense of inner peace. Rather than being grateful for what we have, we become focused on what is wrong. We try to fix it as promptly as we can. This leads to dissatisfaction and discontent.

Listen to the conversation among some colleagues in an office canteen. There is a good chance that the obnoxious traits of bosses and colleagues who are not within earshot are getting discussed. But the more the group dwells on the imperfections of others, the more negative becomes the thinking of its members. Moreover, since people can never be taken at face value, one would not be surprised to find someone from the group gleefully hobnobbing with, and even pampering, the very person being criticized, once back on work.

Consider the case of the hapless souls whose profession demands that they live in a fishbowl, with the media chasing them 24x7. Politicians. Movie stars. Celebrities in other fields of life. Their dress must be perfect. Their bodies must be perfect. Their utterances must be perfect. Their manners need to be impeccable. Their private life must bear the strictest investigation. If not managed smartly, the relentless pressure of perfection can take its own toll in the long run.

The suggestion here is not to cease from doing our very best in a given set of circumstances. Rather, the idea is to detach ourselves and take a balanced view of things. By eliminating the need for absolute perfection in all spheres of our lives, we tend to become more relaxed. We become hotter on our jobs. We end up getting blessed with a surge in our creative juices.

Beth Kempton, in her enlightening book *Wabi Sabi: Japanese Wisdom for a Perfectly Imperfect Life* sums up the unique concept of Wabi Sabi as under:

- An intuitive response to beauty that reflects the true nature of life.
- An acceptance and appreciation of the impermanent, imperfect and incomplete nature of everything.
- Recognizing the gifts of simple, slow and natural living.

The Japanese concept represents a treasure trove of wisdom which places a premium on tranquillity, harmony, beauty, and imperfection. It strengthens one's resilience in the face of modern ills. It encourages one to do one's best but not make oneself stressed out in pursuit of an unattainable goal of perfection.

**We Don't Have to Be Right All the Time!**

Yet another manifestation of our inner urge towards perfection is to believe that we are God's gift to civilization. In other words, the party of the other part is invariably wrong. Well, not necessarily, and surely, not always. Let us be patient listeners. As suggested by Stephen R. Covey, let us first seek to understand the argument being put forward by the other person.

Let us be gracious in accepting defeat, if necessary. Winning an argument could often mean losing a friend and well-wisher. When it comes to maintaining harmonious interpersonal relations, it could be a recipe for disaster. After all, affection is a better gravitational force than perfection!

It would be worth recalling yet again what Lord Krishna has to say about accepting defeat:

सुखदुःखे समे कृत्वा लाभालाभौ जयाजयौ |
ततो युद्धाय युज्यस्व नैवं पापमवाप्स्यसि || 2.38 ||

*Having attained equanimity in happiness and sorrow, in gain and loss, in victory and defeat, then come out to fight. Thus, you will not incur sin.*

## The Perks of Perfection

Perks of perfection are many—better market share, shimmering brand equity, more favourable terms from suppliers, and an enhanced capacity to attract and retain talent. Gadgets marketed by Apple Inc. are held to be perfect. Even at premium prices, customers eagerly look forward to owning them.

In the realm of fine arts as well, unless an artist attains a sense of perfection based on a feeling of inner contentment, the work of art is not considered as finished.

There are three mighty powers within one—the power of the mind, the power of one's skills, and the power of knowledge one possesses. By working tirelessly, a master sculptor like Michelangelo would keep striking blows and chipping away at a slab of marble, till the time a magnificent piece of work like *Pieta* manifests itself.

***(We had touched upon the subject of resilience and detachment in chapters 10–11, and 13–16, respectively.)***

# 36

# Lassoing a Wild Horse Called the Mind

Reining in a mind that keeps galloping off to random places of its own free will is not easy. Those of you who have had the chance to catch up on a movie by the name of *Spirit: Stallion of the Cimarron* (2002, Directors: Kelly Asbury, Lorna Cook), would appreciate what yours truly is trying to convey.

One of the several ways to rein in the mind is to not fall for the mirage of multi-tasking; instead, to go in for monotasking!

## Multi-tasking and the Loss of Productivity

The random-access memory of one's brain has a limited ability to retain information. This worsens further when the amount of information increases. With the advent of 24x7 connectivity, the information overload for CEOs and managers has only gone up. Multitasking has often been touted as a panacea for this ill.

However, several studies done by subject experts over the last two decades have shown that multitasking is not a healthier option. Laboratory-based studies of multitasking indicate that one motivation for switching between tasks is to increase the time spent on the task that produces the most reward (Payne, Duggan and Neth, 2007). This reward could be progress towards an overall task goal, or it could simply be an opportunity to pursue a more interesting or fun activity. A French functional magnetic resonance study published in 2010 indicated preliminary support for the hypothesis that the brain can pursue at the most two goals simultaneously, one for each frontal lobe (which has a goal-oriented area).

Many studies and organizations stress the fact that multitasking of any kind reduces productivity and/or increases the rate of errors, thus generating unnecessary frustrations.

Sure enough, technology, if not used in moderation, could take one far off from a state of bliss and happiness. As technology seeps in more and more into one's life, our attention spans see a drastic reduction. As the number of gizmos at one's disposal goes up, the level of attention per task also nosedives. A clear example is that of talking over a cell phone when driving a car. Those who indulge in this luxury often get to meet God much earlier in their lives.

Contrast this with what Lord Krishna says when He offers a technique to work right.

## Monotasking: The Technique of Working Right

The *Bhagavad Gita* places a premium on the single-minded pursuit of one's objectives, sans any distraction and attachment to results. The recommendation is to concentrate on the task at hand and offer it to one's guardian angels.

सङ्कल्पप्रभवान्कामांस्त्यक्त्वा सर्वानशेषतः |
मनसैवेन्द्रियग्रामं विनियम्य समन्ततः || 6.24 ||

*Completely renouncing all desires arising from thoughts of the world, one should restrain the whole group of senses with the mind from all sides.*

शनैः शनैरुपरमेद्बुद्ध्या धृतिगृहीतया |
आत्मसंस्थं मनः कृत्वा न किञ्चिदपि चिन्तयेत् || 6.25 ||

*Slowly and steadily, let him attain quietude by his intellect; having made the mind established in the Self, let him not think of anything else.*

Herein lies the secret of bringing one's mind to single-pointedness and concentrate on one's work. Obviously, this needs a deliberate and conscious attempt by an aspirant. Once distracting desires have been renounced, one's mind gains strength to assert itself. It can not only tame the wild horses of the sense-organs but also restrain all the sense-organs from all sense objects from all sides.

The next step involves controlling the mind through an appropriate use of one's discriminatory intellect. A steady contemplation of the Self helps. Finally, knowledge is the weapon with which one may succeed in controlling one's mind.

**Casting Off the Veil of Ignorance**

The thoughts of *Homo sapiens* are configured by their minds, their intellect, their consciousness, and their ego.

The mind keeps doing its job—that of always throwing up different ideas. Let us say one sees a movie and gets besotted with a particular actor. Ego, which is the enjoyer as well as the sufferer, behaves like an old defective gramophone record and gets stuck with the actor's image projected on the screen. One's consciousness keeps travelling hither and thither, eagerly anticipating the next interaction with the actor in question. The ego keeps enjoying such forays, whereas one's intellect keeps cautioning if the virus of infatuation is distracting one from one's goals in one's life or career. The only solution is to control the mind with knowledge.

In fact, ignorance, the opposite of knowledge, has no real basis at all. If one encourages it, it assumes various forms—obsession, infatuation, anger, frustration, sorrow, and so on, and deludes the senses, mind, and intellect. But when it is ignored, it loses its power, just like negativity, which, when treated as an unbidden guest, simply melts away.

By its very nature, the mind is restless and unsteady. The speed of its thought flow often exceeds even the speed of light, possibly leaving a genius like Albert Einstein turning in his grave. Much like a wild horse which must be lassoed and brought back to the stables, the mind must be consciously tethered and advised to relax, and let go of its feverish activities.

> यतो यतो निश्चरति मनश्चञ्चलमस्थिरम् ।
> ततस्ततो नियम्यैतदात्मन्येव वशं नयेत् ॥ 6.26 ॥

> *Whatever makes the unstable and unsteady mind wander forth, from that it should be disciplined and brought under the control of the Self alone.*

Those who have perfected this art within excel at whatever task they happen to undertake. Once they are determined to achieve a goal which benefits all stakeholders, their energies get channelled and focused on cracking a target. Often, they find the whole universe conspiring to support their endeavours, resulting in remarkable successes. They also happen to speed up their journey on the path of spiritual evolution.

Einstein himself is reported to have expressed a similar thought:

> Everything is energy and that is all there is to it. Match the frequency of the reality you want, and you cannot help but get that reality. It can be no other way. This is not philosophy. This is physics.

## The Maggi Noodles Imbroglio

Most businesses apply their mind and learn from serious setbacks, let go of their sense of invincibility, and adopt a more pragmatic approach, adjusting to the new market reality. They learn to rein in their corporate egos, remove their blinkers, and improve their responses to a challenge. In the process, they rediscover their innate strengths—the strength of values which have shaped their dealings with diverse stakeholders in the business.

Maggi faced a serious setback in the Indian market in 2015 but was quick to respond to a serious market challenge and rebound within six months' time.

Maggi, one of Nestle's oldest and largest global brands, dates back to 1863. When the company decided to introduce it in India in 1983, noodles were not a part of an Indian's food basket. But the masala spice mix made the taste familiar, and the two-rupee price point made it widely affordable. The company worked hard to market it as a children's snack and gradually transformed it into a mainstream comfort food. By 2015, Nestle was manufacturing Maggi at five of its eight Indian factories. Test reports from a government laboratory surfaced, creating a doubt that these were a health hazard.

When the crisis unfolded, Nestle management was proud and confident of its stand. While dealing with government bodies, it displayed arrogance. It attempted to treat the issue as a purely technical one, relating to product quality, neglecting the undercurrent of bias Indians have for 'foreign' companies. The importance of customer perception—that the product is not safe for human consumption—was realized only in a gradual manner. The decision to voluntarily recall Maggi noodles off the shelves and relaunch these later took its own time coming, thereby denting the company's brand image.

In May 2015, food safety regulator Food Safety and Standards Authority of India banned Maggi noodles because test results showed amounts of lead far exceeding legally permissible limits. However, by November, the company relaunched the product. It worked hard to win over the hearts and minds of customers yet again and quickly started gaining leadership in the market, which, in the interim, had shrunk, allowing inroads to competition from newer entrants.

The company's suppliers stood by it. So did their distributors. Nestle eventually emerged stronger and fitter.

The change in the Nestle management's focus—from a merely technical issue to one that impacted consumer perception—took some time. But what matters is that it came about.

In a media interview in 2016, Suresh Narayanan, then chairman and managing director of Nestle India, is reported to have remarked thus:

> There are very few companies which have been tested, shaken, twisted or turned the way Nestle has been (in the past one year). We gained strength and confidence from that and Nestle will grow further.
>
> We are now more focused on being a fast and flexible company, which can take such challenges head-on. Our decision-making takes less time, and we can launch products faster.

It stands to reason that when change is the only constant, values happen to be the keel on which the mighty ships of businesses run. Organizations which have a focused mindset eventually succeed in keeping customer interest alive and ticking.

# 37

# Of Effective Communication

Speech is a powerful tool in the hands of a smart CEO. It reflects her intellectual calibre, mental discipline, and physical self-control. Above all, it reveals her inner thoughts and intentions to a listener. At a broader level, even body language, eye contact, and speech modulation play a crucial role in improving the effectiveness of communication.

> अनुद्वेगकरं वाक्यं सत्यं प्रियहितं च यत् |
> स्वाध्यायाभ्यसनं चैव वाङ्मयं तप उच्यते || 17.15 ||
>
> *Words that do not cause distress, are truthful, pleasant, and beneficial, as well as the regular recitation of the Vedic scriptures—these are declared as the austerity of speech.*

The *Bhagavad Gita* speaks of three kinds of austerities. One is that of the body, by which it implies due respect to one's teachers and wise persons, purity, straight-forwardness, celibacy, and non-injury. Another is that of the mind, which captures serenity, good-heartedness, self-control, and purity of thought. We shall consider austerity of the mind in Chapter 43, where we touch upon the issue of shoring up our Spiritual Quotient.

Yet another it places a premium on is the austerity of speech. Specifically, it speaks of:

- Speech that causes no shock
- Which is true, agreeable, and beneficial
- Avoiding a waste of this energy
- Recommends its deployment towards self-development

The implication here is that rather than saying a truth which is disagreeable to the listener, one may consider the option of

**"...and never forget that if something is worth communicating, it is surely worth over-communicating!"**

resorting to a discreet silence instead. Even otherwise, there are indeed times when silence is more powerful than speech!

We briefly touched upon the role of 'austerity of speech' in Chapter 24, 'The Angry Birds in Management'.

## The Harsh Reality Could Be Otherwise

However, in the business world, as well as in life, several unpleasant decisions need to be taken. When a pink slip is to be handed over, even an unpleasant truth must be carefully conveyed, so as not to undermine the self-confidence of the hapless employee who happens to be at the receiving end. Factors which help in the communication of this kind could be several:

- An unbiased and positive image of the person conveying the decision.
- A feeling that the intention of the person conveying the bad news is benign.
- If the person at the receiving end has been good at his job, an advanced study of the background, strengths, and weaknesses can help the person at the conveying end to suggest some alternative employment avenues. Even efforts can be made to out-place the person.
- In other words, the psychology of the individual must be invariably borne in mind. After all, people are as different as chalk and cheese, and need to be spoken to accordingly.

Everyone has a unique style of communication, but very few people get to master effective communication. Breakdowns in communication occur all the time, with consequences ranging from stark differences in the problem-solving approach, to hurt egos which generate negative feelings, anger and even violence. When a jaundiced view gets taken of a person, one may hear things being said by the person, but it is not easy for one to really listen to what is being conveyed.

What helps to improve the effectiveness of one's communication is to establish and maintain eye contact while a dialogue is on, clarity of message being conveyed, being a good listener to the party of the other part and, of course, allowing the other person to finish when he or she chooses to speak.

## The Lingering Sweetness of a Separation Well-handled

What is it that makes a professional fondly look back and remember the time spent with a particular organization?

The initial package sounds jaded after some time. The Law of Diminishing Utility eventually kicks in. The seniority for which one so adroitly negotiated at the entry stage fails to charm after some time unless backed by further achievements, recognition, rewards, added responsibilities and advancements. Time also takes the glow and shine off the social prestige which goes with being associated with one of the better-known brands in the industry. Corporate warts start becoming visible.

So, what is a professional left with after having left an organization?

Much after the association with an organization has come to an end, the everlasting impression one carries in one's mind depends on two simple factors. One, professional achievements which were individually attained but facilitated and enabled by the support systems ingrained in the culture of the organization. Two, the way one was treated as a human being and the quality of communication one received from superiors, peers, and subordinates.

Organizations happen to be made up of people of all sizes, shapes and temperaments. But the treatment received at the hands of key people one comes in touch with determines whether the aftertaste remains sweet or sour—also, how long it lingers in the taste buds of one's memory cells.

## Winding Up with Minimal Resistance

In one of the organizations, I had once worked with, a strategic business unit had fallen on hard times, primarily owing to changes in the market dynamics. Eventually, management decided to wind up the operations which directly employed more than 1,000 people. The unit was in an area which had seen a multifold increase in labour disputes of all kinds over the past decade. There was hardly any unit which did not sport a red flag on its main gate, declaring the union which was controlling its workforce.

However, the unit under reference was an exception. Being in a small government-administered territory, there was a high risk of complications arising out of government intervention of an obnoxious kind. The possibility of political interference was high.

Effective internal as well as external communication brought home favourable results. A well-thought-out separation package was planned and rolled out. Most of the management staff got either relocated or outplaced. A well-rehearsed PR campaign got underway with all the key government functionaries to ensure adequate and effective communication.

The eventual outcome was a meticulously designed initiative which ensured that there were no unpleasant obstructions to the winding up plans of the company. Also, no regulatory authority had the dubious pleasure of subsequently claiming that it could have done something to stop the loss of employment to a plethora of people, had they only been told of it beforehand!

One of the key takeaways from this experience was that if something is worth communicating, it is worth over-communicating!

## Some Pitfalls Which Are Best Avoided

- Communication which does not consider the psychology of the hapless recipient.

- Communication which is obnoxious and points fingers at one of the recipients, rather than making suggestions as to how the situation at hand could be handled better.
- Messages which are way too long, repetitive in nature and do not sum up the basic proposition in the very first few lines.
- Critical issues being discussed threadbare over cold e-mails rather than over a steaming hot cup of coffee, or even over a warm phone call.
- A tendency to play to the gallery by gleefully clicking on the 'reply all' button, thereby dragging several unwilling souls into a discussion where they have nothing to contribute.
- Falling to the temptation of responding to official mails even while being on a vacation, when all that would be required would be a simple auto-reply message to the effect that one happens to be vacationing on Mars these days, that connectivity there leaves much to be desired, and suggesting another person who could possibly assist the sender in providing an intermittent solution!

Good communication skills happen to be a powerful weapon in the arsenal at the disposal of a CEO.

# 38

# When Life Hurls Big Rocks at One 1.0

Life is not necessarily fair. Occasionally, when one's guardian angels appear to have gone off to enjoy a long furlough, it decides that merely throwing some brickbats at one is not enough. Instead, it appears to derive a sadistic pleasure in hurling huge rocks at one, leaving the clueless soul wondering what it has done to deserve the honour. 'Why me' is invariably the query which reverberates in one's consciousness.

These are instances when it is no longer a question of one's ego to be kept on a tight leash or just managing one's basket of desires. The challenge in such cases is that of meeting one's basic needs; of keeping one's body and soul together. Even one's survival could be at stake.

On one of those not-so-fine mornings, one simply gets a curt message from the CEO. The proverbial pink slip follows. One is told that given advances in technology, one's services are no longer required. Thanks to the need for the organization to downsize its operations, one's career goes for a toss.

Or, a CEO who has built an enviable reputation for herself over the years comes under the cloud of a corporate scandal which gets eagerly sniffed at by various regulatory agencies. This prompts her to put in her papers and face the legal consequences. The media, of which she was a darling till the other day, decides to start shaming her. A severe loss of prestige comes about. A glorious career comes to a sudden halt. Her feelings in a situation of this kind could not be much different than those of Napoleon after his Waterloo debacle.

Think of the mighty challenges faced by businesses owing to the product having reached the end of its lifecycle. One may recall extinct products and services and notice how technology-driven disruptions make some businesses simply vanish from one's radar—telephones, long play records, audio cassettes, audio CDs, typewriters, telex machines, pagers, telegrams...the list just goes on and on.

### The Coronavirus Challenge

The year 2020 turned out to be an extraordinary challenge for individuals, families, and businesses. Coronavirus spread several other viruses—those of fear, uncertainty, hunger, jobs, lack of physical interactions in education as well as in life, and the like. Sources of income simply vanished overnight. It exposed the fault-lines in our health and social infrastructure. Businesses shut shops. Industries with some core strengths diversified into newer markets and products. Economies the world overtook a severe beating.

In retrospect, those who had a positive attitude not only survived the virus but also discovered new dimensions in their lives. They re-skilled themselves and learnt other trades. For many, especially in countries like India, where a deep faith brings about a sense of acceptance, patience and resilience, survival tactics supported them through the churning that was taking place. New business models emerged. An example is that of the entertainment sector which saw the emergence of OTT platforms, giving movie distributors sleepless nights. Eventually, content came to rule the roost.

### Some Once-in-a-blue-moon Experiences

Allow yours truly to share some experiences from his personal life.

*A Low Point in the Career*

While working in a company which was steadily going downhill due to very high overheads and an unhealthy level of internal bickering and politics, a highly embarrassing moment had to be faced. In a meeting of all senior managers, I was somehow singled out to be publicly lynched for much of what was going wrong with the operations. The unfairness of it, and that too delivered in wide public view, left me shaken to my core. Whereas all those who know me personally can vouch for my chin-up attitude towards life, on this occasion, I confess that suicidal thoughts plagued my mind. Always appreciated for my work and sincerity, this was indeed the lowest point in my career.

Late evening, though, in the privacy of his office, my boss offered his sincere apologies. Gradually, thoughts of a spiritual nature and a dash of equanimity helped me to regain my mental balance. A few months down the road, I moved on to a much better position in another outfit.

### *The Kidnapping Fiasco*

While working in a very senior position with a company located in a small town in India, on one fateful night, I and my son were kidnapped by a gang of four, and kept in captivity overnight. They were under the impression that I was the owner of the business I was employed by at the time. They had a ransom demand which I had no way of fulfilling.

While held in captivity, I could imagine the sequence of events if they decided to bump me off and dump the body at a desolate location. Concerns about my son's safety reigned supreme. But faith in a higher power saw me regaining my confidence. Despite a language barrier, I could explain my financial constraints to them. We could eventually manage to get released without much physical harm by the time the next day dawned.

Swift police action followed. Based on my cell phone records, the miscreants were identified and nabbed. But it took me a very long time to mentally recover from the trauma suffered.

## Crucial Enabling Factors

With the benefit of a 20/20 hindsight, one can analyse and identify the crucial underlying factors which enabled a successful handling of such challenges. If the low point in career could be handled with the help of humility and one's job knowledge, skills and attitude, the kidnapping incident could be overcome with faith and an inclination to surrender to a higher power.

It is not difficult to discover traces here of what the *Bhagavad Gita* proposes.

अमानित्वमदम्भित्वमहिंसा क्षान्तिरार्जवम् |
आचार्योपासनं शौचं स्थैर्यमात्मविनिग्रहः || 13.7 ||

इन्द्रियार्थेषु वैराग्यमनहङ्कार एव च |
जन्ममृत्युजराव्याधिदुःखदोषानुदर्शनम् || 13.8 ||

असक्तिरनभिष्वङ्गः पुत्रदारगृहादिषु |
नित्यं च समचित्तत्वमिष्टानिष्टोपपत्तिषु || 13.9 ||

मयि चानन्ययोगेन भक्तिरव्यभिचारिणी |
विविक्तदेशसेवित्वमरतिर्जनसंसदि || 13.10 ||

अध्यात्मज्ञाननित्यत्वं तत्वज्ञानार्थदर्शनम् |
एतज्ज्ञानमिति प्रोक्तमज्ञानं यदतोऽन्यथा || 13.11 ||

*Absence of pride, unostentatiousness, non-violence, forbearance, simplicity, worship of the teacher, purity, stability, self-control; Dispassion towards the objects of the senses and absence of ego also, seeing the miseries of birth, death, old age and diseases; non-attachment and absence of feeling of possession in son, wife, home, and so on; always being even minded in favourable and unfavourable circumstances; unswerving devotion to Me through exclusive yoga, resorting to solitude and non-involvement with company of persons; constancy of the knowledge of self, perception of the essence of knowledge—all this is called knowledge. What is other than this is ignorance.*

Here, one has a virtual ready reckoner of certain mental and emotional attributes, moral attitudes, and ethical principles. Vacillations of the mind are a strict no-no. One is told that one's mind should be 'un-prostituting' with its point of contemplation. In other words, the mind needs to remain focused on a chosen single ideal. When faced with mighty challenges, basic needs rule supreme.

These attributes and principles are held to be the essential pre-requisites for one to discover—and act in tandem with—the Self within. In turn, this makes one discover and deploy the inner reservoirs of innate strength one possesses and meet a challenge head-on.

We explore this theme further in Chapter 39.

# 39

# When Life Hurls Big Rocks at One 2.0

In its concluding chapter, the *Bhagavad Gita* goes on to extol the virtue of surrender to a higher power. It does not ask one to necessarily believe in a higher power or follow a particular religion or sect for the purpose. Nor does it specifically state that surrender is useful only when a CEO is facing a monumental challenge in her career or life.

However, it is my belief that an attitude laced with liberal doses of surrender, duly backed by the personality attributes listed in the previous chapter, becomes the most crucial enabling factor which facilitates the successful handling of mighty challenges.

> तमेव शरणं गच्छ सर्वभावेन भारत |
> तत्प्रसादात्परां शान्तिं स्थानं प्राप्स्यसि शाश्वतम् || 18.62 ||
>
> *Take refuge in Him alone in every disposition, O Bharata. By His grace you will attain supreme peace and eternal abode.*

Much like a senior vice president who gets promoted as a CEO after the seniors notice a potential in her to shoulder a higher responsibility, coupled with a match between the value system of the incumbent and that of the business, and a deep sense of loyalty (read surrender) to the organization, Lord Krishna also stipulates the condition under which His grace would help a person to attain perfect peace—exclusive surrender. A conscious realization that it is not one's efforts alone which get success in life and that one's destiny also plays a crucial role, helps one to surrender in such a manner.

There are no free lunches in life, as the wise men say!

## Challenges and Evolution

Each of the demeaning experiences faced by yours truly and shared in the previous chapter led to some inner growth. A public rebuke made me learn the value of sensing dangerous turbulence on the flight path in advance and punching the eject button in the cockpit before things spun out of control. Likewise, the kidnapping incident taught me the importance of having some acquaintance with the law and order and regulatory agencies in the area. As an additional perk, each incident revealed the true friends and foes of those around me at the time. An enriching string of experiences, one would say in retrospect.

When a pink slip gets dished out, one finds an opportunity of reassessing one's strengths and weaknesses and act on them. A fall from grace eventually ends up increasing the depth of one's inner reservoirs of patience, equipoise, and fortitude.

## When Kunti Seeks Challenges as a Boon!

In one of the post-war episodes narrated in the *Srimad Bhagavatam*, when Krishna is about to depart for his kingdom of Dwarka, Uttara, the bereaved wife of Abhimanyu and the daughter-in-law of Arjuna, comes running to seek His protection for the son in her womb who has been killed by a mighty weapon unleashed by Ashwatthama. Krishna then brings the child back to life, at which time Kunti, the mother of the Pandavas and an aunt of Krishna, prays thus:

विषान्महाग्नेः पुरुषाददर्शनाद् असत्सभाया वनवासकृच्छ्रतः ।
मृधे मृधेऽनेकमहारथास्त्रतो द्रौण्यस्त्रतश्चास्म हरेऽभिरक्षिताः ॥ 1.8.24 ॥

*My dear Krishna, You have protected us from a poisoned cake, from a great fire, from cannibals, from the vicious assembly, from sufferings during our exile in the forest and from the battle where great generals fought. And now You have saved us from the weapon of Ashwatthama.*

विपदः सन्तु ताः शश्वत् तत्र तत्र जगद्गुरो ।
भवतो दर्शनं यत्स्याद् अपुनर्भवदर्शनम् ॥ 1.8.25॥

*I wish that all those calamities would happen again and again so that we could see You again and again, for seeing You means that we will no longer repeat births and deaths.*

Apprehending that she and her children would subsequently miss being in touch with someone of the stature of Krishna, Kunti seeks a blessing from Him—that her family is always surrounded by some trouble or the other. Krishna is surprised and bemused at someone seeking a negative blessing!

## Of Challenges, Deprivation and Humiliation

Sri Ram Chandra Maharaj, affectionately referred to as Lalaji Maharaj by his followers the world over, was the original master of the spiritual organization Sri Ram Chandra Mission which is spear-heading the practice of Heartfulness Meditation globally these days. He has stated in one of his messages that there are three factors in one's life which lead to spiritual evolution: *Illat* (challenges, adversity in general), *Quillat* (deprivation in material resources) and *Zillat* (deprivation in fame, like humiliation).

In other words, to have a little less money than necessary; to have a little less than good health; and to always have critics around one. Those who are on the path towards an inward growth would do well to receive such brickbats and rocks as fragrant bouquets which life bestows on one.

Saint Kabir echoes a similar sentiment in one of his couplets.

निंदक नियरे राखिए, आँगन कुटी छवाय।
बिन पानी, साबुन बिना, निर्मल करे सुभाय।।

*Keep your critics close. Give them shelter in your courtyard and listen to their criticism without annoyance,*

> ***because critics are not your enemies; instead, they help you to clean the rubbish from your life without soap and water.***

The real examples quoted earlier in this context aptly justify this sobering thought.

**Negatives Support Us Better!**

Swami Vivekananda, in his notes on karma yoga, has the following to say:

> Good and evil have an equal share in moulding character, and in some instances, misery is a greater teacher than happiness. In studying the great characters, the world has produced, I dare say, in the vast majority of cases it would be found that it was misery that taught more than happiness, it was poverty that taught more than wealth, it was blows that brought out their inner fire more than praise.

Perhaps, if Mahatma Gandhi had not been kicked out of a train for travelling first class at Pietermaritzburg in 1893 in South Africa, the history of the Indian continent might have been quite different!

The argument here is not that one should willingly court challenges and negativity in life. It is merely to state a basic truth in life—that challenges have an upside too.

**When Adversity Nudges One to Turn to Spirituality**

In their thought-provoking book *Rajarshi Leadership: The Saving Role of Authentic Spirituality*, S.K. Chakraborty and Debangshu Chakraborty cite the example of Mr R.K. Talwar (former chairman of State Bank of India and Industrial Development Bank of India) who became aware of *Bhagavad Gita* in his childhood. As his career progressed, so did his understanding of this scripture.

At one stage in his career, he faced undue political pressure in respect of a decision taken by him in his professional capacity. Gradually, he sought retirement and shifted his base to the Sri Aurobindo Ashram at Puducherry, offering voluntary services to the organization.

Professionals could turn to spirituality for various reasons. Some could get prompted by people in their inner circle whose influence they trust. Others could be either exploring ways of destressing themselves or continuing their journey towards self-actualization and happiness within. Many others get nudged by the disasters they face in their lives orcareers.

## The Rhinoceroses of Challenges

Challenges come in all sizes, shapes, kinds and severity on the Richter scale. Each challenge faced by one in life eventually results in speeding up one's progress on the tricky path of evolution. One gains maturity and experience. One learns to be grateful when one is feeling unduly elated, and graceful when feeling down and out. One learns to be more careful and patient.

Challenges are blessings that bring about changes which uplift and enrich one. Our guardian angels would never desert us. Instead, they plan their furloughs in such a way that while they are having a rollicking time on a distant planet, one gets precisely the kind of challenges which enable one to become more humane, more pragmatic and more professional in one's dealings with people and with situations.

One's fight with mighty challenges in career and life could be decisively won by using the firepower of the tools in one's arsenal—a relentless drive to keep upgrading one's *knowledge* base and *skill sets*, and to have *faith* in a higher power. An attitude of *surrender* enables one to march on in life, with one's chin up, a smile lighting up one's face, and a steely resolve to make the approaching rhinoceroses-like challenges wilt and retreat into their own comfort zones.

*(Sources:* The Spider's Web, Vol. 3, *'Attitude', Shri P. Rajagopalachari;* Karma Yoga: The Yoga of Action, *'Karma In Its Effect on Character', Swami Vivekananda,* Rajarshi Leadership: The Saving Role of Authentic Spirituality, *S.K. Chakraborty and Debangshu Chakraborty)*

# 40

# Of Free Will, Destiny, and a Dash of Humility

Many CEOs who believe they rule their domains with an iron fist—delivering results quarter after quarter and manipulating people like puppets—could really use a dose of humility. Success and failure alike demand honest introspection. Often, success hinges on factors beyond their control, while failure reveals lessons they might have missed. Realizing that we can act but never fully control outcomes is a key step towards humility.

The idea that humans have complete free will is debatable. The *Bhagavad Gita* teaches that while we are free to act, the results belong to destiny. Neuroscience studies even suggest our brains can be influenced externally, meaning we sometimes act as if part of a grand plan, surrendering free will temporarily. Employees bullied by bosses or captives showing Stockholm syndrome are real-life examples of this surrender.

Take the story of yours truly: as I finished business school, my career launch in the Tata group wasn't solely my doing—it was a mix of effort and chance. I couldn't control the company, my bosses, or colleagues, but the values and ethics of that group shaped me deeply. This blend of personal action and destiny highlights that success is rarely just one's own—humility and openness to life's mysteries are essential.

However, this is the experience of a lesser mortal like yours truly. The *Bhagavad Gita* offers a fresh perspective. Depending upon my soul's past karmic account, and the need for future evolution in this lifetime, the family I was born into and the country I was born in, were both decided. Whatever followed in life came about owing to the choices I had made, including education, work, and the subsequent occurrences. We touched upon this theme in Chapter 32, 'The Karma Operating System'.

**A Hall of Mirrors Called Free Will?**

The notion of free will is an illusion. According to the *Bhagavad Gita*, the will that drives one's thoughts and motives is itself a product of one's past, one's heredity and one's environment. When it comes to the choices one makes at any given moment, the buck stops only at one's own desk. One has the power, as well as the responsibility, over the choices one makes in life, sans the results thereof. What drive one in making choices collectively are the three modes of nature—sattva, rajas or tamas.

The scripture speaks of the 'I Am the Doer' syndrome which afflicts most CEOs, and goes on to assert that 'it is the modes of nature that are acting on the modes' (*gunah gunesu vartante*):

> प्रकृतेः क्रियमाणानि गुणैः कर्माणि सर्वशः |
> अहङ्कारविमूढात्मा कर्ताहमिति मन्यते || 3.27 ||
>
> *In every way, actions are performed by the gunas of nature. One who is deluded by ego supposes I am the doer.*
>
> तत्ववित्तु महाबाहो गुणकर्मविभागयोः |
> गुणा गुणेषु वर्तन्त इति मत्वा न सज्जते || 3.28 ||
>
> *But he who knows the truth about the divisions of three gunas and (their) actions, O mighty armed, knowing that the gunas (in the shape of the senses, mind, and so on) act upon the gunas (in the shape of the objects of perception), remains unattached to them, Arjuna.*

A wise CEO who has realized that her actions belong to the world of the mind is no more anxious for the fruits thereof. Successes and failures belong to the mind, and so do likes and dislikes, and love and hatred. She behaves like a true sportsperson where the very enjoyment is in the game being played well and not in the score.

A true warrior is only she who can act tirelessly to fight with her inner demons of mental preoccupations and worldly attachments and gain a victory in the business world's battlefield of actions.

> स्वभावजेन कौन्तेय निबद्ध: स्वेन कर्मणा |
> कर्तुं नेच्छसि यन्मोहात्करिष्यस्यवशोऽपि तत् || 18.60 ||

> *O Arjuna, that action which out of delusion you do not wish to do, you will be driven to do it by your own inclination, born of your own material nature.*

A smart CEO who has suddenly faced a mighty challenge in her career simply cannot afford the luxury of not handling the same. Her innate faith and inclination would drive her actions. Unlike Arjuna at the beginning of the Manual of Motivation we allude to as the *Bhagavad Gita*, she would be digging her heels in, cancelling all other engagements, and focusing her entire energies on meeting the challenge head-on. Her material nature would make her do this, come what may. Even while believing that she is acting out of her free will, she would perhaps realize that she is in the right place at the right time, fulfilling her destiny:

> ईश्वर: सर्वभूतानां हृद्देशेऽर्जुन तिष्ठति |
> भ्रामयन्सर्वभूतानि यन्त्रारूढानि मायया || 18.61 ||

> *The Lord, O Arjuna, resides in the heart of all beings whirling them by Maya as if (they were) mounted on a machine (made of material energy).*

Here is the 'Serenity Prayer', which perhaps captures the reality quite well:

> God,
> Grant me the serenity to accept things I cannot change,
> The courage to change the things I can,
> And the wisdom to know the difference.

We will explore this theme further in Chapter 41.

# 41

# Of Free Will and Destiny (Part 2)

**Going with the Flow: Different Perspectives**

In life, one does not control one's own birth or death. Nor does one control the kind of parents, extended family, and friends one may merit. One merely goes with the flow, so to speak. The society one gets born in shapes one's values, likes and dislikes. The country of one's origin determines the land and culture one gets to own.

Yes, one's flow is determined by the choices one makes, which is determined by one's own personality characteristics, prejudices, preferences, and one's station in life. The choices one makes could also be random occurrences. But perhaps the choices one makes and the external circumstances one faces are also governed by an invisible hand which propels one through life. When one looks back and evaluates the choices made in life, one is apt to discover a pattern which may reveal the kind of enriching experience our soul has been desirous of going through.

In his poem 'The Road Not Taken', Robert Frost touches upon this facet of our lives. Likewise, in the poem 'If', Rudyard Kipling speaks of humility when he says that:

> ...If you can talk with crowds and keep your virtue,
> Or walk with Kings—nor lose the common touch...

To participate in, and to submit to, the collective rhythm of creation is to attain bhakti (devotion), *Narada Sutra* says. This marks progress towards humility and brings in the thought of surrender.

Omar Khayyam thought one is no better than water, flowing

willy-nilly, '...where destiny with men for pieces plays'. He proposed that one merely follows an unalterable script in one's life, as dished out by one's guardian angels.

As per Marcus Aurelius:

> Does aught befall you? It is good. It is part of the destiny of the universe ordained for you from the beginning. All that befalls you is part of the great web.

However, the *Bhagavad Gita* proposes that the soul makes free choices and moves along its chosen path freely. Outcomes are irrelevant for the soul, except when it develops an attachment towards them. On a mundane plane, effort is always under one's control but not the outcome.

Classical physics had always viewed the universe as being mechanistic, pre-determined and hence predictable, devoid of uncertainty of any kind. But quantum physics subsequently turned the logic upside down by bringing in uncertainty, thanks to Heisenberg's principle. Albert Einstein has said that 'It is entirely possible that behind the perception of our senses, worlds are hidden of which we are unaware.'

Most management decisions need to be taken in an environment which has a high degree of unpredictability, whether in the form of markets, inputs to operations like supplies, labour, transport facilities, government policy, international trade barriers and such threats as the sudden onset of a pandemic, and the like.

At a much higher spiritual plane, Sri Aurobindo points out that behind the visible events of the world, there is always a mass of invisible cosmic forces at work that are unknown to the outward minds of men. We are blind to their action because our ego-sense creates in us the illusion of a coherent personality (*The Life Divine,* Chapter XI, 'The Boundaries of the Ignorance').

Contrast this with the traditional view of Judgment Day of Judaism, Christianity and Islam. This view is based on the conviction that each person is wholly responsible for his or her conduct in life.

But the Bard says that:

> The fault, dear Brutus, is not in our stars, but in ourselves,
> that we are underlings.
> (*Julius Caeser,* Act 1, Scene 2).

The Hindu view of karma also supposes choice for individual human beings but shows a way out for one to attain a state of freedom. It even proposes that just like the Newton's Third Law of Motion, there is a cause-and-effect relationship between our karma and our destiny, a theme which we shall soon explore.

## Freedom from the Giant Wheel of Destiny

All this is not to say that one needs to give up making choices in life. Work one must. Choose one should. However, the endeavour should be to transcend the modes of nature and attain true freedom:

> प्रकाशं च प्रवृत्तिं च मोहमेव च पाण्डव |
> न द्वेष्टि सम्प्रवृत्तानि न निवृत्तानि काङ् क्षति || 14.22 ||
>
> उदासीनवदासीनो गुणैर्यो न विचाल्यते |
> गुणा वर्तन्त इत्येवं योऽवतिष्ठति नेङ्गते || 14.23 ||
>
> समदु:खसुख: स्वस्थ: समलोष्टाश्मकाञ्चन: |
> तुल्यप्रियाप्रियो धीरस्तुल्यनिन्दात्मसंस्तुति: || 14.24 ||
>
> मानापमानयोस्तुल्यस्तुल्यो मित्रारिपक्षयो: |
> सर्वारम्भपरित्यागी गुणातीत: स उच्यते || 14.25 ||
>
> *(He who) does not hate the light and tendency of activity and the delusion when they arise, nor desires them when they recede, O son of Pandu... Who, sitting indifferently, is not disturbed by the gunas, who (realizing that) gunas alone function, is steady, does not waver... Even in*

*pleasure and sorrow; regarding a lump of earth, a stone and gold as equivalent; healthy, balanced with respect to agreeable and disagreeable, steadfast, and balanced in praise and blame to him... Balanced in honour and dishonour, balanced towards friend and foe, renouncer of all tendencies, he is said to be beyond the gunas.*

Quite a tall order, as one can see. The Mother of Sri Aurobindo Ashram explains this in the following manner:

> If you remain in a consciousness which functions mentally, even if it is the highest mind, you have the notion of an absolute determinism of cause and effect and feel that things are what they are because they are what they are and cannot be otherwise. It is only when you come out of the mental consciousness completely and enter a higher perception of things—which you may call spiritual or divine—that you suddenly find yourself in a state of perfect freedom where everything is possible.
>
> [The Mother, *Questions and Answers (1957–1958)*]

The good news is that the probability of one experiencing free will increases as one becomes more conscious of one's true Self (*Atman*). Krishna assures us that enlightened souls are not tied by the bonds of karma.

### Of Enlightened Souls

Becoming a truly enlightened soul is akin to one's journey to a state of perfection. One may strive to be an aspirant to the manner of living recommended by the *Bhagavad Gita*. However, it is important to know, remember and try to imbibe the kind of qualities which an enlightened soul is associated with.

ब्रह्मण्याधाय कर्माणि सङ्गं त्यक्त्वा करोति यः ।

लिप्यते न स पापेन पद्मपत्रमिवाम्भसा || 5.10 ||

*He who acts dedicating all actions to God, abandoning attachment, is not involved with sin (just) as a lotus leaf (is uncontaminated) by water.*

An aspirant who has realized that she is neither the doer nor the enjoyer of what she does and that the fruits of her actions are not to be concerned about is likely to remain happier in her life and career. The art of constant remembrance assists her in worldly pursuits—that is, always remembering inwardly that she is merely an instrument in the hands of the Divine, performing actions on the latter's behalf.

न कर्तृत्वं न कर्माणि लोकस्य सृजति प्रभुः |
न कर्मफलसंयोगं स्वभावस्तु प्रवर्तते || 5.14 ||

*God creates neither the authorship of actions, nor the actions of man, nor does He create the link between the action and the fruit. (One's) Nature alone prevails.*

Our guardian angels are not the ones who decide what one should do in which kind of a situation. Such mundane affairs are taken care of by one's own disposition. One takes full responsibility of doing what one does.

Indeed, there are advantages of being a managing agent of a higher power. One realizes one's potential better. One becomes more objective in assessing oneself. Thus, one's effectiveness improves.

Above all, when things go wrong, one could be delusional and believe that it is the higher power which should take the rap, leaving one free of guilt and despondency! However, the stark reality is that the motives behind our actions alone make or mar our successes.

## The Way Out

The best way out for a manager is to perform the assigned duties without attachment and expectation; and then accept whatever happens. A state of intoxication induced by success could lead to recklessness borne out of overconfidence. Likewise, frustration arising out of failure could undermine efficiency.

One would therefore do well to do one's best and leave the rest. During the effort phase, one needs to forget about destiny and focus only on punching the right buttons with confidence. In other words, exercising one's free will. When the outcome crystallizes, one may accept it with a dash of humility, realizing that one's destiny has a hand in shaping it. Keep repeating this cycle with each new task that one gets entrusted with.

The higher one is placed in a hierarchy, the higher the possibility of one using one's free will to visualize and choose one's actions. Self-motivated employees who act in the mould of Douglas McGregor's Theory Y are invariably appreciated.

*(Related, Chapter 32: 'The Karma Operating System')*

# 42

# Shoring Up One's Spiritual Quotient (Part 1)

It would not be wrong to say that in today's world, a relentless pursuit of wealth and material belongings has left a deep scar on our souls. Many of us are twiddling our thumbs trying to figure out either how to de-stress ourselves or how to keep fighting those depressive blues. Despite all signs of external prosperity, there is a nagging emptiness within. The mind boggles as to why and how it has come about. Most of us have no clue as to what could be done about it.

**Redefining 'Success' and 'Happiness'**

One way out of this dilemma is to perhaps redefine our concepts of 'success' and 'happiness'. What do these terms really mean? When we dig deeper, we might find that these two are not dependent on external factors alone. There is also an inner connection somewhere.

Something very elaborate, say a long well-planned vacation, might not yield the emotional high that we expected. On the contrary, a post-dinner spontaneous outing for a late-night ice cream binge could leave us elated.

Why do some things make us happy, and others do not? We love beauty. We cherish humour. We like being appreciated and being loved. We love doing something 'different'. Anything which connects us to our inner selves tends to make us happy. A movie or a work of fiction which we can relate to relaxes us. Exploring new frontiers and visiting new places often makes us happy. Perhaps the soul revels in reliving its earlier experience

SQ
EQ
IQ
SB

of exploration when we were cave-dwellers and hunters!

A paradigm shift could perhaps help. If 'success' ceases to be about the property we own, the social respect and fame we enjoy, and the high and mighty 'connections' we boast of, we might arrive at a different picture of ourselves. The quality of sleep we get. The inner glow of satisfaction we have when we leave our place of work for the day. The vibrant relationships we have with other people at work. The love we get at home after a hard day's work. The kind of legacy we leave behind when we kick the bucket.

A change in perspective brings about a stupendous transformation in how we think and feel. Our attitude becomes positive.

## Materialism, Big Data and Perception Management

This is not to say that materialism is bad, per se. To satisfy one's needs is a basic requirement of life. Indian scriptures do recognize the fact that materialism and spirituality go hand in hand. Both are like the mighty two wings of the aeroplane assigned to us to soar higher in this life of ours.

In its ninth verse, the *Isha Upanishad* clearly says that:

> Those who cultivate only material science go to hell. But those who cultivate only spiritual science go to an even darker hell.

If materialism is essential for the maintenance of our physical bodies, spirituality is necessary for the manifestation of thc internal divinity within us. We must balance both in our lives to reach the goal of life.

Almost all the Vedas have accompanying scriptures which capture the materialistic part of our lives. For example, *Atharva Veda* has Ayurveda which speaks in detail of what, why and how of maintaining our physical bodies in good shape.

The imbalance arises when we end up laying a greater

emphasis on the material part of our lives. Even if we become aware of the spiritual part, we relegate it to the back of our minds, believing it to be more useful in the later years of our lives. The fact remains that those who take to spirituality early in their lives enjoy the journey of their lives better. We soar like Jonathan Livingston Seagull which can flap both its wings—material as well as the spiritual—with equal ease. We realize that we then have the power to live the life we want to live. We fly higher, fly faster, and live longer.

Most of the time, we fail to distinguish between our needs and our desires. Needs may be satiated easily. But desires tend to regenerate and evolve, keeping us engaged. Desires keep making us run after an illusory rainbow which forever keeps drifting away from us.

Marketing professionals invariably target their products, services, and communications to our desires. With the advent of Big Data, promotional campaigns are becoming far more segment focused. We hear of 'evidence-based decision making' or 'actionable information'. Even public policies get framed and aggressively communicated by governments to promote the feel-good factor, whereas ground realities might reveal a different scenario.

Managing perceptions is essentially about catering to the desires of the average person. Organizations routinely window-dress their accounts and Corporate Social Responsibility initiatives to earn brownie points with diverse stakeholders. Governments do it all the time, especially when the next round of elections are due. Unfortunately, fulfilling the genuine needs of the have-nots of society, say in the realm of public health, education, employment and environment, takes a back seat.

## Enter: Spiritual Quotient

Another way of striking a balance between materialism and spirituality is to become aware of our Spiritual Quotient (SQ);

that is, our ability to understand and comprehend the spiritual aspects of life. In other words, moving on from the world of mind and heart to the realm of our inner Self.

Those who have a high SQ have this uncanny ability to be creative and insightful in their approach to problem-solving. They build up their level of self-awareness and intuitive faculties. They realize that there is a realm of intelligence that is beyond the five senses our bodies are endowed with.

Intelligence Quotient (IQ) is what sees us through academic pursuits. Emotional Quotient (EQ, or Emotional Intelligence) is what we gain by experiencing life. SQ is something of which we become aware a little later in our life.

IQ can be readily measured. EQ can also be estimated, though not with the same level of precision that IQ can be. However, SQ does not lend itself to easy measurement. All its attributes happen to be subjective in nature. By observing a person for a long time, one can perhaps estimate her SQ more realistically.

When we move on from Intelligence Quotient (IQ) to Spiritual Quotient (SQ), we move from the gross to the subtle, from the finite to the infinite, and from the tangible to the intangible.

**Some Components of Spiritual Quotient**

The *Bhagavad Gita* de-mystifies the concept of SQ with the assistance of the following components:

- Abandonment of slavery of clinging to results
- Improving one's vertical mobility; practising equanimity
- Tapping into the calm energy within
- A premium on the austerity of the body, the mind and speech

*(We will try and explore these aspects further in Chapter 43.)*

# 43

# Shoring Up One's Spiritual Quotient (Part 2)

**How Relevant Is SQ to a Business?**

SQ has several components: gratitude, empathy, self-esteem, self-awareness, consciousness, compassion, surrender, service and an ego that is under control. Let us attempt to examine its relevance in the lives of individuals and business entities.

As to gratitude, wise men point out the utility of maintaining a journal of gratitude. Like in a personal diary, if one were to make regular entries about one's experiences wherein one felt the power of gratitude towards others, life would suddenly be seen through a positive lens.

The undercurrent of most of the tips dished out by Lord Krishna to live a balanced and happier life also gives us a clear clue as to what really constitutes a CEO's spiritual quotient.

*Abandonment of Slavery of Clinging to Results*

> त्यक्त्वा कर्मफलासङ्गं नित्यतृप्तो निराश्रयः ।
> कर्मण्यभिप्रवृत्तोऽपि नैव किञ्चित्करोति सः || 4.20 ||

> *Having cast off attachment to the fruit of action, ever contended; depending upon nothing, even though fully engaged in action, he does not act at all.*

The proposition here is not to renounce the results of one's actions; it is merely to give up one's intellectual clinging to expected results. If a grand merger and alliance being planned does not fructify, one does not merely sulk and get into a state of intellectual impotency. Rather, having learnt from experience, better efforts are put in to close the next deal which fits into the strategic vision of the organization.

Consider the case of Nano, the 'world's cheapest car' launched by Tata Motors in 2009. It was a brilliant effort at frugal innovation and creativity based on detailed studies of consumers' needs and wants. The whole effort apparently cost the company between USD 380 million and USD 435 million. However, customers in the aspirational bracket of the Indian economy did not respond favourably. The promotional focus on the product being 'cheap' apparently created a perception that the car was of poor quality. The product failed to satisfy the social aspirations of families who were trying to move on to a four-wheeler from a two-wheeler occupancy. Even though the management demonstrated its penchant for agility and equanimity and went on to introduce newer models in the normal price range, customers were not enthused. The brand could not create a ripple in the market. Eventually, the project was abandoned.

*Improving One's Vertical Mobility: Equanimity*

> विद्याविनयसम्पन्ने ब्राह्मणे गवि हस्तिनि |
> शुनि चैव श्वपाके च पण्डिता: समदर्शिन: || 5.18 ||
>
> *The truly learned, with the eyes of divine knowledge, perceive alike a Brahmin, a cow, an elephant, a dog and a dog-eater.*

It is common knowledge that CEOs who venture to go out of their way to encourage and motivate others across the organization are invariably more popular. What also goes on to improve their following is to swim against the tide, like adopting a deferential approach towards board members but taking a principled stand when the actions recommended by them go against the basic values on which the organization is run. Likewise, a pat on the back for someone who does a fine job, even if the person happens to be five rungs down in the hierarchy, helps. So does a chat with the liftman to check how his daughter is doing at school, or an occasional enquiry from a junior in the shipping department as to how his newborn baby is doing. All this needs a dash of concern and empathy.

*Tapping into the Calm Energy within*

> यस्मान्नोद्विजते लोको लोकान्नोद्विजते च यः |
> हर्षामर्षभयोद्वेगैर्मुक्तो यः स च मे प्रियः || 12.15 ||
>
> *From whom the world is not perturbed and who is not perturbed by the world, free from elation, jealousy, fear, and anxiety—he is dear to Me.*

A super boss would be one who would be firm and polite. She would spread clarity and cheer around herself, appreciating over-achievers in public while ticking off under-performers in private. If she creates agitation in the minds of others, it is only with the purpose of eventually finding a harmonious solution to a vexing problem. To her, the tornados of business challenges are like charging lionesses which need to be looked in the eye and tamed and prompted to beat a retreat by appropriate measures. The fire of fear does not affect them, nor do the leaping flames of anxiety.

> अनपेक्षः शुचिर्दक्ष उदासीनो गतव्यथः |
> सर्वारम्भपरित्यागी यो मद्भक्तः स मे प्रियः || 12.16 ||
>
> *(One who is) without expectation, clean, efficient, unbiased, unperturbed, (and) who has renounced all actions; a devotee of this kind is dear to Me.*

When trying to solve a problem, she might seek suggestions from many, but act independently of their opinions, based only on her own intuition and gut feeling. She is well-disciplined and systematic. Her office and her working table reveal the kind of no-nonsense person she happens to be. Her enthusiasm and mental agility are seldom found wanting.

The advent of 'Conscious Leadership', which has been on the rise in the recent past, is but a manifestation of corporates looking within and deciding to use their power to give back to society in imaginative ways, even in the absence of regulatory laws.

When an IT major like Infosys decides to compensate its carbon footprints by providing green products to rural households, it makes eminent sense.

At its new campus in Nagpur in India, Infosys endeavoured to create structures which could house up to 20,000 employees, but with a net-zero balance of energy and water, and nil transfer of waste to landfills.

When a multinational corporation like Hindustan Unilever decides to use a government scheme like MNREGA to create water potential for farmers in one of the most water-starved areas of India, it is serving the society it draws its inputs from.

At the headquarters of Kotak Mahindra Bank in Mumbai, meeting rooms now have glass water jars and disposable paper cups, thereby avoiding the consumption of 4,30,000 plastic bottles per annum.

When an Air Asia flight goes down killing all passengers on board, and its CEO resorts to Twitter to keep the anxious relatives updated, it is a humane gesture which deserves to be applauded.

When the Tata group sets up a Centre of Performing Arts, as also institutions like the Indian Institute of Science, Tata Institute of Fundamental Research, and Tata Institute of Social Studies, the group's value of giving back something to society becomes manifest.

In 2018, Taj Hotels of the group decided to phase out plastic straws at its hotels and aviation catering units, thereby eliminating two million straws each year.

These instances illustrate a heartening and accelerating trend among companies—to listen to their conscience within and be thoughtful of the impact of their operations on the planet and the people around them, including employees, customers, partners, and communities.

*A Premium on the Austerity of the Body, Mind and Speech*

We have already touched upon the austerity of body and speech in Chapter 37, entitled 'Of Effective Communication'. Let us now explore the concept of austerity of mind.

> मनः प्रसादः सौम्यत्वं मौनमात्मविनिग्रहः |
> भावसंशुद्धिरित्येतत्तपो मानसमुच्यते || 17.16 ||
>
> *Mental bliss, serenity, kindness, silence, self-control and purity of thoughts are said to (constitute) austerity of the mind.*

Conscious leaders practise austerities of body, speech and mind, steadily, with no clinging attachment to, or anxiety for, the fruits of their actions. Thus, they act like well-integrated persons who come to be seen as being dependable and sincere, thereby beefing up their brand equity over time.

They are aware that a new business vertical which utilizes a core competency of the group may need to be entered into, even though a downsizing becomes necessary in another part of the organization. There is no place for personal agendas in the scheme of things.

## An Inwardly Gaze

By nature, we tend to be outward-looking. We try to find the threats, challenges and other factors outside ourselves. We blame others and our external circumstances for our failures. Often, what we do not realize is that when we point a finger at others, there are three others which point towards us.

Lord Krishna points out that our real threats and challenges are inside ourselves, arising out of our desires, anger, greed, selfishness, attachments and so on. When we start seeing our own faults, weaknesses and mistakes rather than gleefully siding with these, then we can say that our SQ is on the increase. Regular practice of meditation helps us to develop this inner connection.

**The Age of Spiritually Evolved CEOs is Already Upon Us!**

Technology is changing the way we live, think, behave and feel. Thanks to pandemics, and even otherwise, the rate of change is only going to go up in future. Leaders, managers and even individuals with a high level of SQ are bound to have a better chance of tasting success in the decades to come.

Dr Ian Marshall and Danah Zohar, in their 2001 book *SQ: Connecting With Our Spiritual Intelligence*, say that 'while computers have IQ and animals can have EQ, it is essentially an SQ that sets human beings apart.'

It follows that to have a smooth ride in life, all three—IQ, EQ and SQ—need to be relied upon equally by all of us—whether in our personal lives or in our businesses.

It is time to still our brains, rein in our emotions, desires, prejudices and egos, and start shoring up our Spiritual Quotients.

Those of us who decide to progress on this path would boost our professional shelf lives manifold. The demand for spiritually evolved leaders, businessmen, CXOs and managers is only going to rise in the years to come!

*(Related chapters: #30: 'The Option of Rewiring Oneself' #46: 'Can the* Bhagavad Gita *Help Us to Cope with the Challenges Posed by Industrial Revolution 4.0?')*

# 44

# The Challenges of Industrial Revolution 4.0 (Part 1 of 3)

The first Industrial Revolution used water and steam to mechanize production; the second used electric power and the third one used electronics and IT as its springboard. The fourth one fuses various technologies such as artificial intelligence (AI), the Internet of Things (IoT), autonomous vehicles, 5G telephony, nanotechnology, biotech, robotics, quantum computing and the like.

Exciting days are indeed ahead!

Disney World now has an app and supplies a visitor with a Magic Band which is to be worn on one's wrist. The customer can choose and book rides and is tracked through a web of beacons scattered throughout the park. Booking at the hotel is on one's fingertips, and so is reserving tables at any of the restaurants.

Amazon Go has already started a cashier-less store in the US. The sales staff is there merely to assist a customer in choosing a product. Japan already boasts of retail chains where there is hardly any human interface.

Rolls Royce makes the Trent engine used in the Boeing 787 Dreamliner. Their latest ones come with 25 IoT sensors that track fuel flow, pressure and temperature. On top of that, the company provides technology to track the aircraft's altitude, speed and air temperature, as well as ways to analyse the data to figure out maintenance patterns and better routing. With increasing crowding in the air space, such innovations make it possible to avoid mid-air disasters, thereby rendering air travel relatively safer.

Edge computing, generative AI, AI-driven applications in healthcare, manufacturing, finance, predictive analytics, natural

"The Chairman and I feel that with the arrival of Artificial Intelligence, Data Analytics and Robotics, you and your entire department shall get replaced by the next month end."

language processing, and autonomous decision-making are here to stay. Quantum computing has evolved rapidly over the past five years, especially with companies like IBM and Google leading the charge in quantum supremacy. It can potentially revolutionize such industries as cryptography, logistics and material science.

Blockchain is already bringing trust and transparency to many facets of our lives. Consumers can now ascertain the sourcing history of the food on their tables to check its authenticity and environmental impact.

Robots are already taking over routine jobs. Leading companies are already pursuing the promise of a driverless car with much gusto. Chatbots in the realm of e-commerce, education, entertainment, finance, health, news and productivity are already changing the character of white-collar jobs.

Companies like ABB, Airbus, Bosch, Schneider Electric, Siemens and many others are already using Industry 4.0 technologies to change the way they are marketing and manufacturing products and services. This includes smarter customer solutions, value-added services, innovative pricing models, increased aftermarket support, stronger network collaboration and better efficiencies on the shop floor.

By deploying IR 4.0 technologies, economies can align themselves better with Sustainable Development Goals (SDGs). Smart grids, energy-efficient AI systems, and decarbonization technologies could make the world greener.

The possibilities are mind-boggling, indeed. However, if the delectable aroma of the roses of rapid technological advances has to be savoured, we also need to handle the many thorns these present to us.

## The Perils of Advances in Technology

What concerns the sceptics is the purpose for which we embrace these advances. Developments in technology need to be evaluated on two parameters: the cost-benefit ratio of utility for the masses, and its ethical and moral dimensions. The latter brings into focus the motives behind each of the developments and its subsequent deployment.

So far, Industrial Revolution 4.0 has brought to the fore the following challenges:

- Widespread changes in the skill sets required by commercial enterprises, already leading to severe joblessness.
- Dehumanization of the *Homo sapiens*.
- Leadership and ethical challenges.
- Values being compromised, both at the development and at the implementation stage; training (or re-skilling) of the workforce being accorded a lower priority than investments in upcoming technological advances.
- An unholy nexus between revenue-hungry businesses and governments, facilitating the promotion of technologies that may harm flora, fauna and even human beings.
- Regulatory frameworks are several steps behind developments being rolled out.
- The digitization of individuals and the resultant threat to data privacy.

Cybersecurity is another area of serious concern. With the rise of ransomware attacks and breaches, our brainy geeks need to create sturdier firewalls.

Let us consider these challenges and eventually check how some of the basic tenets of the *Bhagavad Gita* could assist business managers in handling the same.

**Skill Sets of the Future: A Premium on Softer Skills**

The World Economic Forum (WEF) was the first one to use the term Industrial Revolution 4.0 in 2016.

As per WEF's *Future of Jobs Report 2023*, cognitive skills

top the list of the skills deemed to be of greatest importance for workers in 2023. Analytical thinking is considered a core skill by more companies than any other skill, making up, on average, 9.1 per cent of the core skills reported by companies.

Creative thinking comes second, ahead of three self-efficacy skills—resilience, flexibility, and agility; motivation and self-awareness; and curiosity and lifelong learning—which recognize the importance of workers' ability to adapt to disrupted workplaces.

The *World Economic Forum's Framework for Preparing Workers for Dynamic Job Transitions* proposes four key levers to prepare workers for transitions. It highlights the roles that public and private sectors can play in enabling these transitions. The four pillars of the framework read as follows:

- Re-skilling and upskilling for new opportunities.
- Improving employee-employer matching.
- Worker safety nets.
- Multistakeholder collaboration to break through industry barriers.

One thing which stands out is the need for businesses to follow a more humane approach to handling team members. In turn, this would presuppose a higher Emotional Quotient and a much higher Spiritual Quotient, especially at the leadership level. Even as the reliance on artificial intelligence grows for the analytical part of decision-making, the importance of practising the art of remaining connected with one's inner Self would go up quite a few notches.

*When Creativity and Human Values Rule Supreme*

What can be more relevant than to consider the case of a hapless pilot who, when faced with a mid-air crisis, reacts quickly, based purely on her intuition and the concern for passenger safety?

On 17 April 2018, Southwest Airlines Flight 1380 took off from New York's LaGuardia Airport and was headed to Dallas

Love Field. The Boeing 737-700 experienced an uncontained engine failure, damaging the fuselage and a cabin window which led to rapid depressurization. One passenger got partially ejected from the aircraft and died later. Eight others were injured. The flight had 144 passengers and a total of five crew members on board.

Tammie Jo Schults, a former US Navy pilot, was in command. With her intuitive skills and an abiding concern for human safety, she managed to steer the ill-fated plane to safety. The crew conducted an emergency descent and decided to land at Philadelphia International Airport.

On 1 May 2018, the US president welcomed the crew and selected passengers in a ceremony at the Oval Office of the White House, thanking them for their heroism.

*The Evolving Relationship between Machines and Homo Sapiens*

Machine learning systems, which process vast quantities of data and make decisions based upon that data, are incapable of such competencies as compassion and empathy, which are the firm foundations of human values.

Already, technology has evolved to enable robots to be highly effective at collaborating with humans. Yet, humans continue to be much more resilient and possess the unique ability of flexibly changing their plans to cope with unpredictable events.

Unlike thought so far, the human-machine relationship shall become more integrated with each other in the near future. As a result, the combined force of processing billions of data points for efficient decision-making by machines, and contextual, emotional and intuitive aspects of decision-making by human beings, would be, to that extent, higher and greater in its impact—for good or bad.

## Dehumanizing Humans

Glitzy offices, sleepover spaces, a gym, a food court, flexible work hours and many more carrots get dangled before the best and the brightest. But overwork often ends up disturbing the work-life balance of hapless employees. Burnouts, depression, anxiety and suicidal thoughts soon start snapping at their heels.

A July 2024 study by the Confederation of Indian Industries and Medibuddy reported that around 62 per cent of Indian employees experience burnout, which is three times the global average of 20 per cent.

The buck stops at the top. Shareholder value, stock price, profit and potential decide the fate of CEOs and boards of companies. Faster, better, cheaper to stay ahead of the pack is the sacred mantra. The idea is to keep whipping the horses to run faster. In the process, some horses perish. The advent of Industrial Revolution 4.0 appears to have accentuated this issue.

In their relentless pursuit of wealth and market share, corporations are willing to ignore the human cost of achieving their business targets. HR honchos depend on such formalities as rules, SOPs, and committees but fail to enable a culture of respect and empathy all across their organizations. Any attempt by white-collar employees to either unionize themselves or resort to any other form of collective bargaining is nipped in the bud.

However, it appears that CEOs with a Western mind and an Eastern heart are configured somewhat differently. Microsoft CEO, Satya Nadella, sounds passionate about leadership and transformation, but the route he chooses is based on ethos, empathy, empowerment and democratization. In his book *Hit Refresh*, he concludes that 'the choice of leading through consensus versus fiat is a false one.'

He goes on to propose that the 'C' in the CEO represents culture, thereby implying that culture building forms the core of his leadership style. In his leadership paradigm, hubris gives way to humility and envy to empathy. A CEO is as much responsible to the investors as he is accountable to the citizens.

# 45

# The Challenges of Industrial Revolution 4.0 (Part 2 of 3)

## Leadership and Ethical Challenges

*Algorithmic Bias in AI*

As AI becomes more ingrained in decision-making (e.g., hiring, loan approvals, law enforcement), there are growing concerns about how biased data can perpetuate social inequities. Facial recognition technologies and recruitment algorithms pose this challenge.

*Global Inequality and Technology*

The disparity between the Global North and Global South in terms of access to technology and related infrastructure is a topic that is gaining attention. The debate about whether AI can exacerbate or help reduce global inequalities remains inconclusive.

*Diversity, Equity and Inclusion (DEI)*

Over the past five years, the corporate world has placed a stronger emphasis on DEI initiatives, acknowledging the role diversity plays in driving innovation and ethical decision-making.

## When Leadership Deficit Leads to a Compromise on Values

The truth is that no technology is inherently good or bad. Its potential to be beneficial or damaging to society depends entirely on how we choose to use it. The onus is on our leaders.

Regrettably, most business leaders keep biting their nails trying to beat the competition. But when they chase business goals by compromising on their core values, they eventually get caught in a regulatory web and start losing customers and goodwill. Their brand image takes a serious hit.

Consider the following instances:

*The 1986 Space Shuttle Challenger Disaster*

For a space exploration agency of the stature of NASA, revenues and profit were not the motives, but it appears that deviations were indeed made from standard safety protocols because the top leadership put a higher premium on expediency. The now infamous O-ring pressure seals, supplied by a Utah-based contractor, served as the cause of the crash.

The O-rings had been tested to perform in 40 degree Fahrenheit or above weather conditions. On that fateful morning in Florida in 1986, it was only 18 degrees. NASA knew it was an issue, but hours before the launch it pressed the contractor to 'green light' the launch. Robert Ebeling, heading a team of the concerned contractor's employees experienced with the O-rings, debated whether they could knowingly approve that the O-rings would not fail.

In the end, the team wanted NASA to wait until the afternoon when temperatures would be closer to 53 degrees Fahrenheit. Due to the pressure exerted by NASA—in addition to the wilting of the contractor's senior managers—the company reversed its original decision and ended up giving the go-ahead for launch.

Alas, Challenger broke apart 73 seconds into its flight, killing all seven members on board.

*The Boeing 737 Max Issue*

In October 2018, Indonesia's Lion Air flight plummeted to the ground shortly after taking off, killing all 189 people on board. Subsequently, in March 2019, a crash happened in an eerily comparable manner in Ethiopia, killing all 157 persons aboard.

Boeing claims to work on such 'enduring values' as integrity and safety. The company defines integrity as taking 'the high road by practising the highest ethical standards.' Likewise, safety is captured thus: 'We value human life and well-being above all else and take action accordingly,' the company suggests, and that 'by committing to safety first, we advance our goals for quality, cost, and schedule.'

But to match the launch of A320neo by Airbus, said to be 15 per cent more fuel efficient, Boeing moved fast and launched the 737 MAX nine months after Airbus's announcement. Regulatory approvals were apparently rushed through, by simply declaring the 737 MAX to be merely a 'derivative' model of the company's cash cow—737. Technical changes of a material kind were apparently made, but the need for pilot training was never prioritized. The *Flight Crew Operating Manual* was not modified to reflect the changes. If this had been done, perhaps the pilots might have been in a better position to know what to do should the plane begin to behave unpredictably after taking off due to the bad sensor data.

During July 2024, Boeing pleaded guilty to both air disasters, branding itself a convicted felon. It is also supposed to pay a criminal fine of $243.6 million. Boeing has pleaded guilty to making knowingly false representations to the Federal Aviation Administration about having expanded a key software feature used on the MAX to operate at low speeds. The new software saved Boeing money by requiring less intensive training for pilots.

The Manoeuvring Characteristics Augmentation System (MCAS) is a software feature designed to automatically push the airplane's nose down in certain conditions. It was tied to the two crashes that led to the FAA's grounding the plane for 20 months, an action that cost Boeing $20 billion, and the government lifted in November 2020.

All this is not to forget the tragic June 2025 crash of Boeing's

Dreamliner 787-8 at Ahmedabad, India. The plane crashed 32 seconds after take-off, killing 12 crew members and 228 passengers on board. On the ground, 19 people were killed, and 67 others were seriously injured. As of November 2025, a conclusive inquiry report was still awaited. However, the fact that the crash occurred flies in the face of the company's avowed vision of its 'enduring values' wherein passenger safety is held to be of supreme consideration.

The common thread running through all these instances is the leadership deficit these organizations faced at the time. When values become mere words on a company's website, disaster just lurks around the corner. As technology advances, the human angle can only be ignored at the risk of a great cost to the organization as well as to society at large.

### Of Revenue-hungry Businesses and Governments

World over, history has repeatedly taught us that when it comes to the rajasic world of commerce, truth is a casualty. Cigarette and liquor manufacturers contribute to the exchequer and keep their stakeholders happy. Pharmaceutical companies keep peddling drugs which may have serious side effects on hapless patients. After holding up cholesterol as the main villain for cardiac problems for a very long time, medical research now tells us otherwise.

A recent example has been that of the mad rush to bring in 5G which rides on a much stronger dose of radiation. In a research paper published in 2018, Martin L. Pall, PhD, Professor Emeritus of Biochemistry and Basic Medical Sciences, Washington State University, USA, summed up the grave side effects of non-thermal microwave frequency electromagnetic fields on *Homo sapiens.* These range from attacks on our nervous systems, our hormonal balances and our DNA to cancer and lower male and female fertility levels.

Nowhere did one notice a reasoned debate on the incalculable costs of imminent health degradation that the coming generations are bound to face owing to sustained exposure to high doses of radiation.

## Regulatory Controls Playing Catch Up

Regulatory frameworks continue to lag behind the rapid advancements of Industrial Revolution 4.0 technologies. While groundbreaking regulations like Europe's GDPR addressed early data privacy concerns, they now struggle to keep pace with the complexities of AI, autonomous vehicles and blockchain. As innovations in areas like generative AI and cryptocurrencies outstrip existing laws, policymakers remain largely reactive, leaving businesses and consumers exposed to risks, such as ethical breaches and security vulnerabilities. This widening gap underscores the urgent need for proactive, adaptive regulation to safeguard the future of technology.

## The Risk of Data Privacy

As businesses and governments go in for higher levels of digitization, lay citizens who avail of products and services end up living in more transparent fish bowls. Individuals cease to matter. Somewhere in a data repository, they become mere numbers, coded by a binary system, and mercilessly crunched into big data; data which is eagerly lapped up by the corporate world.

Hapless customers and citizens are no longer kings and queens; they are jacks of all trades who master none, let alone themselves or their own thought processes.

Caveat emptor (or buyer beware) is the only way forward!

## The Alice-in-Blunderland Syndrome

One thing is certain. Things are not changing at a constant rate. With each passing year, the rate of change is also increasing. Much like Alice in Wonderland, *Homo sapiens* are discovering that they need to keep running faster and faster, with nary a respite in sight.

Alvin Toffler might have labelled this as Future Shock 4.0!

## Some lessons from the *Bhagavad Gita*

Smart CEOs can perhaps look up to this ancient scripture to find ways to avoid getting entrapped in a quagmire of this kind. We explore this theme in the next part.

# 46

# The Challenges of Industrial Revolution 4.0 (Part 3 of 3)

## How Coronavirus Accelerated Technological Progress

When businesses resumed operations after having been forced to remain shut during lockdowns in 2020, they woke up to the kind of belt-tightening they could do by increasing their dependence on artificial intelligence, machine learning, and many other technological advances. Cheer-bots and bot-dogs gradually became the norm for brightening up life for sports persons and patients. In Japan, in stadiums bereft of human presence, robot cheerleaders had perked up players on the field. Robotic priests had started popping up in Buddhist temples. Therapy dogs had started spreading sweetness and light amongst patients.

Large companies which place a premium on employee goodwill responded by hiking salaries, promoting good performers, and facilitating work-from-home. Quite a few others had no other option but to resort to issuing pink slips and giving people a compulsory break from work. Some had slashed salaries temporarily to manage their cash flows better.

The pandemic led to an accelerated adoption of remote work and hybrid-work models, reshaping workforce expectations. It increased reliance on digital infrastructure and accelerated the adoption of digital tools, automation, and upskilling.

What the virus had thrown up was a challenge to human beings to live, work and become smarter; to respect nature and environment better and to focus on living sustainably. It prodded us in the ribs to be more flexible in our thinking and to expect the unexpected. It brought home the basic truth that we need to keep acquiring newer skill sets on a lifelong basis. Platforms like Coursera and Udemy proved to be the enablers of this shift. It made us realize that we would do well to review our life priorities and focus on what is essential.

In other words, it opened new windows for our species to evolve faster.

### Kinds of Business Leaders Embracing IR 4.0 Well

A Deloitte 2019 study which was a part of the agenda for World Economic Forum's annual meeting, indicated then that four kinds of business leaders will thrive in the IR 4.0 scenario.

1) **Social Supers:** Social Supers consider social initiatives fundamental to their businesses, and their optimism about creating societal impact influences their outlook in several ways. Companies with leaders who identify as Social Supers are also growing more than those who haven't successfully found the balance between doing good and making a profit.
2) **Data-driven Decisives:** Some C-level executives are overcoming challenges by taking methodical, data-focused approaches to strategic decision-making. In the past year, almost half of such organizations generated annual revenue growth of five per cent or more while only a quarter of other organizations saw such results.
3) **Disruption Drivers:** These leaders understand that investments in disruptive innovations set their organizations apart from competitors. Disruption Drivers' organizations typically have more defined decision-making processes, and they are more likely to make data-driven decisions with input from diverse sets of stakeholders.

4) **Talent Champions:** These executives are more likely than others to invest in employee retraining for the future of work. They are also committed to societal impact and are seeing early returns from their progressive efforts—and 64 per cent have already generated new revenue streams for their organizations through socially driven initiatives.

These are the modern-day Arjunas, who would go on to embrace the tectonic shifts triggered by Industrial Revolution 4.0. Besides being focused on the action to be taken, they would be keenly aware of the contribution of employees and the society at large to facilitate the process of transition.

## The Prometheus-Cassandra Syndrome

The brainy coves who ingeniously develop something new for humanity occasionally suffer from this syndrome. They get torn between a human desire to achieve and an impulse to reflect on the consequences of their discovery.

J. Robert Oppenheimer and Albert Einstein did ground-breaking research and gave us the atomic bomb. But they were subsequently worried about its destructive consequences. Alfred Nobel, the inventor of dynamite, became so concerned over his legacy that he formed a foundation to award the Nobel Prize to those who did exemplary work for humanity.

Geoffrey Hinton won the 2024 Nobel Prize in physics for his work in developing neural networks, the technology that underpins AI.

Over the past year, Hinton, dubbed 'the godfather of AI', has repeatedly and emphatically warned about the dangers the technology unleashed by his discovery could cause.

Much of Hinton's worry arises from the fact that we know very little about artificial intelligence; also, that machines may outsmart humans. In an interview with National Public Radio, he is reported to have said:

> These things could get more intelligent than us and could decide to take over, and we need to worry now about how we prevent that happening.

## Lord Krishna May Be Able to Help

Machines are far more objective than humans, who often indulge in emotions and attachments. Unlike humans, machines don't have the luxury of self-pity or emotional ties, making some of Lord Krishna's teachings irrelevant to them. However, humans must still face challenges in ensuring machines are programmed with ethical and moral values.

Unlike *Ramayana* which speaks of *Ram Rajya* and *Thirukkural* which elaborates upon the duties of a king, the *Bhagavad Gita* does not directly address such issues as the manner in which either businesses or governments need to be run. Nor does it directly touch upon the subject of taking better care of human resources—a key factor in management. Yes, when it places a premium on work being done with benign motives, it hints at the desirability of getting work done with malice towards none. The scripture is primarily focused on the need to do one's duty with a sense of detachment and equanimity.

Let us consider the kind of indirect clues it offers which could perhaps be of some use to CEOs and managers who are trying to grapple with the challenges posed by rapid advances in technology.

### *The Promise of Sattvic Actions*

To recapitulate what *Gita* says, it is work which is taken up for work's own sake, in an attitude that work itself is worship. Actions performed in a spirit of inspiration and with benign motivation would fall in this category. So would actions which are propelled neither by love nor by hate. These are acts of grace which are not acts of obligation. These are not actions arising out of one's likes and dislikes.

नियतं सङ्गरहितमरागद्वेषतः कृतम् ।
अफलप्रेप्सुना कर्म यतत्सात्त्विकमुच्यते || 18.23 ||

*The assigned action, which is done without attachment, attraction (or) repulsion and without clinging to (its) fruit that is called 'sattvic'.*

Business leaders who mostly operate at the rajasic plane, if they were to consider working in this manner, the issue of wrong motives—whether at the development or the implementation stage—would not come up. Eventually, they would end up steering their business along sustainable lines.

*The Perils of Rajasic and Tamasic Actions*

Machines have serious limitations, especially when it comes to human connection—people often miss the warmth of human interaction in robot-run services or automated customer support. They struggle with unquantifiable values and can't guide CEOs on complex choices like balancing profit with human safety. While machines excel at processing data and aiding decisions, even with evolving algorithms, their 'thinking' remains fundamentally different from human judgment. Machines could therefore assist at either the rajasic or the tamasic level of actions. Lord Krishna cautions that such actions eventually lead to problems.

कर्मणः सुकृतस्याहुः सात्त्विकं निर्मलं फलम् ।
रजसस्तु फलं दुःखमज्ञानं तमसः फलम् || 14.16 ||

*The fruit of virtuous action is said to be sattvic and pure; the fruit of rajasic action is sorrow; ignorance is the fruit of tamas.*

*Overcoming Leadership Deficit*

The responsibility on the shoulders of a leader is rather heavy. She must walk the talk and set an example for others to follow.

If she is prone to using her expense account to accommodate outings for her loved ones, others will lose no time to sniff it out and follow in her footsteps.

कर्मणैव हि संसिद्धिमास्थिता जनकादय: |
लोकसंग्रहमेवापि सम्पश्यन्कर्तुमर्हसि || 3.20 ||

यद्यदाचरति श्रेष्ठस्तत्तदेवेतरो जन: |
स यत्प्रमाणं कुरुते लोकस्तदनुवर्तते || 3.21 ||

*By performing their prescribed duties, King Janak and others attained perfection. You should also perform your duties to set an example for the good of the world. Whatever standard great persons set, the world follows it.*

The scripture does not specifically talk of leadership qualities. But it explains well the qualities of those who are great and whose conduct deserves to be emulated. Verses from 3.21 to 3.27 do so. So do verses 13.7 to 13.11.

*The Pink-slip Syndrome*

For someone who ends up getting a pink slip suddenly due to the organization having adopted a newer set of technologies could find that the *Bhagavad Gita* has already highlighted the importance of doing work skilfully and sincerely, thereby pursuing excellence.

यस्त्विन्द्रियाणि मनसा नियम्यारभतेऽर्जुन |
कर्मेन्द्रियै: कर्मयोगमसक्त: स विशिष्यते || 3.7 ||

*But he who, controlling the senses with the mind, without attachment engages the organs of action in the yoga of action, he excels, O Arjuna.*

It exhorts one not to overtly fall for the temptation of the senses which get continuously exposed to the delectable offerings of life—pleasures of the table, inclination for a variety of amorous endeavours, addiction to social media, and the like.

Keeping one's desires under check and avoiding undue intoxication with power and pelf is another crucial idea that it recommends. It advises one not to live a life of delusion which makes one undertake a perennial but futile search for an everlasting pampering of one's ego. Practising equanimity and being steady inside is highly recommended. So are regular meditative practices.

*In Praise of Self-control*

The *Bhagavad Gita* does not recommend a boring, listless, and monochromatic life to a spiritual aspirant. It merely says not to get swayed by the temptations of life and to gratify one's senses and fulfil one's desires with a strict sense of moderation. Self-control is the keyword. In case a confrontation comes about, empathy and the ability to put oneself in the shoes of the other person is spoken of.

> यथा दीपो निवातस्थो नेङ्गते सोपमा स्मृता |
> योगिनो यतचित्तस्य युञ्जतो योगमात्मन: || 6.19 ||
>
> *A lamp which does not flicker in a windless place, to such is compared the Yogi of a disciplined mind who remains steady in meditation on the Self.*

## The Need for Leaders with a Higher Spiritual Quotient

All of these are proactive measures that could enable a CEO to scale greater heights in her career, delivering results with greater efficiency and composure. These are not quick fixes. Instead, these are long-term solutions which have the potential of enabling one to not only face the challenges of technological advancement but also to utilize technology to the best of one's advantage, rather than becoming a slave to it.

The future would thus see a much higher demand for business leaders whose heads are screwed on right and who take decisions using not only a commercial compass but also a Spiritual one, guided by the values of the organization. Several companies already have chief ethics officers. Those who have thrived in such roles are the ones who have enjoyed support from the very top.

## Of Jackals, Cobras, Giraffes, Elephants and Tortoises

To run a business well, wily jackals and cobras are required; but so are friendly giraffes, elephants and tortoises. In the days to come, conscious managements would do well to assign the role of conscience keepers to any competent and willing full-time director on the board who would help to keep the business afloat without running into a collision with massive icebergs of targets which involve a hidden mass of compromise on core values and ethics. A culture of encouraging dissent and listening to whistle-blowers would also help in a business being steered right.

# 47

# What Would Lord Krishna Share with Students of the Harvard Business School?

All of you are welcome to join me on this journey!

From depths of doubt to action bright,
From storm to calm, from wrong to right.
From shadow's grip to steady flame,
I rise renewed, no more the same.
No longer lost in fear's domain –
I walk with values, clear and sane.

From stress and strain to peace of mind,
From chasing time to being kind.
From ego's noise to blissful tone,
The mind once wild – now mine, my own.
No longer trapped in an endless fight,
I act with heart, not just with might.

From chaos born, I find my ground,
Where balance and purpose are both found.
From profit's chase to purpose pure,
Intent made clean, of that, I'm sure.
From holding wealth to letting flow,
To serve, to give – and humbly grow.

From 'me and mine' to 'we and us',
From greed to grace, from pride to trust.
From loud control to gentle art,
I speak my truth with an open heart.

OFFICE

I'll stand for right, defy the wrong,
And lift the weak where they belong.

From a selfish dream to a selfless deed,
From want to give, from haste to heed.
From passion fierce to kindness deep,
From fire to light the soul can keep.
From anger's storm to grace's air,
The Self within — forever there.

From fear to faith, from rush to rest,
From envy's sting to love expressed.
From restless thoughts to a centred soul,
From half to whole, from part to whole.
Each wound a teacher, each loss a gain,
Each scar a mark of wisdom's reign.

From outer masks to inner truth,
From fleeting joy to timeless proof.
From silence cold to the voice of right,
To guard the good, defend the light.
From grasping hands to letting be,
From 'mine' to 'ours', from 'want' to 'free'.

From craving much to calm content,
From reason's pride to heart's consent.
From knowing facts to wisdom's glow,
From dim to bright, from seed to grow.
Awake, aware, both strong and kind,
With noble aims and a peaceful mind.

With motives pure, with actions fair,
With faith that binds us everywhere.
No harm shall come, no fear remain,
Struggle shaped my soul through pain.
Each trial taught, each loss refined —
The path to peace, in heart and mind.

### Consider My Own Life

Born in a prison, I was separated from my parents within a few hours of my birth. For my own safety, I grew up in the loving care of my foster parents. When the call of duty came from the tyrant king of Mathura, my birthplace, I left my adopted home and its soothing environment, including my beloved Radha, never to return.

When Kansa, the king who also happened to be my maternal uncle, was killed, I freed my parents and my maternal grandfather, all of whom had been wrongfully imprisoned by Kansa. My family had then expected me to take up the task of governing the kingdom, a suggestion I politely declined. My suggestion to hand over the charge back to my imprisoned maternal grandfather was accepted by the assembly.

Overthrowing a kingdom and assuming its charge was never my idea of fun in life. What appealed to me instead was to replace kings who had swerved from the path of righteousness by replacing them with any of their own worthy descendants. I overthrew a lot of unjust kingdoms later in my life, but I was always a kingmaker. When I killed Narakasura, I anointed his son as his successor. I never had ambitions of becoming a king myself, for I wished to be free to pursue higher goals in my life.

When the mighty armies of the dead king's father-in-law kept attacking the kingdom of Mathura repeatedly, I decided to build a small kingdom with myself and my clan, far away, in Dwarka. Beating a strategic retreat was the best way to spare the trauma of the lay citizens of my homeland.

The grave injustice being meted out to my cousins, the Pandavas, by the ruling dispensation, comprising the Kauravas, made me side with the former. I realized they were on the path of righteousness. They were being denied their rightful share in the kingdom. Several unsuccessful attempts were made to disarm them, either by killing them or by cheating them in a game of dice, thereby deferring and denying their right to get their due share in the kingdom. Their wife was insulted in the royal court and an attempt was even made to disrobe her in the presence of all family seniors, who, despite their wisdom, did not object.

If you face a formidable enemy who continues to be patently unjust to a fair-minded party, what are your options? You either go into an oblivion of sorts, or you look him in the eye and challenge him in combat. Sceptics among you may label me a warmonger. Of course, wars are disastrous and against basic human values. But the fact remains that even while knowing there was no hope for avoiding a war, I did make a last-ditch attempt to reconcile the two factions. Not only was my offer rejected but even an attempt was made to arrest me, much against the standard norms.

And when the two armies were standing face to face, my friend Arjuna, one of the Pandava brothers, who was always keen on waging a war, suddenly started having self-doubts. That is how the *Bhagavad Gita* came about.

What I conveyed to my friend Arjuna on a battlefield a long time back can inspire you to face mighty challenges while running or managing a business.

From a despondent being, I could somehow succeed in persuading him to becoming a highly charged-up warrior, ready to fight for his rights.

I merely re-packaged the rich lessons of eternal wisdom embedded in Indian scriptures and presented a highly distilled version of the same for the use of all of you.

I have also held out a specific assurance in the *Bhagavad Gita*, that of my being available to humanity as and when the situation on this planet gets very grim. I consider it my duty to protect the ones who follow their dharma, and to vanquish those who do not.

यदा यदा हि धर्मस्य ग्लानिर्भवति भारत |
अभ्युत्थानमधर्मस्य तदात्मानं सृजाम्यहम् || 4.7 ||

परित्राणाय साधूनां विनाशाय च दुष्कृताम् |
धर्मसंस्थापनार्थाय सम्भवामि युगे युगे || 4.8 ||

*Whenever dharma decays and adharma flourishes, O Bharata, then I create Myself. To protect the righteous and destroy the wicked, to establish dharma firmly, I come into being age after age.*

Never lose hope in life!

If you wish to deliver miraculous results, keep your saw always sharpened, put in extraordinary effort, and have unwavering faith. There is no other way to success.

**How Faith and Devotion Work**

The *Bhagavad Gita* has its origin in the Indian Vedas and Upanishads, but the message it gives is universal in nature.

When it was composed, the term religion, as we understand it today in a much narrower sense, did not exist. The *Bhagavad Gita* is based on one following one's own dharma, or the path of righteousness. In other words, it takes a binary approach to living—one either follows dharma, or one does not. Anything other was held to be adharma, or the absence of righteousness. In short, it expects everyone to have a valid code of conduct (*Bhagavad Gita*—Chapter 16).

Today, you have choices of so many religions, should you decide to go that way. But what I have conveyed is the way of leading a spiritual life, the cornerstones of which—human values, fairness, empathy and so on—are extolled by all religions.

If religion today has the potential to create disharmony, spirituality is there to unite mankind in its search for true happiness.

**A Strategist, Not a Warmonger**

I am not a warmonger, as believed by some of you. Nor am I a devious diplomat. To me, upholding dharma is a strategy, for sustainable success—whether in leading a nation or a business empire. In turn, this has three components:

1. Upholding the larger righteous interest; taking care of the welfare of humanity,
2. Decisive action and not passivity, and
3. Action which is independent, without fear, external pressure, and attachment of any kind.

Take the case of J. Robert Oppenheimer who spearheaded the drive to develop the first atomic bomb. As he witnessed the first nuclear test in July 1945, the following verse of mine is said to have come to his mind:

कालोऽस्मि लोकक्षयकृत्प्रवृद्धो
लोकान्समाहर्तुमिह प्रवृत्तः ।
ऋतेऽपि त्वां न भविष्यन्ति सर्वे
येऽवस्थिताः प्रत्यनीकेषु योधाः ॥ 11.32 ॥

*I am mighty Time, the source of destruction that comes forth to annihilate the worlds. Even without your participation, the warriors arrayed in the opposing army shall cease to exist.*

Even though Oppenheimer supported this development against fascism, he opposed the production of a thermonuclear hydrogen bomb during the Cold War.

**A Doubt over My Self-praise!**

Many of you take a jaundiced view of the fact that I have often elaborated upon my own qualities. You are left wondering as to how someone, who appears to be so knowledgeable, could praise himself so very lavishly!

But when I use the term 'I' rather liberally, I am not referring to myself, but to the ultimate godhead, who is beyond both *saguna* and *nirguna* (either having a physical form or an abstract one) and who can be attained by either a judicious combination of Karma Yoga, Gyan Yoga, Bhakti Yoga and Raj Yoga, or through following either Gyan Yoga or Bhakti Yoga.

If you are aware of what I have said in the *Bhagavad Gita*, Karma Yoga, in any case, is compulsory. Gyan Yoga is essentially about the knowledge of the real Self. When combined with Bhakti Yoga, a combination of devotion and surrender, it becomes a critical success factor in this quest of an aspirant. Throughout my dialogue with Arjuna, you will notice an undercurrent of Raj Yoga.

If you choose the first option, that of using a judicious combination of all the four kinds of yogas, you would be a balanced practitioner who keeps knowledge in the heart, performs actions with the physical body and does so in a spirit of surrender and devotion.

If you choose the second option, that of not only performing all necessary actions but also following either Gyan Yoga or Bhakti Yoga, as exemplified by Jagadguru Shankaracharya and Chaitanya Mahaprabhu respectively, success will be yours.

You could be from any religion (as we understand the term these days) but you just need to focus yourself on whichever superior power you have faith in. Faith, devotion and surrender come highly recommended, though not to me in person, but to the ultimate godhead, of whom I am merely another form.

Admittedly, to someone who does not subscribe to such concepts as reincarnation and the karmic theory, the *Bhagavad Gita* is not an interesting scripture to be considered.

Life is a unique opportunity for all of you to use it wisely and move up the ladder of spiritual evolution. Pray do not waste it while you are busy chasing materialistic goals.

Follow the *Bhagavad Gita* and you would surely excel in all spheres of your life and thrive in the corporate jungle!

# 48

# Post-script: Of Autonomous Cars and the *Bhagavad Gita*

Those of you who do not take a jaundiced view of the proposition of reincarnation may consider the example of a brand-new shimmering car being allotted to us in the form of a new body at the beginning of each of our lives. The car does not come with any time-limited warranty and could conk off any day. Its longevity is determined by the quality of its engine, the love with which one maintains it, the way it is handled while being driven around the sunlit streets of life, and several other factors.

The *Bhagavad Gita* gives one a realistic manual which describes what one can do to utilize this car to its optimum level. The more one injects the fuel of hopes and desires into its system, the faster it may run, though there is a range of speed within which its engine efficiency is at its best. Regular application of brakes—on one's senses, one's mind and one's desires—is a necessity, so one does not meet one's ruin while driving. Brakes need to be used effectively, so the three factors mentioned above are kept on a tight leash and deployed only in moderation. This way, the mileage one gets is the best possible under the driving conditions that one faces. The lubricants of skills, knowledge, faith and sincerity help to maximize engine efficiency. The coolant of detachment assists quietly in its own way. This would be the best way to enjoy the ride of life.

Try and visualize a driver-less car of the future, duly armed with artificial intelligence, and practically run by a complex array of programmable logic controllers and other technological marvels. It can take one from point A to point B in a far less stressful manner. It can manage to park itself even in a bumper-to-bumper situation. Assuming that it is a hybrid model which works on conventional fuel as well as also on its battery, whenever brakes are applied to keep its sensors and desires under check, a part of the kinetic energy gets utilized to charge the battery as well.

Now, if the supreme analytical skills of this car lead its 'mind' to believe that it is indeed the real driver and not the human being who 'owns' it and decides its destinations from time to time, the car could be said to be living in a delusion of its own. In fact, the soul would be held to be the real driver!

This indeed is the tragedy of all of us, as well as CEOs and managers. We believe that we alone are the doers as well as the enjoyers of the delightful journey called life. What we fail to realize is that it is the 'soul' which is the real driver. Once this realization has dawned, a sense of conscious detachment comes about, making one realize one's true place in the overall scheme of things.

Those of you who have accompanied the author on this unique voyage through the deep waters of the *Bhagavad Gita*, exploring the evergreen conceptual islands of eternal wisdom encountered on the way, may now feel enthused to devour the original scripture itself.

Wishing you all an enlightened future hereafter!

# 49

## The *Bhagavad Gita*: The Esoteric Scheme of Things

For the enthusiasts amongst you who may like to explore the *Bhagavad Gita* better, it consists of 18 chapters, which may be said to comprise of three broad segments. The first set of six chapters describes Karma Yoga. the second set describes the glories of Bhakti Yoga. For the nourishment of bhakti, this set also dwells upon the opulence of the supreme godhead. The third set of six chapters expounds upon Gyan Yoga, or *tattva jnana* (knowledge of scriptural terms and principles).

Here is a chapter-by-chapter summary.

### Chapter 1: Despondency Has Arjuna in Its Grip

As the opposing armies stand poised for battle, Arjuna, the mighty warrior, sees his intimate relatives, teachers and friends in both armies ready to fight and sacrifice their lives. Overcome by grief and pity, Arjuna fails in strength, becomes befuddled, and gives up his determination to fight. He starts eulogizing the benefits of avoiding the war and even questions its rationale.

### Chapter 2: A Management Summary of the *Gita*

Lord Krishna starts his motivational discourse by explaining the fundamental distinction between the temporary material body and the eternal spiritual soul. He explains the process of transmigration, the nature of selfless service to the Supreme and the characteristics of a self-realized person.

### Chapter 3: Of the Karma Operating System

Everyone must engage in some sort of activity in this material world. But actions, irrespective of whether these are good or bad, can either bind one to this world or liberate one from it. By acting for the pleasure of the Supreme, without selfish motives, one can be liberated from the law of karma (action and reaction) and attain transcendental knowledge of the Self and the Supreme.

### Chapter 4: The Supreme Knowledge

Transcendental knowledge—the spiritual knowledge of the soul, of God, and their relationship—is both purifying and liberating. Such knowledge is the fruit of selfless devotional action (Karma Yoga). The Lord explains the remote history of the *Gita*, the purpose and significance of His periodic descents to the material world, and the necessity of approaching a guru, a realized teacher.

### Chapter 5: The Wise Man

Outwardly performing all actions but inwardly renouncing their fruits, the wise man, purified by the fire of transcendental knowledge, attains peace, detachment, forbearance, spiritual vision and bliss.

### Chapter 6: Techniques and Benefits of Meditation

*Ashtanga Yoga*, a mechanical meditative practice, controls the mind and the senses and focuses concentration on *Paramatma* (the Super-soul, the form of the Lord situated in the heart). This practice could lead one to a state of *samadhi*, when one becomes fully conscious of the Supreme and leads one's life accordingly.

### Chapter 7: Knowing the Absolute

Lord Krishna is the supreme truth, the supreme cause and sustaining force of everything, both material and spiritual. Advanced souls surrender unto Him in devotion, whereas unrighteous souls divert their minds to other objects of worship.

### Chapter 8: Reaching the Supreme

By remembering Lord Krishna in devotion throughout one's life, and especially at the time of death, one can attain to His supreme abode, beyond the material world.

### Chapter 9: Knowledge for Your Eyes Only

Lord Krishna is the supreme godhead and the supreme object of worship. The soul is eternally related to Him through transcendental devotional service (bhakti). By reviving one's pure devotion one returns to Krishna in the spiritual realm.

### Chapter 10: Krishna—The Supreme Object of Worship

All wondrous phenomena showing power, beauty, grandeur, or sublimity, either in the material world or in the spiritual, are but partial manifestations of Krishna's divine energies and opulence. As the supreme cause of all causes and the support and essence of everything, Krishna is the supreme object of worship for all beings.

### Chapter 11: The Cosmic Form

Lord Krishna grants Arjuna divine vision and reveals His spectacular unlimited form as the cosmic universe. Lesser mortals like us may accuse Him of indulging in an act of unabashed self-praise, but the fact remains that this form reveals not only the brighter but also the darker side of the all-encompassing divinity in Him. Krishna explains that one can perceive this form only by pure devotional service.

**Chapter 12: Of Devotion**

Bhakti Yoga, pure devotional service to Lord Krishna, is the highest and most expedient means for attaining pure love for Krishna, which is the highest end of spiritual existence. Those who follow this supreme path develop divine qualities.

**Chapter 13: Nature, the Enjoyer and Consciousness**

One who understands the difference between the body, the soul, and the Super-soul beyond them attains liberation from this material world.

**Chapter 14: Three Modes (Gunas) of Material Nature**

All embodied souls are under the control of the three modes, or qualities, of material nature: goodness, passion and ignorance. Lord Krishna explains what these modes are, how they act upon us, how one transcends them and the symptoms of one who has attained the transcendental state.

**Chapter 15: The Importance of Surrender to a Higher Power**

The ultimate purpose of Vedic knowledge is to detach oneself from the entanglement of the material world and to understand Lord Krishna as the supreme personality or godhead. One who understands Krishna's supreme identity surrenders unto Him and engages in His devotional service.

## Chapter 16: Of Divine and Demoniac Natures

Those who possess demoniac qualities and who live whimsically, without following the regulations of scripture, attain lower births and further material bondage. But those who possess divine qualities and regulated lives, abiding by scriptural authority, gradually attain spiritual perfection.

## Chapter 17: Three Kinds of Faith

There are three types of faith, corresponding to and evolving from the three modes of material nature. Acts performed by those whose faith is in passion and ignorance yield only impermanent, material results, whereas acts performed in goodness, in accord with scriptural injunctions, purify the heart and lead to pure faith in Lord Krishna and devotion to Him.

## Chapter 18: Conclusion—Perfection in Renunciation

Krishna explains the meaning of renunciation and the effects of the modes of nature on human consciousness and activity. He explains *Brahman* realization, the glories of the *Bhagavad Gita* and its ultimate conclusion, that the highest path of religion is absolute, unconditional loving surrender unto Lord Krishna, which frees one from all sins, brings one to complete enlightenment and enables one to return to Krishna's eternal spiritual abode.

*(Source: http://www.krishna.com/info/bhagavad-gita-it-chapter-summary)*

# Part 50

## Suggestions for Further Reading


1. Covey, Stephen R, *The 8th Habit, From Effectiveness to Greatness*, Simon & Schuster, USA, 2004.
2. Lala, R M, *Beyond the Last Blue Mountain*, Penguin India, New Delhi, 1992.
3. Gopalakrishnan, R, *Six Lenses: Vignettes of Success, Career and Relationships*, Rupa Publications, New Delhi, 2015.
4. Mourkogiannis, Nikos, *Purpose: The Starting Point of Great Companies*, Palgrave Macmillan, New York, 2006.
5. Zak, Paul J., *Trust Factor: The Science of Creating High-Performance Companies*, AMACOM, New York, 2017.
6. Clinton, Bill, *Giving: How Each of Us Can Change the World*, Knopf, New York, 2007.
7. Sharma, Robin S, *The Monk Who Sold His Ferrari*, Jaico Publishing House, Mumbai, 1999.
8. Getz, Isaac, and Robert Davids and Brian Carney, *Leadership Without Ego*, Springer Nature Switzerland AG, Cham, 2019.
9. Lama, Dalai, and Howard C Cutler, *The Art of Happiness*, Riverhead Hardcover, New York, 1998.
10. Rao, Professor G P, *I am Something : Developing a New Leader Mindset: A step by step approach to being a more humane leader*, Amazon Kindle Edition, 2019.
11. Moi, Justin, *The Giraffe and Jackal Within*, SWP Publishing, Amsterdam, 2012.
12. Kempton, Beth, *Wabi Sabi: Japanese Wisdom for a Perfectly Imperfect Life*, Harper Collins, London, 2018.
13. Redfield, James, *The Celestine Prophecy*, Warner Books, New York, 1993.
14. Nelson, Dr. Noelle, *Make More Money by Making Your Employees Happy*, MindLab Publishing, 2012.

15. Tolle, Eckhart, *The Power of Now: A Guide to Spiritual Enlightenment*, New World Library and Namaste Publishing, Novato, 1997.
16. Rajagopalachari, Shri P, *The Spider's Web, Volume 3*, Shri Ramachandra Mission, Chennai, 2004.
17. Vivekananda, Swami, *Karma Yoga: The Yoga of Action*, Shri Ramakrishna Publications, Kolkata, 1896.
18. Marshall, Ian, and Danah Zohar, *SQ: Connecting with our Spiritual Intelligence*, Bloomsbury, London, 2000.
19. Bhat, Nilima, and Raj Sisodia, *Shakti Leadership: Embracing Feminine and Masculine Powers in Business*, Penguin Random House, New York, 2016.
20. Rappaport, Alfred, *Saving Capitalism From Short-Termism: How to Build Long-Term Value and Take Back Our Financial Future*, McGraw-Hill Education, New York, 2011.
21. Chakraborty, S K, and Debangshu Chakraborty, *Rajarshi Leadership: The Saving Role of Authentic Spirituality*, Sri Aurobindo Society, Puducherry, 2012.
22. Gnaur, Jens, *Being One: The Vision and Way of the Bhagavad Gita*, BoD, Copenhagen, 2017.
23. Nadella, Satya, et al., *Hit Refresh: The Quest to Rediscover Microsoft's Soul and Imagine a Better Future for Everyone*, Harper Business, New York, 2017.
24. Bhat, Harish, *#Tata Stories: 40 Timeless Tales to Inspire You*, Penguin, India, 2021.

# Part 51

## Some Comments on the *Bhagavad Gita*

*The Gita is one of the clearest and most comprehensive summaries of the Perennial Philosophy ever to have been done.*

Aldous Huxley

*The Gita is a bouquet composed of the beautiful flowers of spiritual truths collected from the Upanishads.*

Swami Vivekananda

*My last prayer to everyone, therefore, is that one should not fail to thoroughly understand this ancient science of the life of a householder, or of worldly life, as early as possible in one's life.*

Lokmanya Tilak

*The Gita is a book that has worn extraordinarily well, and it is almost as fresh and still in its real substance quite as new, because always renewable in experience, as when it first appeared in or was written into the frame of the Mahabharata.*

Sri Aurobindo

*When disappointment stares me in the face and all alone, I see not one ray of light, I go back to the Bhagavad Gita. I find a verse here and a verse there, and I immediately begin to smile in the midst of overwhelming tragedies – and if they have left no visible, no indelible scare on me, I owe it all to the teaching of Bhagavad Gita.*

Mahatma Gandhi

*The teaching of the ancient battlefield gives guidance in all later days, and trains the aspiring soul in treading the steep and thorny path that leads to peace.*

Dr Annie Besant

# Index